MW00805902

Navigating Complexities in Leadership

Moving Toward Critical Hope

A Volume in
Contemporary Perspectives on Leadership Learning

Series Editor:
Kathy L. Guthrie, *Florida State University*

Navigating Complexities in Leadership

Moving Toward Critical Hope

Edited By

Kathy L. Guthrie
Florida State University

and

Kerry L. Priest
Kansas State University

Information Age Publishing, Inc.
Charlotte, North Carolina • www.infoagepub.com

Library of Congress Cataloging-in-Publication Data

CIP data for this book can be found on the Library of Congress website:
http://www.loc.gov/index.html

Paperback: 978-1-64802-788-8
Hardcover: 978-1-64802-789-5
eBook: 978-1-64802-790-1

Cover art provided by Danielle Seago.

Copyright © 2022 IAP–Information Age Publishing, Inc.

All rights reserved. No part of this publication may be reproduced, stored in a retrieval system, or transmitted in any form or by any electronic or mechanical means, or by photocopying, microfilming, recording or otherwise without written permission from the publisher.

Printed in the United States of America.

DEDICATION

To those who continue to navigate the complexities of leadership with hope of a better future. Thank you for being in this work with us.

CONTENTS

PART I:
EXPANDING DYNAMIC LEADERSHIP FRAMES

PART II:
LEADERSHIP PRACTICE IN HIGHER EDUCATION

PART III:
HIGHER EDUCATION AS A PARTNER IN LEADERSHIP PRACTICE

PART IV:
IDENTITY

PART V:
GLOBAL CONTEXT

ACKNOWLEDGMENTS

When we (Kathy and Kerry) began talking in May 2020 about the complexities we were dealing with as leadership educators, we had no idea this project would be one to emerge from those reflective meetings. We acknowledge no book is ever constructed in isolation, especially when it is focused on the sheer complexities around us. We all know 2020 and beyond has been challenging because of the multiple complexities we were and still are all dealing with. Being able to make meaning from all that is going on around us takes countless conversations, listening, thinking, reflecting, and learning to build upon each other's ideas and concepts into something worthy of others reading. Acknowledging all of the educators, practitioners, and scholars who have gone before us in tackling the tough aspects of complexity, we thank you. You gave us a lens. When we think about all of the individuals who have taken us up on engaging in the tough conversations about leadership, we could probably write a book on just what we have learned from those conversations. We are so grateful to a special group of colleagues, our coinquiry team: Jessica Chung, Michael Gleason, Christie Navarro, Darren Pierre, Michelle Steele, and John Weng. You have become family during these challenging times. Thank you for not shying away from the hard conversations, leaning into the discomfort together, for the laughter, encouragement, and teaching us more than we can express.

Also, we cannot miss the opportunity to mention several people who directly influenced this book. Chapter authors, we acknowledge we asked for the impossible—to enter into an emergent inquiry process with us, exploring the complexities being faced, searching for critical hope, and do it in minimal pages. You answered the call and provided such powerful insight. Thank you for being cocreators and teaching us all. Anna Van Gurp, thank you for your support in a time of extreme complexity. Your thoughtfulness, dedication, passion, and support in helping us frame the book and recognize how the writing process can be a form of healing.

Brittany Devies and Julie LeBlanc, thank you for all your support and assisting in getting this book to the finish line. Danielle Seago, thank you for sharing your brilliant artistic ability with us. The cover artwork so beautifully captures the themes of this book: even in the clouds of complexity we can see patterns—colors and form. As we interpret the patterns, we find new meaning and insight. The sunlight shining through represents the critical hope we all need, and beacon of possibility and light to guide our ongoing journey.

Kathy wants to first thank her coeditor, Kerry. Kerry, this has been such a journey and I am so thankful we were navigating it together. You are such a brilliant, passionate, and caring person. I am a better person because you are in my life. I would also like to thank the professionals in the Leadership Learning Research Center, students in the Higher Education Program, and the Division of Student Affairs at Florida State University. I am thankful, everyday, for being able to work collectively with such an intelligent, passionate, fun group of people, especially in times of extreme complexity. Team Guthrie, I am forever thankful for you. Brian, you have always been the love of my life, my biggest fan, and the greatest partner I could ask for. Kinley, you have sharpened my focus, given me purpose, and motivate me every day to be the best version of myself.

Kerry wants to first thank her colleagues and students at the Staley School of Leadership Studies and Leadership Communication Doctoral Program at Kansas State University. You truly model what it means to be a learning community. You inspire me to stay on my "edge" in my leadership and scholarship. I am grateful to be part of the Humans Systems Dynamics community. Your vision inspires me to keep looking for the patterns, seeking understanding, and acting with courage in the face of uncertainty. To my family, thank you for teaching me much about resilience and hope. And finally, to my coauthor, Kathy, I cannot thank you enough for this opportunity. You have been a mentor and a friend. Your legacy as a scholar is in how you live now—the voices you lift up, the powerful questions you ask, the collective insights you emerge, the compassion and humility by which you lead, teach, and live—and in the work that you inspire beyond this moment.

—*Kathy L. Guthrie and Kerry L. Priest*

CHAPTER 1

PARTING THE CLOUDS

Navigating Complexity in Leadership

Kerry L. Priest and Kathy L. Guthrie

The dynamics of the 21st century have been described as volatile, uncertain, complex, and ambiguous (VUCA; van der Steege, 2017). The conditions of VUCA create disruption while triggering fast-paced innovation (2017). While many leadership researchers, educators, and practitioners situate their work within these dynamics, we still found ourselves unprepared and overwhelmed by the total disruption of the COVID-19 pandemic. Global communities, organizations, and higher education institutions have experienced unprecedented challenges and tensions. Long-time problems were confounded with emerging crises: public health and wellbeing, inequity and injustice, racial tension, political polarization, economic insecurity, and more.

The confluence of complexities we experience can surround us like heavy clouds. Clouds of injustice, concern for the health and safety of those we love, trying to meet expectations and commitments, lead teams and teach in virtual environments, maintain households, and support our neighbors. The multiple pandemics may have felt like walking or driving in a dense fog—the clouds are thick and feel dangerous, unsettling. We feel our hearts pounding, and fear and worry may hold us back from even

Navigating Complexities in Leadership: Moving Toward Critical Hope, pp. 1–13
www.infoagepub.com
Copyright © 2022 by Information Age Publishing
All rights of reproduction in any form reserved.

venturing out onto well-known paths, let alone new ones. We cannot see what is ahead, and it is scary. Yet, like the cover of this book illustrates, what at first seems like only clouds are full of patterns and forms. When we search for meaning in complexity, the clouds begin to part, and we can see possible paths forward.

Living and working within the context of multiple pandemics surfaced humanity's interconnectedness and brought into sharper focus the role and responsibility of leaders and the need for leadership. For those who teach, study, and practice leadership, the relevance—and gaps—within our work became clearer. This book was born out of questions: What complexities face those of us who engage in leadership learning and development? What is important? To what do we need to pay attention? What powerful questions need to be asked? And, how can higher education continue to change in response to a changing world?

In their call for socially just leadership education, Guthrie and Chunoo (2021) frame leadership education in culturally relevant ways (Guthrie et al., 2016) and from critical perspectives (Dugan, 2017). They assert that "action is long overdue for justice, fairness, and equity" (Guthrie & Chunoo, 2021, p. 280).

Engaging in socially just leadership requires shifting the mindset of the dominant perspectives and approaches of research, teaching, and practice. The work of socially just leadership is situated in complexity. Perhaps a barrier to action is feeling overwhelmed or stuck by the complex nature of the challenge(s). Applying conventional thinking to chronic, complex social problems undermines good intentions to improve social systems (Stroh, 2015). Systems thinking is needed; it is a catalyst for social change. Through this volume, we propose that complexity combined with systems thinking and socially just leadership offers insights for courageous action. Critical, culturally relevant, complexity, and systems perspectives provide frameworks and tools that help us to see injustice in systems and develop strategic interactions to influence change across levels, from individual and whole systems. The purpose of this book is to (1) bring to light patterns of complexity in current times as experienced by leadership educators and practitioners in higher education, (2) make meaning of the uncertainty around us and share our learning and insights with one another, and (3) build our collective adaptive capacity to live and work in critical hope and possibility.

COMPLEXITY IN LEADERSHIP

There have been many books written about complexity theory and its application to leadership research and practice. We draw from inspiration from the scholars who have gone before us (e.g., Hazy et al., 2007; Uhl-

Bien & Marion, 2008; Wheatley, 2006, 2017). Dugan (2017) asserts, "Complexity leadership theory is incredibly innovative and impressive in its comprehensive treatment of how leadership emerges in systems. It's also so insanely complex that it borders on unusable" (p. 291). Our desire was for this book to model leadership learning *praxis*: engaging in practice with theoretical understanding, learning by doing, reflection and action that leads to transformation (Friere, 1972; Harvey & Jenkins, 2014). Dugan identifies several cognitive shifts required to engage complexity theory in practice: (1) seeing problems as complex rather than complicated, (2) the ability to see a whole system, and (3) critical sense-making perspectives. These shifts help leadership educators and practitioners to acknowledges interdependence, see the embedded nature of systems and how systems socially construct norms and engage all parts of a system in "meaning making and action that addresses the ways in which the system may reproduce forms of social stratification and inequity" (Dugan, 2017, p. 292). Next, we share a brief overview of key concepts to build understanding and provide a conceptual frame for our praxis goal: to make collective meaning of our lived experiences of complexity, generate insight, and move into new possibilities with hope and courage.

Complexity and Complex Adaptive Systems

In this book, we explore complexity as a systems concept. The term complexity can describe a state or quality of being (it was a challenge of great complexity) or the many factors involved in situations or processes (the complexities of leadership). When a system has many individual parts that can be taken apart and recognized as separate parts, it is considered to be *complicated*—the many parts work together to make the whole (Holladay & Tytel, 2011). A *complex* system is different, as it is composed of many interdependent parts that interact in unpredictable ways. When you change one part of a complex system, it can have unexpected or unintended consequences in different parts. It is impossible to predict or control how the parts will interact at any given time, and if you take them apart, they cannot be reconstructed in the same way. It is like a net or web that is deeply entangled, cannot separate one part from another. In this way, the whole is "more than the sum of its parts" (Holladay & Tytel, 2011, p. 23). Complex systems are dynamic, meaning things change and emerge over time. And they are nonlinear, meaning that there are no clear root causes to problems, and change cannot be attributed to any single person or action. Causality is multidirectional. In these conditions, the future is unknowable, and "the best you can hope for is to build adaptive capacity to coevolve with the system as it changes over time" (Eoyang & Holladay, 2013, p. 25)

Eoyang and Holladay (2013) conceptualize complex adaptive systems as "a cluster of individual parts that interact with each other, and over time systemwide patterns appear" (p. 15). *Parts* refer to a collective of semiautonomous, unpredictable agents—people and things that follow system rules and expectations but have the freedom to choose what to do next in the context of their surroundings. Their *interactions* are dynamic and produce systemwide *patterns*. Patterns can be defined as "similarities, differences, and relationships that have meaning across space and time" (Eoyang & Holladay, 2013, p. 43). Patterns subsequently influence behaviors and ongoing interactions. In this way, systems are *adaptive,* expressing the capacity to make changes, reactions, or adjustments individual or system responses to pressures, actions, behaviors, or conditions of the system's environment (Holladay & Tytel, 2011). The purpose of adaptation in a complex system is to sustain the system. The continual process of adapting and responding to changes in its environment is called self-organizing (Holladay & Tytel, 2011).

Leadership Through Adaptive Action

From a complex systems point of view, leadership is an emergent phenomenon produced through dynamic interactions that lead to changes in the ways agents relate to one another (Hazy et al., 2007). Emergent dynamics, such as conflicting across tensions or linking across networks, are forms of collective action that transform the system (Uhl-Bien & Arena, 2018). Reflecting on the complexities of the COVID 19 pandemic, Uhl-Bien (2020) suggests research, education, and practice must focus on how to enable leaders and organizations to adapt more quickly in the face of challenges and pressures. Enabling adaptive responses is an emergent dynamic through which to develop ideas for action that can be scaled into the system. There is a need for organizations and institutions to open "adaptive space"—creating the conditions within systems that enable adaptive processes to occur (Uhl-Bien, 2020; Uhl-Bien & Arena, 2018).

Leadership in complex systems is not located in the characteristics or actions of any one person; however, individuals can pay attention to patterns as they emerge, critically examine the meaning of the patterns, and take intentional action to influence new patterns (and then, repeat)—what Eoyang and Holladay (2013) call the process of adaptive action. Adaptive action (see Figure 1.1) is a human systems dynamics approach to navigating complex adaptive challenges.

Figure 1.1

Adaptive Action

Source: © 2016 Human Systems Dynamics Institute. Used with permission.

The adaptive action process is guided by three relatively simple questions that support individual and collective decision making and action in complexity.

- **What?** This question is an opportunity to collect data and describe what is happening around you in the system. *What do you see? What is happening? Who is part of this system? How did the current situation come to be? Where is the power located in this system?*
- **So what?** This question prompts meaning making, identifying patterns and conditions that are shaping the world as you see it. *So what patterns emerge? So what are the similarities? So what differences make a difference? So where are the tensions? So what surprises me? So what are the risks or benefits, and for whom? So what options are emerging?*
- **Now what?** This question generates a plan of action to shift the situation and bring about change. As you choose one action to try next, you learn and adapt by repeating the cycle. *Now what will I/we try? Now what will I/we communicate? Now what support or resistance will there be? Now what are the most important questions?* (adapted from Mennin et al., 2020).

The adaptive action process reflects similar elements of the observe-inter-intervene process of adaptive leadership (Heifetz et al., 2009) and the experiential learning cycle (Kolb, 2015). Using critical perspectives as interpretive tools in the adaptive action process allows us to deconstruct— or deeply examine taken-for-granted assumptions, power, and inequity— and reconstruct our leadership research, teaching, and practice in more just ways (Dugan, 2017). Adaptive action can be used to build adaptive capacity and support transformation at all scales of human systems (Eoyang & Holladay, 2013). For the purpose of this book, we utilize adaptive action as an organizing principle. Adaptive action is reflected in the purposes of this volume (1) to bring to light patterns of complexity in current times through the lens of leadership educators and practitioners in higher education (what?), (2) make meaning of the uncertainty around us and share our learning and insights with one another (so what?), and (3) to build our collective adaptive capacity as leadership educators to live and work in critical hope and possibility (now what?).

EMERGING VOICES, EMERGENT PATTERNS

This inquiry project emerged from interactions across and within institutions, programs, classrooms, professional conferences, and personal conversations. For this book, we invited emerging voices of doctoral students and faculty colleagues within higher education who are engaging in emerging scholarship. Drawing from their lived experiences, as well as observations within their context and communities, the authors in this volume were tasked with describing complexities as they were living them. The questions, examples, insights, meaning, and recommendations within this volume capture meaning for this moment in time and offer insight for the future. The chapters were created through dynamic interactions between our collaborators—and now between authors and readers. Each chapter represents a cycle of adaptive action unique to the author(s) and their context(s) and contributes to the broader inquiry. Next, we will describe the five parts of this book, which are organized by the themes, or patterns, that emerged across and within the chapters.

Expanding Dynamic Leadership Frames

Making progress on complex issues and challenges is difficult because there are many ways to frame both problems and solutions, and stakeholders often hold radically different frames and worldviews for understanding the problem (Mennin et al., 2020). The first part of this book raises consciousness of how paradigms and perspectives influence leadership research, education, and practice. In Chapter 2, Chelsea D. Shore provides an overview of paradigms in leadership studies and illuminates the tensions between completing ontological assumptions, questions, and methods. She advances the idea of paradigm interplay, or the ability to share, hear, and hold differing perspectives that support whole-system work in complexity. Rian Satterwhite, Katherine Sheridan, and Whitney McIntyre Miller bring paradigm interplay to life in Chapter 3. Through the lens of sustainability, they introduce a tension leadership model as a framework for addressing complex challenges facing humanity and the planet. The tensions of dualities are bridged through dialectical thinking (holding competing truths), criticality and critical hope, and commitment to shared work across generations.

Brandon W. Kliewer also speaks to theoretical and practical tensions that result from various ontological frames in Chapter 4. Ontological assumptions represent choices about what is included, and what is left out, in the conceptual boundaries of leadership. Kliewer invites readers to reconsider leadership learning and development through a biopolitical lens, which is especially important for work that advances justice and the common good. O'Juan Edwards' critical reflection in Chapter 5 prompts leaders and leadership educators to consider the lens of bad leadership as a tool for analysis and accountability. It is essential to acknowledge history's legacy of ineffective, unethical, and evil leadership and how that plays out in modern-day injustices. Edwards calls for leaders and educators to be more conscious, adaptable, and compassionate concerning humanity and the experiences of those around us.

In Chapter 6, Martinella Dryburgh, Elizabeth Goryunova, Carol Clyde Gallagher, Trent Grundmeyer, and Cristina de Mello e Souza Wildermuth model collective adaptive action as they engage the tensions experienced as leadership education scholars in a changing higher education landscape. Through personal examples and research, they generate insight and questions to guide more inclusive and innovative scholarship practices. In summary, the chapters in this first section challenge us to reflect on the assumptions and beliefs guiding our practices, and shift patterns within institutions and across academic systems to support different paradigms and encourage new forms of scholarship.

LEADERSHIP PRACTICE IN HIGHER EDUCATION

One way to understand the conditions within complex adaptive systems is as a "container" that holds parts together in such a way that they interact to create patterns (Eoyang & Holladay, 2013). These chapters reflect leadership practice within the container of higher education. The pattern holding these chapters together is a shared vision—a belief that higher education can develop leadership capacity to realize social change. The authors highlight pedagogies, tools, and strategies to facilitate engagement across scale, from individuals to classrooms, programs, and institutions.

Ciera Fluker takes a praxis approach in Chapter 7, applying practices from Brown's (2017) emergent strategy framework to navigate the many tensions and complexities within and across higher education institutions. For example, she highlights the fractal nature of institutional patterns. Realizing justice and liberation at an institutional level begins by practicing it at an individual level. In Chapter 8, Cassandra R. Kepple explores shares how social media in higher education can be used to respond to changing conditions and crises, and as an opportunity to influence change beyond the walls and hallways of the institution. Kepple applies systems and complexity frames to followership. She suggests that students, educators, and administrators can apply followership to engage more effectively and prepare for the unknown.

In Chapter 9, Marissa Mainwood speaks from experience as a practitioner, working closely with students and observing dynamics. She notices how in times of complexity, roles shift, and different relational dynamics emerge. Mainwood scales into the level of the individual, helping us understand system forces and stressors on the people within it and what that means for leadership education. Brittany Devies, Chapter 10, invites educators to consider the role of observation in leadership learning. Classroom systems reflect broader dynamics at play in society. Observation is a pedagogical approach that helps students recognize their interconnectedness with each other and societal issues. Devies illustrates how observation creates the conditions for critical conversations on power in leadership processes. In summary, these chapters help educators in higher education to consider our roles and opportunities to engage in new and meaningful ways and influence shifts in thinking and practice across multiple levels of the system.

Higher Education as a Stakeholder in Leadership Activity

This next section shifts the lens of discussion from higher education as the site of leadership practice to higher education as a stakeholder and partner in leadership activity that addresses broader societal challenges. Community engagement includes forms of collaboration between institutions of higher education and their larger communities for the mutually beneficial exchange of knowledge and resources (Driscoll, 2008). From the lens of complex adaptive systems, an "exchange" is a connection between parts of a system that transmits information, resources, and energy and helps shape system patterns (Eoyang & Holladay, 2013). In Chapter 11, Julie B. LeBlanc describes how the dynamics of complex adaptive systems offer a lens for leadership educators to consider shaping conditions for community engagement to address inequity and injustice in communities. LeBlanc describes tensions and considerations among common forms of community engagement: one-day events, short-term programs, and long-term programs. She examines how community engagement is a form of interaction that either replicates or influences patterns in a system.

In Chapter 12, Susan Metzger and Russell Plaschka insight from their experience as practitioners and community-engaged researchers. They describe tensions facing rural and agricultural communities, and propose that a higher education, through engaged research and leadership development, can partner with community stakeholders to generate solutions for sustainability and growth. Entering relationships with communities requires recognizing the cultural patterns that exist and building trust to cocreate new approaches. Mac T. Benavides, Saya Kakim, and Jurdene Coleman, in Chapter 13, examine the U.S. healthcare system's legacy of medical oppression, Western modes of efficiency that do not align well with other cultural frameworks, and ways of operating within a system of racial capitalism. They describe the need for community-engaged strategies, or exchanges, like community conversations, and listening to and centering the perspectives and experiences of communities of color who have historically been ignored or silenced. These chapters emphasize how university-community partnerships and programs can develop learners' ability to examine issues from a systemic lens, bolster adaptive capacity within communities, and foster more equitable and just practices within systems.

Identity

Identity is critical to personal and system-level understandings of leadership processes (Guthrie et al., 2021). The culturally relevant leadership learning model is a framework for addressing the advantages and disadvantages difference creates (Bertrand Jones et al., 2016); it addresses how external forces influence contexts for leadership development and practice. In complex adaptive systems, patterns emerge from difference. Essential to adaptive action is asking both "What are the differences?" and "What differences make a difference?" (Eoyang & Holladay, 2013). For our authors, aspects of identity that emerged as important within current complexity was related to race and gender.

In Chapter 14, Jesse R. Ford and Brandy S. Propst explored the experiences of Black students navigating racial injustice amplified by the COVID-19 pandemic. They share insights into how leadership educators can engage, support, and retain Black students. Fostering communities of care, acknowledging student identities in educational spaces, and self-care for students and educators are necessary pathways that build critical hope. Brittany Brewster, in Chapter 15, unpacks patterns of hidden tax of leadership for Black women. She describes how advocacy for Black women has served as a gateway for transformation and liberation from suffering within inequitable systems. She offers insight for disrupting the tax, such as centering and celebrating Black womens' experiences leadership and making self-care a core leadership practice.

In Chapter 16, Sherrina S. Lofton points to the historical legacy of athlete activism and the role of athlete activism today, particularly those with African Black identities. Lofton raises critical considerations and important questions for higher education leaders and educators supporting student athletes in their personal and professional development. The chapter offers insight to support student athletes who desire to engage in activism against social injustice.

Brittany Devies and Julie E. Owen, in Chapter 17, illuminate how the COVID-19 exacerbated issues of gender disparities, inequity, and violence on a global scale. They invite readers to interrogate how systems thinking might move everyone closer to embracing feminist leadership to move from disconnection to interconnectedness, toward valuing wholeness and cultivating critical hope. R. J. Youngblood, Tess Hobson, and Roberta Maldonado Franzen take up this challenge in Chapter 18. They explore how leadership educators and developers can equip both themselves and learners with critical perspectives, approaches, and tools to address complex social issues.

Global Context

The last group of chapters highlight the fractal nature of complex adaptive systems—the infinitely complex patterns across different scales (Brown, 2017), as well as the importance of point of view. The pattern of global context may refer to a planet-wide challenge, or it may refer to how that challenge manifests as a local issue in any organization, institution, or community across the world. As is the nature of complexity, the themes of prior sections (expanding dynamic frames, leadership in and through higher education, and identities) are also inextricably connected to and through global context.

In Chapter 19, Yang Li makes a critical case for leading with a global mindset. She unpacks the complexities that makes up a global mindset and how to exercise leadership in an uncertain and changing world. Yi highlights how the constraints of Western-centric thinking limits leaders' ability to recognize and integrate diversity across borders and offers insight for educators to develop a transnational scope in developing the next generation of global leaders.

In Chapter 20, Pei Hu deconstructs complexities of international student leadership experiences on U.S. campuses, highlighting unique challenges during COVID-19 pandemic. There is a need to understand the diverse experiences and cultures of international students, in order to expand opportunities for them. Hu proposes a conceptual framework for international student leadership development that honors cultural identities to create inclusive environments.

In Chapter 21, Trish Gott, Mary Tolar, Salif Kanouti, and Seydi Ndiaye connects the role of higher education to the development of global leaders through programs and partnerships, offering examples from their experience with a leadership development program and grassroots movements in Senegal. "In higher education, by engaging the processes and principles of democracy, we create a container for critical hope, grassroots movements, and leadership education and development" (p. 221).

Onyedikachi Ekwerike also speaks to the power of social movements to create change in justice systems. In Chapter 22, Ewerike shares a case study of #EndSars, a leaderless movement in Nigeria against police brutality. He offers Drath et al.'s (2008) ontological framework of direction, alignment, and commitment to understand the complex nature of leadership enacted within leaderless movements and inform the ways higher education can develop the capacity for people to exercise leadership without power or positional authority.

Finally, in Chapter 23, Kathy L. Guthrie and Kerry L. Priest reflect on the ways these chapters move us from complex problems into patterns. The insight and understanding gained from these chapters and themes become possibilities for ongoing conversation and courageous action.

Collectively Navigating Complexity

Navigating is an action word that implies journey, challenge, and crossing boundaries and borders. The complex conditions created by multiple pandemics reflect what Carse (1986) describes as an "infinite game" –ambiguous boundaries, changing rules, no clear ending, multiple ways to keep score, and shifting positionalities. We can longer approach leadership learning and development as a finite game (conditions of stability and certainty to predict and replicate practice). Instead, we need to culti-vate mindsets and tools that are agile, sensitive, and responsive to com-plexity, change, and disruption. We invite you to join us in engaging with these chapters from an inquiry stance (Holladay & Tytel, 2001). Through curiosity, shared exploration, self-reflection we hope you will discover pat-terns and insight that resonate and challenge your own experiences, find energy to engage the complexities you are facing, generate new questions, and build your adaptive capacity live and work in critical hope and possi-bility.

REFERENCES

Bertrand Jones, T., Guthrie, K. L., & Osteen, L. (2016). Critical domains of cultur-ally relevant leadership learning: A call to transform leadership programs. In K. L. Guthrie, T. Bertrand Jones, & L. Osteen (Eds.), *New Directions for Student Leadership: No. 152. Developing culturally relevant leadership learning* (pp. 9–21). Wiley & Sons. https://doi.org/10.1002/yd.20205

Brown, A. M. (2017). *Emergent strategy: Shaping change, changing worlds*. AK Press.

Carse, J. P. (1986). *Finite and infinite games: A vision of life as play and possibility*. Free Press.

Dugan, J. P. (2017). *Leadership theory: Cultivating critical perspectives*. Jossey-Bass.

Drath, W. H., McCauley, C. D., Palus, C. J., Van Velsor, E., O'Connor, P. M., & McGuire, J. B. (2008). Direction, alignment, commitment: Toward a more integrative ontology of leadership. *The Leadership Quarterly*, *19*(6), 635–653. https://doi.org/10.1016/j.leaqua.2008.09.003

Driscoll, A. (2008). Carnegie's community-engagement classification: Intentions and insights. *Change*, *40*(1), 38–41.

Eoyang, G. H., & Holladay, R. J. (2013). *Adaptive action: Leveraging uncertainty in your organizations*. Stanford University Press.

Freire, P. (1972). *Pedagogy of the oppressed*. Herder and Herder.

Guthrie K. L., & Chunoo, V. S. (2021). *Shifting the mindset: Socially just leadership education*. Information Age.

Guthrie, K. L., Bertrand Jones, T., & Osteen, L. (Eds.). (2016). *New Directions for Student Leadership: No. 152. Developing culturally relevant leadership learning*. Jossey-Bass.

Guthrie, K. L., Beatty, C. C., & Wiborg, E. R. (2021). *Engaging in the leadership pro-cess: Identity, capacity, and efficacy for college students*. Information Age.

Harvey, M., & Jenkins, D. M. (2014). Knowledge, praxis, and reflection: The three critical elements of effective leadership studies programs. *Journal of Leadership Studies*, *7*(4), 76–85. https://doi.org/10.1002/jls.21314

Hazy, J. K., Goldstein, J. A., & Lichtenstein, B. B. (Eds.) (2007). *Complexity systems leadership theory: New perspectives from complexity science on social and organiza-tional effectiveness*. ISCE.

Heifetz, R. A., Linsky, M., & Grashow, A. (2009). *The practice of adaptive leadership: Tools and tactics for changing your organization and the world.* Harvard Business Press.

Holladay, R., & Tytel, M. (2011). *Simple rules: A radical inquiry into self, going beyond self-help to generate self-hope.* Gold Canyon Press.

Human Systems Dynamics Institute. (2016). *Adaptive action.* https://www.hsdinstitute.org/resources/adaptive-action.html

Kolb, D. K. (2015). *Experiential learning: Experience as the source of learning and development* (2nd Ed.). Pearson Education.

Mennin, S., Eoyang, G., & Nations, M. (2020). *Leadership: The future of the health professions workforce.* Human Systems Dynamics Institute.

Stroh, D. P. (2015). *Systems thinking for social change: A practical guide to solving complex problems, avoiding unintended consequences, and achieving lasting results.* Chelsea Green.

Uhl-Bien, M. (2020). Complexity and COVID 19: Leadership and followership in a complex world. *Journal of Management Studies.* https://doi.org/10.1111/joms.12696

Uhl-Bien, M., & Arena, M. (2018). Leadership for organizational adaptability: A theoretical synthesis and integrative framework. *The Leadership Quarterly, 29*(1), 89–104. https://doi.org/10.1016/j.leaqua.2017.12.009

Uhl-Bien, M., & Marion, R. (Eds.). (2008). *Complexity leadership, Part 1: Conceptual foundations.* Information Age Publishing.

van der Steege, M. (2017). Introduction. In R. Elkington, M. van der Steege, J. Glick-Smith, & J. Moss Breen (Eds.), *Visionary leadership in a turbulent world: Thriving in the new VUCA context* (pp. 1–12). Emerald.

Wheatley, M. J. (2006). *Leadership and the new science: Discovering order in a chaotic world* (3rd ed.). Berrett-Koehler.

Wheatley, M. J. (2017). *Who do we choose to be? Facing reality, claiming leadership, restoring sanity.* Berrett-Koehler.

PART I

EXPANDING DYNAMIC LEADERSHIP FRAMES

CHAPTER 2

RAISING CONSCIOUSNESS IN PARADIGM INTERPLAY IN LEADERSHIP

Chelsea D. Shore

Tensions around what constitutes "good" or "bad" leadership affect the relationality between leaders and followers. The perspective of whether something is good, bad, sufficient, or effective lies with our paradigmatic stance—how we view and make sense of the world. It is difficult to openly discuss our perspectives of complexity when the very nature of the complexity is understood and experienced differently; however, a greater understanding can be achieved through a transformative process called paradigm interplay (Uhl-Bien & Ospina, 2012). Paradigm interplay requires engaging in open dialogue with others who hold different assumptions about the nature of reality. Providing clarity of one's perspective allows for new and creative ways to understand leadership from a whole-system view and work through complexity with innovation. This process relates to leadership as it concerns the transactional nature and relationality of leaders-*and*-followers, or leaders-*or*-followers (Uhl-Bien & Ospina, 2012).

This chapter begins with a brief overview of research paradigms, waves of leadership scholarship, and the influential relationship between the two. Next, a synopsis of the innumerable questions being asked through

Navigating Complexities in Leadership: Moving Toward Critical Hope, pp. 17–25
www.infoagepub.com
Copyright © 2022 by Information Age Publishing
All rights of reproduction in any form reserved.

multiple lenses showcases how paradigm interplay (Sanchez et al., 2020) propels us through the complexities add new layers to the leadership process. This chapter concludes by discussing the challenges leaders face when rethinking how to do leadership differently in the face of incomparable times and affords us new ways of relationality between leaders and followers.

LEADERSHIP THROUGH AND BEYOND CURRENT COMPLEXITIES

Leadership researchers and practitioners face what Day and Antonakis (2008) refer to as "a crises" when attempting to package an integrative theoretical framework for leadership. However, accepting that leadership is socially constructed (Dugan, 2017; Uhl-Bien & Ospina, 2012) means that no universal definition of leadership can satisfy every facet or social predicament. To accept the necessity that leadership must be performed differently across disciplines and issues requires us to become comfortable with ambiguity and discomfort. Consider the competing philosophical concepts of absolutism and relativism, as seen in Figure 2.1.

Absolutists believe that absolute principles, or a single truth, exists. This belief is called into question when individuals experience the same physical reality yet ascribe different meanings or interpretations to this reality (Denzin & Lincoln, 2003). On the contrary, relativists believe in overlapping realities; there is no absolute truth. However, the irony of

Figure 2.1

Philosophical Concepts

Absolutism	*Relativism*

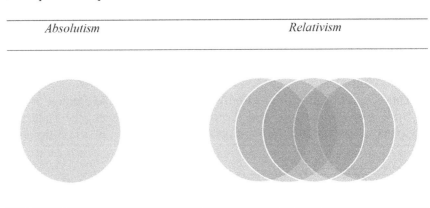

only believing in relativism equates a singular, or absolute, thought. The challenge is not to hold so tightly to the philosophy that one reinforces the limitations of beliefs; instead, relativism creates conditions for the curious exploration of differences that open up possibility. This relates to the process of leadership within current social complexities. Believing there is a best way to do leadership, the way that feels familiar and true, may no longer be sufficient in solving unfamiliar and intersecting crises. Emerging crises require emerging solutions brought about by rethinking and expanding paradigms of leadership studies.

WAVES OF LEADERSHIP

The multifarious history of leadership studies is defined in numerous places (Day & Antonakis, 2008; Dugan, 2017; Owen, 2020; Rost, 1993) and it would be haphazard to repeat it here. However, some background knowledge about the various waves of leadership studies is necessary for answering the guiding questions of this chapter. The "story most often told" (Dugan, 2017) is socially constructed in waves or decades that are not necessarily definitive but rather illustrative of influential theories and aspects of the leadership process. This historic overview is intended to lay the foundation for elevating our consciousness on doing leadership differently as various worldviews are simultaneously at play in the new complexities of here and beyond.

The story most often told begins with the great man theory of the 1900s, which asserted good leaders were born and the thought evolved into good leaders could be taught (Rost, 1993). The 1930s lent attention to group theory, and the 1940s was trait theory, then behavior theory in the 1950s, and situational leadership or contingency theories in the 1960s. By the 1970s, leadership scholars finally packaged the holistic framework of excellence theory which contextualized leaders as having particular traits that allowed them to choose the correct behaviors and do the right things in the right situations with authority which made for good leadership (Rost, 1993). The next era of postindustrial theories includes servant leadership (Greenleaf, 1999), adaptive leadership (Heifetz & Linsky, 2002), relational leadership (Sanchez et al., 2020), and shared leadership. The late 1990s brought about authentic leadership (Miao et al., 2018), emphasizing a moral dimension where leaders' and followers' interactions develop over time. The historical discussion on chaos or systems leadership (Dugan, 2017) covered the relational processes that occurred without control and "within the context of a complex, rapidly changing world" (p. 74). Current fourth wave leadership studies (Owen, 2020) emphasize critical theory and leadership as a social construct to incorporate conversations of "ideology, hegemony, social location, power, and agency in leadership development" (p. 46). The social complexities brought about in 2020 arguably propel our field into a new era that requires a shift in, or expansion of, paradigms that cultivate new knowledge and new practices of doing leadership.

PARADIGMS IN LEADERSHIP STUDIES

Guba and Lincoln (1998) describe paradigms as a belief system based on certain ontological, epistemological, and methodological assumptions representing one's worldview. Ontological questions ask: What is there? And what can be known about it? Epistemological questions inquire about the relationship between the knower and what can be known. And methodological questions advance how knowers uncover whatever they believe can be known. The four commonly referenced paradigms are *positivism*, *post positivism*, *critical theory*, and *constructivism*. Table 2.1 offers an overview of how the paradigms influence presumptions about the nature of leadership.

How leadership is best performed as a process is largely determined from the lens leadership is being viewed; leaders-*and*-followers or leaders-*or*-followers (Uhl-Bien & Ospina, 2012). The social and relational construction of leadership processes requires acknowledging that leadership is an activity between and among people, spaces, and environments. Roles are taken up based on these interactions.

Intersecting or mixing paradigms can generate new or alternative paradigms. For example, Guba and Lincoln (2005) expanded their discussion of paradigms to include a *postmodernism* paradigm that accepts truth as partial due to the unclear referent system of language. It is neither realism nor relativism but rather views science as a social construction (Hosking, 2006). Hosking points out this worldview has had little attention from leadership studies but can "open us up to multiple, simultaneous, realities such as power-to and participatory ontology" (p. 252). What is lacking in the literature is this bridge in language for how competing paradigms inform one another (Fairhurst & Grant, 2010; Hosking, 2006; Sanchez et al., 2020). The question is not, *what questions should we be asking during this new era?* But instead, it is, *how can we ask current questions in ways that bridge the language between competing paradigms of thought?* The next section of this chapter explores how approaching leadership with an open mind for intersecting paradigms can stimulate praxis within the field.

Table 2.1

Overview of Paradigms in Leadership Studies

Paradigm	Ontological Assumption	Epistemological Assumptions	Methodological Assumptions	Presumption About Leadership*
Positivism	Naïve realism: reality is absolute	Objectivist: research findings are true	Quantitative; hypothesis testing	"Goal of leadership research/theory is to provide prescriptive answers"
Postpositivism	Critical realism: we can only know reality to the extent that our methods work	Objectivist: research findings are probably true	Hypothesis testing using mixed methods	Leadership theory provides prescriptive answers to the leadership process with some margin of nuance
Critical theory	Historical realism: culture shapes how we can know reality	Subjectivist: values mediate the findings	Qualitative; dialogue	"Leadership is relational … attention paid to interactions between people in processes"
Constructivism	Relativism: reality is dependent upon social location; fluid	Subjectivist: Research findings were created	Qualitative; hermeneutical	"Power is central to leadership … leadership is defined by and reflects values/beliefs of dominant groups"
Postmodernism	Stratified relativism: objectivity and universalism are impossible	Subjectivist: reality is constructed by how meanings of social world are reproduced	Qualitative; phenomenological	Leadership and its "relative values are challenged to disrupt status quo … built on contradictory concepts"

Note: *Dugan (2017, p. 31).

PARADIGM INTERPLAY:
THE PRAXIS OF RAISING CONSCIOUSNESS

Romani et al. (2011) describe paradigm interplay as "a respectful interaction between analyses performed in different paradigms … that builds upon the tension created by the simultaneous consideration of how the analyses are connected and what differentiates them" (p. 433). They highlight a three-step process: (1) conduct an analysis in preferred paradigm,

(2) contrast with counter analysis in competing paradigm, and (3) assess interaction to indicate possible improvements. Simply put, leaders must critically analyze the problems they face from their preferred worldview then discuss their conclusions with followers and other leaders in similar positions in a way that is open and receptive to new or differing interpretations regarding the performance of leadership. The final step is to perform leadership differently by incorporating diverse understandings of the problem. The incorporation of paradigm interplay into research need not follow this exact structure; but, it is discussed here as a reference to an evidence-based tool for confronting procedural issues of leadership in unprecedented times and at an unwavering intersection of events.

Working through an interplay of paradigms to promote diversity within the field of leadership studies can evolve more tangible implications for leadership theory (Sanchez et al., 2020). Table 2.2 works through this exercise by exhibiting questions asked by various leaders across three social movements: (a) the global pandemic COVID-19, (b) social injustice related to the Black Lives Matter movement (Freelon et al., 2016), and (c) civil unrest during a national election. It is not an exhaustive list of questions, but it is a starting point generated from major news stories and conversations with leaders of each identity group.

Answering each question, individually, through one paradigmatic lens most certainly adds depth to understanding the problem. However, we are not experiencing one problem at one time; each of these dimensions are simultaneously intertwined by leaders, followers, organizations, and communities with varying degrees of salience. Engaging in paradigm interplay facilitates thinking paradoxically and entertaining conflicting truths about each question posed. Each layer of complexity changes the question being asked. As Lewis and Kelemen (2002) affirm, "postmodern philosophers ignore everyone; functionalist ignore workers; critical theorists ignore managers ... multiparadigm inquiry strives to respect opposing approaches and juxtapose the partial understandings to inspire ... reality is at once 'made' and 'in the making'" (p. 358). For example, at the intersection of the presidential election and the COVID-19 global pandemic, higher education leaders ask *Who will control Congress? What will it mean for COVID-19 relief for schools?* Likewise, the two presidential candidates of 2020 fundamentally differed on their opinions of racial inequality and law enforcement, thus creating another layer of complexity that germinates the question, *what are the candidate's opinions on protecting officers during the coronavirus pandemic?* Using Table 2.2 as an example, we cannot look at each column or row of questions individually (as an absolutist) because the social movements are happening simultaneously (such as in relativism). Paradigm interplay can be as simple as engaging in

Table 2.2

Visualizing Questions at the Interplay of Complexities

Perspective	COVID-19	Black Lives Matter	Political Unrest/ Election Year
Higher ed leaders	Who's liable for COVID-19 testing of students? Staff? Faculty?	How do we contribute to systemic oppression and marginalization? What can we do to address issues of racism on our campus?	Will this be a pivot point for federal education priorities?
Students	How do I self-isolate in a dorm? How will I get food if I self-isolate in group housing?	How are institutions assessing current practices in an effort to dismantle racist and racially charge requirements for admission (i.e., ACT/ SAT scores, GRE)?	Can a university revoke my admission for posting a TikTok that supports Trump?
Public health leaders	How can we persuade public adherence to protectionary social distancing and hygiene practices?	How can we ensure that BIPOC community members have access to quality healthcare in their neighborhoods? What role does the FDA play in all of this?	How does each candidate plan to address the Affordable Care Act, care for older Americans and pharmaceutical drug pricing? (Firth & Frieden, 2020)
Community members	When will my business reopen?	When do Black Lives Matter?	Does my vote by mail count?
Law enforcement	How can we get personal protective equipment when they are in short supply?	Why is this even a movement? How can we relate to our communities without misuse of power?	What are each candidate's policing proposals and opinions on use of force?

open, receptive dialogue with our peers at various layers and intersectionality with an empathetic viewpoint.

COCONSTRUCTING THE LEADERSHIP PROCESS

Now, amid intricate, complicated, and intertwined social complexities, the relationality between leaders and followers becomes paramount in the process of leadership. The social construction of leadership accounts for multiple truths and emphasizes relationality and materiality; these considerations open up greater possibilities for people to learn from and with one another. Coconstructing the leadership process requires recognizing how people are leaders-*as*-followers. Leadership processes are community-based (Sanchez et al., 2020), where followers have an equal voice in how leadership is performed. Paradigm interplay incorporating assumptions from postmodernism (Lewis & Kelemen, 2002) and critical theory (Dugan, 2017) allows for multiple truths. A new moral ethic (Greenleaf, 1999) is cultivated when leadership empowers the voices of followers. Educators assume a new paradigm, leader-*as*-follower, when as leaders we ask what our followers need in the leadership process and can imagine a role shift across social complexities through conscious empathy.

Individuals look to leaders to guide the way, to use prior experiences to show us how to navigate the current situation, but there is no roadmap for leaders in unprecedented times. Leaders have no leaders; and if they are not leaders, then they must be followers, but if there is no roadmap, who will they follow? Leadership then, becomes cocreated between leaders-*and*-followers through leaders-*as*-followers and is centered upon the immediate community; *What do we need now to feel safe, supported, and empowered? What can be said or done in the immediate environment to reduce uncertainty?* This is especially true in higher education, particularly as leadership educators. As educators, we cannot broaden our perspective too much that we lose touch with the individual experiences in our immediate interaction. Instead, we must address our immediate space before we can generalize leadership processes in the context of higher education and beyond. Active dialogues between leaders and followers or leaders and leaders across social movements can illuminate how each individual is experiencing the current complex and intersecting reality by painting a holistic road map for moving forward with new ways of doing leadership.

REFERENCES

Day, D. V., & Antonakis, J. (2008). Leadership: Past, present, and future. In J. Antonakis & D. V. Day (Eds.), *The nature of leadership* (pp. 3–26). SAGE. https://www.doi.org/10.4135/9781506395029.n1

Denzin, N. K., & Lincoln, Y. S. (2003). *9/11 in American culture (Crossroads in qualitative inquiry)*. AltaMira Press.

Dugan, J. P. (2017). *Leadership theory: Cultivating critical perspectives*. Jossey-Bass.

Fairhurst, G. T., & Grant, D. (2010). The social construction of leadership: A sailing guide. *Management Communication Quarterly*, *24*(2), 171–210. https://doi.org/10.1177/0893318909359697

Firth, S., & Frieden, J. (2020). *What will a Biden or Trump victory mean for healthcare? | MedPage Today*. https://www.medpagetoday.com/washington-watch/election-coverage/89488

Freelon, D., McIlwain, C. D., & Clark, M. D. (2016). Beyond the hashtags: #Ferguson, #Blacklivesmatter, and the online struggle for offline justice. *SSRN Electronic Journal*. https://doi.org/10.2139/ssrn.2747066

Greenleaf, R. K. (1999). *The power of servant-leadership: Essays*. Berrett-Koehler.

Guba, E. G., & Lincoln, Y. S. (1998). *Competing paradigms in qualitative research*. In N. K. Denzin & Y. S. Lincoln (Eds.), *The landscape of qualitative research: Theories and issues* (pp. 195–220). SAGE.

Guba, E. G., & Lincoln, Y. S. (2005). *Paradigmatic controversies, contradictions and emerging confluences*. In N. K. Denzin & Y. S. Lincoln (Eds.), *The SAGE handbook of qualitative research* (pp. 191–215). SAGE.

Heifetz, R., & Linsky, M. (2002). *Leadership on the line: Staying alive through the dangers of change*. Harvard Business Press.

Hosking, D. M. (2006). Not leaders, not followers: A post-modern discourse of leadership processes. In B. Shamir, R. Pillai, M. C. Bligh, & M. Uhl-Bien (Eds.), *Follower-centered perspectives on leadership: A tribute to the memory of James R. Meindl* (pp. 243–263). Information Age.

Lewis, M. W., & Kelemen, M. L. (2002). Multiparadigm inquiry: Exploring organizational pluralism and paradox. *Human Relations, 55*(2), 251–275. https://doi.org/10.1177/0018726702055002185

Miao, C., Humphrey, R. H., & Qian, S. (2018). Emotional intelligence and authentic leadership: A meta-analysis. *Leadership & Organization Development Journal, 39*(5), 679–690. https://doi.org/10.1108/LODJ-02-2018-0066

Owen, J. E. (2020). *We are the leaders we've been waiting for*. Stylus.

Romani, L., Primecz, H., & Topçu, K. (2011). Paradigm interplay for theory development: A methodological example with the Kulturstandard method. *Organizational Research Methods, 14*(3), 432–455. https://doi.org/10.1177/1094428109358270

Rost, J. C. (1993). *Leadership for the twenty-first century*. Praeger.

Sanchez, I. D., Ospina, S. M., & Salgado, E. (2020). Advancing constructionist leadership research through paradigm interplay: An application in the leadership-trust domain. *Leadership, 16*(6). 683–711. https://doi.org/10.1177/1742715020919226

Uhl-Bien, M., & Ospina, S. M. (Eds.). (2012). *Advancing relational leadership theory: A dialogue among perspectives*. Information Age.

CHAPTER 3

TENSIONS IN SUSTAINABILITY LEADERSHIP

**Rian Satterwhite, Kate Sheridan,
and Whitney McIntyre Miller**

The current context in which we learn, teach, and practice leadership is liminal—a transition space between deeply charged social, political, and economic systems and patterns, and visions of a more collective, humane, just future. In this postmodern context, sustainability is not only a paradigmatic complex problem in itself, it also serves as a framework for the many systemic complex issues in our world, those that are both global and local, individual and collective, and urgent yet slow to change (Satterwhite et al., 2020). Several large international organizations such as the United Nations (2015), World Bank, and World Economic Forum (2020) use sustainability as a core framework for defining and better understanding interwoven complex issues such as education, gender inequality, distribution of wealth, food access and security, holistic wellness, environmental health and justice, and community development. Sustainability itself shapes and is shaped by the way other complex problems are defined, persist, and are addressed. It is a complex container that holds both the complexity of these interdependent issues and the mindsets needed to begin to address them.

This chapter builds upon Priority 5 of the National Leadership Education Research Agenda 2020–2025, which explored the nature of address-

Navigating Complexities in Leadership: Moving Toward Critical Hope, pp. 27–37
www.infoagepub.com

Copyright © 2022 by Information Age Publishing
All rights of reproduction in any form reserved.

ing complex challenges by framing sustainability as a representative complex challenge (Satterwhite et al., 2020). In this chapter, we begin with a discussion of sustainability as an exemplar complex issue. Then, we propose and describe a tensions model as a framework for leadership which incorporates existing dualities of our world. Finally, we offer resources for leadership educators eager to provide for students wishing to engage in the work of leadership.

CENTERING SUSTAINABILITY

As presented in the National Leadership Education Research Agenda 2020–2025 Priority 5 (Satterwhite et al., 2020), sustainability is a frame that centers the biosphere and integrates anthropocentric and ecocentric ideals, builds collaboration across boundaries, develops systems literacy, employs criticality and critical theory, expands time horizons, lives within uncertainty, learns from nature, moves toward cocreation, nurtures adaptive capacity, and honors wisdom from Indigenous and non-Western traditions. The United Nations (2015) defines sustainability as "meeting the needs of the present without compromising the ability of future generations to meet their own needs" (para. 1), which presents a tension between the present and the future; the felt and articulated needs of individuals, communities, and societies in the present versus the unknown but anticipated needs of our descendants. Effective sustainability leadership must inherently navigate these tensions by holding multiple truths and becoming better at leading from multiple perspectives.

Criticality: Tensions Between Critique and Action

Criticality offers another frame for balancing tensions when practicing sustainability leadership. There has been a flurry of work in leadership studies in recent years engaging with critical social theory; yet, Dugan's (2018) assertion still rings true: that "far too often critical perspectives continue to be relegated to the background or met with overt resistance in leadership studies" (p. 5). Utilizing critical theory demands asking uncomfortable questions about hidden assumptions in our work. According to Bronner (2011), critical theory "questions the hidden assumptions and purposes of competing theories and existing forms of practice … [it is] concerned not merely with how things [are] but how they might and should be" (pp. 1–2).

Imagining how things might and should be is a powerful invitation to action and an essential element of sustainability leadership. Western

(2013) further charges that the purpose of critical theory is to "study power and knowledge relations, to challenge dominating structures, and also to prevent leadership becoming another instrumental project, serving only to promote greater efficiency, productivity, profit, with little reflection on its wider impact on society" (p. 8).

Here we suggest that leadership educators must not only be concerned with the wider impact of leadership practice on society, but also on the planet. What does it actually mean to move to a social and economic system that sustains life, affirms equity, dismantles systems of oppression, and advances justice? How might we engage in the work to do so? Two of the essential tools for this critical leadership work are found in the intertwined processes of deconstruction and reconstruction. Deconstruction, the act of examining implicit beliefs and assumptions about that which we hold as true, makes space for the act of reconstruction: recovering, recreating, and evolving knowledge and theory toward justice and equity (Dugan, 2017). Here we find another tension to hold between the processes of deconstruction and reconstruction themselves and what they represent: critique and the often difficult, iterative work of change sustained by a grounded, dogged critical hope in the future.

TENSIONS LEADERSHIP MODEL:
LIVING AND LEADING IN TENSION

Many contemporary resources on leadership highlight how the dominant, mechanistic paradigms have failed us in current, complex environments; but, they do not offer clear tools to move past deep uncertainty and collective anxiety to an envisioned future. Living and leading in tensions build an effective bridge between the strides we have made under existing paradigms and the new paradigms to which we are moving. By learning to live and lead in tension, we can make space for both the known and unknown, failure and learning, logical processes and emotional responses. We can let less useful models fall away and still carry forward that which nurtures or supports emerging paradigms.

The tensions leadership model (Figure 3.1) provides a framework for making the connections within the leadership tensions explicit while still posing questions of *how*: How can we acknowledge and embrace what works about our current ways of being and allow them to help guide us into more ideal future states? How can we give ourselves permission, individually and collectively, to engage in the messiness of this process? How can we sit with both urgency to move quickly and faith that we are moving in the right direction?

Figure 3.1

Tensions Leadership Model

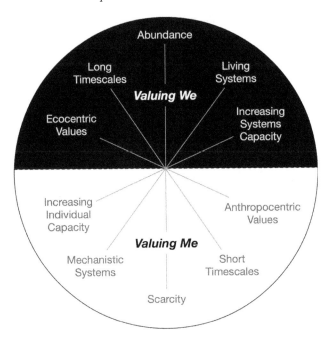

We are often uncomfortable sitting between two dichotomous ideas or perspectives. This means we frequently err on the same patterns of thought rather than embrace the in-between, trusting that doing so will bring us important change. Cultivating the capacity to navigate this ambiguous in-between space is crucial. Through the tensions leadership model, we acknowledge the need to value and question current ways of being and connect current states with those that better allow us to sit with complex issues. The tensions between the values in this framework are characterized by and bridged through (a) dialectical thinking and problem solving (the ability to hold multiple and sometimes competing truths); (b) criticality and critical hope (the ability to honestly assess and understand the problems we face while maintaining a grounded hope in our ability to meet these challenges); and (c) a commitment to shared work that spans generations.

The model does not represent all implicit values underlying our current social, political, economic, and environmental conditions. Many of the values not included are those that we believe should be discarded because they do not serve our collective humanity. The current paradigms and values included in the framework are those that must be recalibrated, limited, and contextualized, but that which we should not lose entirely. It is easy to see how they represent fundamental, ever-present values that have run amok.

Increasing individual capacity (captured best in traditional education models, professional development, and life-long learning) is limited in scope but still essential. When applied in the correct contexts, mechanistic thinking is incredibly useful and has driven problem solving and exploration of the world in recent centuries. Scarcity, when harnessed appropriately, gifts us urgency and drives innovation. Short timescales have become all consuming, limiting our ability to see beyond the horizon and dream big; however, they also ground us in the present reality and root us in our lived experience. Anthropocentric values—centering humans—should not be set aside (if that were even possible). However, these values must be expanded and challenged with a frank recognition of our place within, dependence upon, and responsibility to natural systems.

In contrast with these established paradigms of the present, alternative values and mindsets help decenter the dominant ways of structuring the world. Increasing systems capacity enables us to better ensure that the benefit and purpose of continuous learning and adaptive capacity extend to the communities and organizations we are a part of, not just individual learners. Embracing living systems frameworks breaks us free from the limitations of a mechanistic mindset, enabling new ways of thinking and problem solving by learning from nature. Operating with a sense of abundance balances the limitations of scarcity and recognizes the riches that surround us. Operating within and valuing long timescales help us to appreciate and protect the rights of future generations. Ecocentric values present a vital alternative to the absolute supremacy of operating as though we are the principle or only beings of value.

In this framework, all elements are necessary: they reflect the need to balance opposing thoughts, needs, and actions in response to complex issues rather than choosing among opposing viewpoints. As such, this is not a model of transition from one worldview to another, but rather one of expansion to better represent the whole and build our capacity to hold multiple truths.

Living and leading in tension requires learning to navigate significant and often continuous disequilibrium. These ideas are not unknown to us; we cultivate our capacity for holding competing truths throughout our lifespan. By middle age, most adults have had to make multiple decisions about their life's journey that require weighing significant competing values: a job offer that requires deciding between a salary and a desired geographic location; determining which educational path to pursue based on financial access or the ability to fulfill family responsibilities; political decisions that may require voting for one ideological belief and against another; and many decisions that may be much more personal, impactful, and deeply held. Indeed, adult development is very much characterized by the capacity to hold an expanding sphere of values that both enrich and complicate our lives. Choices between these values, even those with positive outcomes, may instill in us a sense of loss or regret at the path not taken (Wilber, 2005).

It should be noted that balance does not equate to harmony. Holding or seeking balance within these tensions is inherently disruptive and unsettling. We must dwell within and increase our tolerance for processes of discomfort. In order to successfully reshape our social world in a way that integrates responsiveness to these tensions, our focus should be enhancing our capacity to hold complex tensions inherent in our work. Included in this may be knowing the problems are big, wanting to help, but not knowing where to start. To exist as a self-actualized human being requires the ability to hold tensions, which speaks to the value of this work in leadership, particularly in creating a more sustainable and peaceful world.

Living Within Scarcity and Abundance

The global and U.S. economies can be characterized as overwhelmingly extractive: economies that are viewed as places "from which wealth – resources, money, labor, [et cetera]—can be extracted" (Goerner, 2015, p. 2). Over time, "extraction and corruption naturally lead to an ever-more fragile real economy" (Goerner, 2015, p. 2), creating or contributing to problems elsewhere in the social systems of which they are a part. Such an economic reality cultivates a mindset of scarcity and individual competition, which, when balanced, can contribute to the vitality of a free market, but when significantly imbalanced, creates entrenched poverty, diminishes the middle class, and continues the upward flow of wealth while neglecting critical social systems. The scarcity mindset that results from this kind of economic system creates oppressive thought patterns (ideology) that are difficult to overcome when individuals fear being unable to meet basic needs. It is difficult to invest in the future when present needs are threatened. Moving toward a regenerative economic and social system, which cycles resources back into economic, social, and human systems, can create greater vitality and long-term learning and contribute to a collective mindset of abundance. We should operate with humility in the face of natural resources that are scarce and finite and preserve those elements of the economy that generate broad wealth, with a lens toward shifting to economies and mindsets that distribute resources that feed back into economic and social systems.

Embracing Short and Long Timescales

In our 2016 article, "Rediscovering Deep Time" (Satterwhite et al.), we highlighted how leadership theory and practice have long avoided an in-depth discussion of time scales. We shared how we often think of short-term or long-term time, frequently ignoring the nuances, complexities, and depth of time, which are essential in effective decision-making processes, particularly in sustainability leadership. In that article, we proposed a framework for appreciating multiple time scales, which includes (a) present time, that which is 5 years from now; (b) near time, that which encompasses 5 years to several decades; (c) distant time, which is roughly 80–100 years or spanning a few generations; and finally, (d) deep time, which bookends the spectrum and encourages all of us to think about distant hopes and fears for the future and the deep generations of the past. Deep time is multigenerational and is often cited as a seven-generation perspective (though it extends far past that). We propose that leadership scholars and practitioners should consider each level of time in their decision-making processes.

Goleman (2014) also encouraged leading for the long future by changing systems and engaging in big picture leadership. However, the challenge with time is holding both the present and near time in mind while also considering the impacts of distant and deep time. We exist in the tension of having to make decisions today, while understanding these decisions will have lasting impacts on the future, all while knowing that everything informing our decision making is based upon the past. Therefore, those in leadership roles must wrestle with the notion that present-day leadership requires reflection of the past and a constant eye toward the future.

Focusing on Anthropocentric and Ecocentric Values

What we choose to prioritize, and how, has great importance, especially when focusing on our planet and its people. This tension reflects the priorities and needs of humans; our systems, structures, and cultural assumptions; and the priorities and needs of our planet, or the ecosystem(s) that embed and surround us. Anthropocentric values focus solely on the needs of the people who live on this planet. These values prioritize the survival and thriving of humanity. On the other hand, ecocentric values put the focus on our planet, prioritizing the health of ecosystems. Within this tension, we challenge leadership scholars and practitioners to find the balance between anthropocentric and ecocentric values, prioritizing not one over the other but instead finding harmony among these values—ways to thrive as humans with our planet, not in spite of it or by abusing it. Bill Plotkin (2015) speaks to this in his eco-soulcentric development work by stating that fully developed adults experience themselves as members of the Earth community first and human communities second. By considering people *and* the planet, we find ways to align these interests. For example, we may not all be able to live "off the grid." Still, we can invest in renewable energy and infrastructure, ensure that we are limiting our waste, reducing our consumption, recycling all qualifying items, and perhaps most importantly pressuring the systems we are a part of to change systemically.

Operating Within Mechanistic and Living Systems

One of the powers of dominant paradigms—or to adapt the terminology of critical theory: hegemony and ideology—is that we are frequently operating with it even when we do not consciously know it. Such is the power of a mechanistic worldview, which has held sway in Western thought for centuries. Capra and Luisi (2014) explain that the terms "Cartesian," "mechanistic," and "reductionist" can be used interchangeably. All three terms refer to a scientific paradigm crafted by René Descartes in the 17th century in which the universe is seen as a machine. The legacy of this paradigm is both profound and troubling. It has helped to shape and advance innumerable scientific discoveries, significantly advancing understanding of the world. It has also been used as justification for atrocities, both specific and systemic. Living systems, however, is a framework that arises from closely attending to resilient natural systems. It can balance the benefits of the mechanistic worldview while limiting its myopic and problematic impact, focusing on regenerativity. A living systems framework helps us navigate, design, and protect the short-term needs and long-term goals in the systems we are a part of without discarding entirely the benefits that mechanistic thinking has brought.

Increasing Individual and Systems Capacity

Many recent and emergent constructs and applications of leadership identify systems thinking as a critical capacity for both individuals and communities. The ability to distinguish patterns, see deep interconnection, operate nonlinearly, and recognize relationships is increasingly critical to framing and addressing complex problems, such as sustainability. Systems thinking precipitates greater innovation, resilience, and capacity for change, which are critical capacities for navigating the uncertainty of complex problems. "Systems citizenship," as framed by Senge et al. (2008), reflects the ability of a system to conceive of and enact leadership that is the responsibility of the entire system rather than a select few. Similarly, Heifetz (2006) argues that in the "medium and long term, leadership generates new cultural norms that enable people to meet an ongoing stream of adaptive challenges, realities, and pressures likely to come" (p. 76). In both of these framings, leadership is found in the capacity of systems.

As we seek to address complex problems like sustainability, it is crucial that we operate from a systems lens and on behalf of the systems we are a part of; but, we must also do this as individual actors with greater systems literacy. Social systems are, after all, composed of individual actors. We have long ignored the systems dynamics at play in leadership processes but must not lose the importance of individuals as we expand our view. Successfully living and leading in tension with individual and systems capacity will increase our resilience, innovation, and capacity for change. We must center both the individual and the system simultaneously.

IMPLICATIONS OF LIVING AND LEADING WITHIN THE TENSIONS

We are often pulled between poles—between two elements that are both simultaneously true. It is within the tensions of living and leading *in between* these poles that draws our attention here. Navigating these liminal spaces requires new navigational toolkits. As leadership scholars, practitioners, and educators, we must embrace the uncertainty that these tensions provide and do the immense work of finding our place within them—and helping learners do the same—to ensure that we are leading and living for positive, systemic change. Reflecting on where one naturally sits within these tensions, and using feedback from personal and shared reflections to build consciousness, can bring to conscious awareness our natural defaults. Cognitive tools, such as mapping, allow learners to plot their location along these tension spectrums to make conscious choices for the growth and realignment they may wish to pursue in a given tension.

It is the role of leadership scholars, practitioners, and educators to help provide the developmental space through self-reflection and assessment for our next generation of leaders to get us closer to the goal and engage in more sustainable practices and processes on the way. These tensions present an essential foundation for reconstruction and for cultivating critical leadership skills. The skills needed to effectively respond to the wicked challenges that we face—outlined previously, not the least of which is increasing our comfort with ambiguity—are the same that are nurtured by learning to live and lead in tension.

CRITICAL HOPE FOR TENSIONS LEADERSHIP

Criticality and critical hope invite us to navigate between established beliefs, behaviors, assumptions, ideas, and perspectives not represented within those constructs. They present a tension space for us to sit within and help us cultivate the ability to tolerate that tension and the discomfort of moving between points of perceived certainty. Regarding sustainability and the tensions presented in this chapter, criticality and critical hope present important frameworks and platforms for discovering collective ways to move forward and build on practices that have greatly served the progress we have made as a global community. Criticality and critical hope remind us that learning, leadership, and collective evolution are an infinite continuum that we must continue to evaluate and critique as we move through more holistic ways of being, living, and leading. This practice is equally critical for sustainability, ensuring that the approaches we develop to address this wicked problem do not themselves become the ingrained practices and mindsets that get us stuck in damaging patterns.

REFERENCES

Bronner, S. E. (2011). *Critical theory: A very short introduction*. Oxford University Press.

Capra, F., & Luisi, P. L. (2014). *The systems view of life: A unifying vision*. Cambridge University Press.

Dugan, J. (2017). *Leadership theory: Cultivating critical perspectives*. Jossey-Bass.

Dugan, J. (Ed.). (2018). Editor's notes. In *New Directions for Student Leadership: No. 159*. Integrating critical perspectives into leadership development (pp. 1–4). Jossey-Bass. https://doi.org/10.1002/yd.20293

Goerner, S. (2015, September 1). *Regenerative development: The art and science of creating durably vibrant human networks*. Capital Institute. http://capitalinstitute.org/

Goleman, D. (2014). Leading for the long future. *Leader to Leader, 2014*(72), 34–39.

Heifetz, R. (2006). Anchoring leadership in the work of adaptive progress. In F. Hesselbein & M. Goldsmith (Eds.), *The leader of the future 2: Visions, strategies, and practices for the new era* (pp. 73–84). Jossey-Bass.

Plotkin, B. (2015). A short introduction to the eco-soulcentric developmental wheel: Stages of life, rites of passage, and cultural transformation. https://www.animas.org/wp-content/uploads/Intro-to-ESDW-for-Animas-website.pdf

Satterwhite, R., Sheridan, K., & McIntyre Miller, W. (2016). Rediscovering deep time: Sustainability and the need to re-engage with multiple dimensions of time in leadership studies. *Journal of Leadership Studies, 9*(4), 47–53. https://doi.org/10.1002/jls.21426

Satterwhite, R., Sarid, A., Cunningham, C. M., Goryunova, E., Crandall, H. M., Morrison, J. L., Sheridan, K., & McIntyre Miller, W. (2020). Contextualizing our leadership education approach to complex problem solving: Shifting paradigms and evolving knowledge–Priority 5 of the National Leadership Education Research Agenda 2020–2025. *Journal of Leadership Studies, 14*(3), 63–71. https://doi.org/10.1002/jls.21717

Senge, P., Smith, B., Kruschwitz, N., Laur, J., & Schley, L. (2008). *The necessary revolution: How individuals and organizations are working together to create a sustainable world.* Doubleday.

United Nations. (2015). *Transforming our world: The 2030 agenda for sustainable development.* https://sustainabledevel-opment.un.org/post2015/transformingourworld/publication

Western, S. (2013). *Leadership: A critical text* (2nd ed.). SAGE.

Wilber, K. (2005). Introduction to integral theory and practice: IOS Basic and the AQAL map. *AQAL: Journal of Integral Theory and Practice, 1*(1), 1–36.

World Economic Forum. (2020). *The global risks report 2020.* https://www.weforum.org/reports/the-global-risks-report-2020

CHAPTER 4

PREPARING LEADERSHIP ACTIVITY AT THE INTERSECTION OF LIFE AND POLITICS

Brandon W. Kliewer

Efforts to account for and unpack antecedent ontological assumptions are essential to meaningful leadership learning and development. Ontological assumptions assign boundaries to conceptual categories, determine what type of analysis is available to a particular knowledge claim, and is essential to evaluating the relationship between a knowledge claim and fit within specific conceptual categories. Ontological assumptions are never neutral elements of leadership learning, development, and practice; instead, they represent choices about what is included—and what is left out—in the conceptual boundaries of leadership. Leadership learning and application can be improved by acknowledging ontological assumptions operating in learning and development experiences, especially in interdisciplinary contexts connected to some conception of the common good.

The purpose of this chapter is to reconsider the ontological basis of leadership learning and development through a biopolitical lens. First, biopolitics is offered as one possible political ontology that is related to

Navigating Complexities in Leadership: Moving Toward Critical Hope, pp. 39–46
www.infoagepub.com
Copyright © 2022 by Information Age Publishing
All rights of reproduction in any form reserved.

civic and common good frames of leadership. Next, I explore the relevance of biopolitics to leadership learning and development. Finally, I will describe practical implications for attending to bipolitical questions in leadership learning and development experiences that attempt to advance critical hope.

BIOPOLITICS AS AN ONTOLOGICAL LENS: FRAMING THE COMMON GOOD

The ontologies that inform concepts associated with leadership learning and development are wide ranging. The diversity of ontological entry points in leadership learning and development create theoretical and practical tensions. These tensions have implications for how leadership is taught, learned, developed, studied, and exercised. Educators and trainers can improve their practice by connecting teaching methods, content, and curriculum to an ontological foundation.

Recent global events have made antecedent ontological assumptions associated with leadership learning and practice even more pronounced for leadership developers. One political ontology useful to leadership developers is biopolitics. Simply, biopolitics is an analytical and ontological framework that considers the relationship between life and politics. Biopolitical questions consider how operations of power define the boundaries and quality of choice necessary to sustain life.

The COVID-19 pandemic, associated government responses, vaccine development and roll-out efforts, and systems and institutional arrangements that determine different levels of exposure to the virus have biopolitical implications. The contemporary moment has also included increased attention to state-sanctioned violence against Brown and Black bodies. Biopolitics provides a lens to contrast state-sanctioned violence against Brown and Black bodies with the apparent restraint state authority is often able to access when confronting White bodies. For example, during the January 6, 2021 insurrection, White supremacists and alt-right ethnonationalists stormed the U.S. Capitol and delayed Congress from convening a constitutionally mandated meeting. The circumstances seemed to allow White bodies associated with ethnonationalist/alt-right insurrectionists to avoid state violence. In other circumstances that challenge state authority and sovereignty, like the border crisis, we have seen examples of unjust detention and murders at the hands of law enforcement agents. These contrasting circumstances and outcomes raise a series of biopolitical questions for leadership developers and associated common good leadership frames. Leadership teaching methods, content, and curriculum ought to account for biopolitical ontologies in order to better prepare learners to advance nuanced conceptions of the common good.

A biopolitical ontology, particularly as it relates to calls for recognition and justice, is not new. Issues associated with the COVID-19 pandemic, the U.S. border crisis, unjust police murders, and White supremacy have refocused the relevance of biopolitics for leadership learners and developers. These contemporary issues have awakened broader attention to the intersection of biopolitical questions, civic action, and justice. Leadership developers would be remiss not to adjust their lens and practice accordingly. Generic curricular claims to "civic leadership" or "the common good" deserve to be revisited with fresh eyes. For the purpose of this chapter, "civic" is understood to include social (civil society), political (governing systems and institutions), economic (systems that produce and distribute goods and services), and moral spheres (public virtues) of society (Berger, 2011). Leadership for the common good is the continuous effort to define the proper relationship and size of each of these civic spheres (Allen & Somanathan, 2020). In practice, the common good is ephemeral and something that is always already an unfinished project. Leadership activity that remakes systems and institutions through productive contestation is how the common good is advanced, and the requirements of justice are met (Mouffe, 2013). Leadership developers can revisit civic leadership for the common good by unpacking antecedent (political) ontological assumptions that give meaning to core leadership learning and development concepts and experiences through a biopolitical lens.

Teachers and trainers rely on underlying assumptions to set conceptual boundaries and determine what ought to be considered appropriate knowledge within a specific orientation to leadership learning. Underlying assumptions about what leadership is, and what the conceptual boundaries of learning and development include, are linked to antecedent ontological assumptions. These underlying assumptions are sometimes consciously addressed within a leadership learning and development experience, yet often they remain unacknowledged. Intentionally identifying and unpacking antecedent ontological assumptions establishes a solid knowledge and practice foundation for leadership learning and development.

For example, a leader development model that assumes the phenomenon of leadership includes *leader, followers*, and *shared purpose* is just one way, among many, to set the boundaries of what should be considered in the phenomenon of leadership (Drath et al., 2008). Collective or relational orientations to leadership rely on another set of antecedent ontological assumptions that emphasize relational interaction between people, dialogic exchange, and specific sociomaterial relationships (Raelin, 2016). Trainers and educators can improve their practice by acknowledging when and where antecedent ontological assumptions impact and shape their decisions about teaching methods, content, and even the contextual or cultural appropriateness of learning and development included in a specific leadership ontology. Biopolitics is a helpful lens for trainers and educators interested in deconstructing the antecedent ontological assumptions informing their understanding of leadership, approach to teaching leadership, application of leadership activity.

In U.S. higher education contexts, the discourse of "civic" leadership and "leadership for the common good" has found broad acceptance; a frame often operating under the auspices of socially conscious leadership or the social change model of leadership development (Higher Education Research Institute, 1996; Komives & Wagner, 2017). The National Clearinghouse for Leadership Programs and the Multi-Institutional Study of Leadership have helped advance socially responsible leadership learning and development opportunities across the United States. Wide acceptance of leadership learning and development efforts in higher education that work to develop civic-minded graduates and advance the common good ought to be celebrated (Priest & Clegorne, 2015). It is a testament to the hard work practitioners, faculty, and administration have made when institutionalizing leadership learning and development in various spaces of higher education.

However, the field has reached a maturity that makes it appropriate to identify and interrogate the antecedent ontological assumptions of existing curriculum, practices, and experiences. This is not a call to jettison the civic project of leadership; instead, an encouragement to explore available growth opportunities. Practitioners, programs, and more generally the field, have the potential to develop a more nuanced ontology. Ultimately, accounting for a biopolitical ontology in leadership learning and development experiences will deepen the ways learners engage questions of leadership for the common good and define conceptual boundaries of leadership learning and development practice.

IMPLICATIONS OF BIOPOLTICS
IN LEADERSHIP LEARNING AND DEVELOPMENT

Biopolitics is a specific political ontology useful to interrogating the intersection of life and politics. Questions of sustaining and ending life are associated with exploring how sovereignty, systems, and institutions contextualize the possibility of life itself. Politics is a framework to understand how power and choice are determined, negotiated, and contested in systems and institutional contexts. As an object of study and lens to analyze questions of life and politics, biopolitics draws on a range of interdisciplinary perspectives to consider how the possibility of life becomes open to contestation.

Many attribute the idea of biopolitics to Michel Foucault (2004). Bipolitical questions quickly took on an interdisciplinary nature and were applied to a range of issues at the intersection of life and politics. Giorgio Agamben's scholarship solidified biopolitics as a common reference point and a specific political ontology (Agamben, 1998). Agamben argues that the degree to which mass genocide was operationalized using principles of 20th century industrialization has fundamentally reshaped the relationship between life and politics. A biopolitical lens provides a lens to interrogate the antecedent ontological assumptions of leadership learning and development. Here, Agamben's point is that the relationship between life and politics should be considered forever altered as a result of applying leadership and management practice to the systematization of mass murder (Agamben, 1998). Identifying and interrogating how leadership learning and development accounts for a biopolitical ontology is one way to ensure leadership can account for the relationship between life and politics in sustaining and affirming ways (Arendt, 2018). (See Campbell & Sitze, 2013 for a more comprehensive exploration of biopolitics).

Leadership trainers and developers make choices about teaching methods, content, and curriculum. These choices have implications for what is assumed to be appropriate learning and the boundaries of practice. Biopolitics can be used to interrogate political ontologies within leadership learning and development and serve as a mechanism to add depth to the analysis of civic leadership issues. This section will unpack each of these uses, respectively.

The practical function of accounting for ontologies, intentionally and unintentionally held in leadership, is to ensure desirable aims align with theory and practice and that the aims *ought* to be achieved. Accounting for biopolitical onotologies can add depth to analysis and offer a mechanism to evaluate the fit and worthiness of a knowledge claim in relation to teaching methods, content, and curriculum. Worthiness refers to the sense that knowledge claims acknowledge, and exist within, conceptual categories associated with the ontology being considered. Fit refers to alignment between conceptual categories and the types of analysis and knowledge claims someone is making.

The social change model of leadership development (Higher Education Research Institute, 1996; Komives & Wagner, 2017) is often organized as operating at the levels of individual/self, group, and society. Some leadership learning and development experiences offer additional context around each of these categories that indicate conceptual boundaries and what exactly ought to be included as relevant knowledge in each of the levels. As mentioned above, overlaying a political ontology like biopolitics across efforts to learn about self adds depth to analysis and a criteria to evaluate fit and worthiness of knowledge claims. Accounting for biopolitical ontologies helps educators and trainers clearly delimitate conceptual and knowledge boundaries when designing leadership learning and development experiences. One example of how accounting for a biopolitical ontology at the level of self follows.

Imagine the organizers of a residential hall leadership program have intentionally designed an entry-level intervention for students to better understand "self." Students complete the StrengthsQuest assessment (Anderson, 2004). StrengthsQuest is a personal assessment that uses positive psychology to identify, develop, and deploy their talents toward general well-being. Students receive a profile of their "top 5" talents. The results of the StrengthsQuest assessment fall into four domains: executing, influencing, relationship building, and strategic thinking. In this case, the purpose of the leadership activity is to help students actively consider the significance of their new knowledge about themselves (their strengths profile) and how they use this knowledge to make sense of self in the work of leadership.

Applying a biopolitical lens to this leadership learning intervention can offer another frame for analysis and orient how students make sense of self. At the risk of providing an oversimplified example, imagine how the content of StrengthsQuest might be experienced without a clear connection to political ontology. StrengthsQuest could be experienced as deepening self-awareness, marking an understanding of self, and highlighting potential asset-based pathways to leadership learning and development. On its face, StrengthsQuest is not inherently lacking in helping students make sense of self. However, without a clear account of ontology, knowing one's StrengthsQuest assessment results (talent profile, or "my strengths") can become an end in and of itself. If the leadership learning and development experience is working to move learners toward understanding self in relation to larger dynamics of power and advantage across dimensions of race, class, gender, sexuality, and ability in systems and institutional arrangements associated with the common good, then an understanding of self cannot only be connected to the StrengthQuest assessment.

A biopolitical lens allows learners to ask different questions of self. In the StrengthsQuest example, a learner may say: "Most of my strengths are in the executing domain. Therefore, I do not do much in the strategic thinking domain." An account of biopolitical ontologies informs questions that help the learner deepen the focus of their analysis of self and evaluate the fit and worthiness of a knowledge claim. For example, learners might ask the following questions of self through a bipolitical lens:

- What experiences in my life have allowed me to cultivate executing strengths?
- How has my exposure to, or the absence of, precarity shaped how I think about my strengths?
- In what ways has my life and sense of self been shaped by larger systems? How have systems been designed to recognize the circumstances of my life and experience?
- How do executing strengths currently fit within the current biopolitical moment?
- How do my executing strengths acknowledge the lived experience of others?
- What is the underlying driver of my executing strengths? Well-being and abundance? Survival and scarcity? Personal and professional advancement?

Offering a specific biopolitical ontology at the level of self can improve analysis and create frameworks to evaluate the fit and worthiness of knowledge claims at the level of self.

PRACTICAL IMPLICATIONS OF BIOPOLITICAL QUESTIONS AND CRITICAL HOPE

Identifying and accounting for ontological assumptions in leadership experiences improves learning, development, and practice. This is particularly true in situations in which educators and trainers are working to connect leadership learning and development to claims about equity, the common good, and justice. Clear ontological frameworks allow educators and learners to set clear boundaries around relevant concepts, focus knowledge claims, and more deeply analyze leadership learning, development, and practice. Without accounting for ontological assumptions, leadership for the common good, equity, and justice can become unmoored from a shared ontological starting point—rudderless, adrift in a sea of competing claims and no intentional way to analyze, sort, and assign differential meaning to leadership learning, development, and practice.

Accounting for antecedent ontological assumptions helps to frame contestation within a common starting point. Suppose multiple or competing ontological frameworks are at play in the learning and development context. In that case, the leadership learning and development experience or intervention may focus on discovering ontological assumptions educators and learners could reasonably accept when considering the role leadership has in advancing justice aims. Leadership activity that advances a common good and aspires to realize just systems and institutional arrangements will involve creating the conditions for productive disagreement.

Biopolitics offers one (political) ontology to help operationalize different takes on what kind of leadership learning and development advance the common good. Accounting for ontological assumptions prepares educators and learners to analyze competing conceptions of justice, and create the conditions for productive disagreement in ways helpful for evaluating the fit and worthiness of a claim within a specific ontological frame. A critical hope in the possibility for a better future exists insofar as the field works to move learning and practice to solid ontological grounding. Leadership efforts to re-create more equitable and just institutions will rely on negotiating and establishing solid ontological foundations for leadership teaching methods, content, and curriculum.

REFERENCES

Agamben, G. (1998.) *Homer sacer: Sovereign power and bare life*. Stanford University Press.

Allen, D., & Somanathan, R. (Eds.). (2020). *Difference without domination: Pursuing justice in diverse democracies*. The University of Chicago Press.

Anderson, E. C. (2004). *StrengthsQuest: Curriculum outline and learning activities*. Gallup Organization.

Arendt, H. (2018). *The human condition* (2nd ed.). University of Chicago Press.

Berger, B. (2011). *Attention deficit democracy: The paradox of civic engagement*. Princeton University Press.

Campbell, T., & Sitze, A. (Eds.). (2013). *Biopolitics: A reader*. Duke University Press.

Drath, W. H., McCauley, C. D., Palus., C. J., Velsor, P. M. G., O'Connor, C., & McGuire, J. B. (2008). Direction, alignment, commitment: Toward a more integrative ontology of leadership. *The Leadership Quarterly, 19*(6), 635–653. https://doi.org/10.1016/j.leaqua.2008.09.003

Foucault, M. (2004). *The birth of biopolitics: Lectures at the Collège De France*. Picador.

Higher Education Research Institute. (1996). *A social change model of leadership development: Guidebook Version III*. National Clearinghouse for Leadership Programs.

Komives, S. R., & Wagner, W. (2017). *Leadership for a better world: Understanding the social change model of leadership development* (2nd ed.). Jossey-Bass.

Mouffe, C. (2013). *Agonisitics: Thinking the world politically*. Verso.

Priest, K. L., & Clegorne, N. A. (2015). Connecting to experience: High-impact practices for leadership development. In J. E. Owen (Ed.), *New Directions for Student Leadership: No. 145. Innovative learning for leadership development* (pp. 71-83). https://doi.org/10.1002/yd.20125

Raelin, J. A. (2016). *Leadership-as-practice: Theory and application*. Routledge.

CHAPTER 5

REFLECTIONS ON BAD LEADERSHIP IN COMPLEX TIMES

O'Juan Edwards

I think about living in a land of possibility. Like the late Coretta Scott King, I think of a land where leaders will value "human dignity regarding social change who speak out on behalf of racial and economic justice, full-employment, healthcare, gay and lesbian dignity, and educational opportunities" (The King Center, n.d). Throughout history, unethical and ineffective leadership practices have taken place in various contexts, including numerous diverse communities, higher education institutions, and organizations. My perspective is influenced by my ancestors being forced to pick cotton for hundreds of years without pay, benefits, or sick leave. This history is why I must let my voice be heard concerning my community, declaring that Black Lives Matter (BLM) primarily since the BLM movement is deeply rooted during times of slavery to the civil rights movement to the modern-day police brutality and racial profiling that continues to happen.

In recent years, a report from Parker et al. (2019) acknowledges that Generation Z (Gen Z), those individuals between the ages of 13–21 as of 2018, have significantly different views than individuals who are a part of older generations such as the Baby Boomers and Gen Xers (Parker et al.,

Navigating Complexities in Leadership: Moving Toward Critical Hope, pp. 47–55
www.infoagepub.com
Copyright © 2022 by Information Age Publishing
All rights of reproduction in any form reserved.

2019). Moreover, Gen Z values social justice, and they feel comfortable when questioning older generations or individuals in leadership positions, which is beneficial concerning future generations of marginalized individuals.

In this chapter, I will focus on bad leadership, describing practices of unethical and ineffective leadership. In addition, I explain the seven types of bad leadership and provide a case of bad leadership from a higher education perspective. Lastly, the chapter ends with a call for all leaders regarding what we can do moving forward.

BAD LEADERSHIP

Kellerman (2004) declares that sometimes, bad leaders do awful things for personal gain or to please the individuals who follow them. When leaders do not have anyone to hold them accountable, it is easier for them to lose focus and stray away from what they intended to do when appointed or nominated to carry out a particular role. Kellerman (2004) coined the term bad leadership.

For purposes of this chapter, leadership is defined as interactions between leaders and followers. According to Blair et al., "Historically researchers have frequently attributed leaders' proclivity to behave unethically to narcissism, and recent literature in this area has continued to support the claim that understanding narcissism is key to understanding unethical leadership" (2017, p. 333).

Furthermore, "leadership solves the problem of organizing collective effort; consequently, it is the key to organizational effectiveness. With good leadership, organizations (governments, corporations, universities, hospitals, armies) thrive and prosper" (Hogan & Kaiser, 2005, p. 169). I define leadership as a process where leaders and followers engage with one another. Leadership is the process that shows leaders how to lead and when to follow.

The following terms are different ways that leadership can be enacted and put into action by leaders: unethical leadership, bad leadership, and ineffective leadership. Hogan and Kaiser (2005) found that individuals in leadership positions perpetuate bad leadership ideologies, and their subordinates are not off-limits concerning the horrifying retaliation followers may endure if they try to hinder what the leader is trying to accomplish. When defining bad leadership, I think of it as being unacceptable. Bad leadership is not considerate. Another critical thing to remember is, sometimes leaders have a fascination with themselves, and they cannot lead morally. They stop caring about their followers' feelings and concerns, and they despise criticism (Blair, 2017). When an individual gets caught up in narcissism, they lose themselves because they are so focused on doing wrong, which leads me to my next topic of unethical leadership.

Given the complexity, bad leadership cannot be reduced to a singular definition; rather, Kellerman (2004) describes it through two broader patterns of leadership behavior: ineffective and unethical.

Ineffective Leadership

Kellerman (2004) argues that ineffective leadership is when individuals in leadership positions lack competence in planning, setting goals, and lacking the knowledge, skills, and abilities it takes to do their job well. Kellerman defines ineffective leadership as "failing to produce the desired change. For reasons that include missing traits, weak skills, strategies badly conceived, and tactics badly employed, ineffective leadership falls short of its intention" (Kellerman, 2004, p. 33). In other words, Kellerman is saying that ineffective leadership is unsuccessful. Ineffective leadership is the complete opposite of leading with excellence. Leaders can eliminate themselves from falling into the category of ineffective leadership by keeping mentors, having people around them who tell them the truth, and who are forward thinkers who are honest and truthful. This way, they can lead with pride, free from guilt and shame.

Unethical Leadership

Kellerman (2004) argues it is challenging to separate right from wrong concerning unethical leadership. While listening to Barbara Kellerman, author of *Bad Leadership, What It Is, How It Happens, Why It Matters,* on a podcast entitled *Phronesis: Practical Wisdom for Leaders hosted by Scott J. Allen.* Barbara Kellerman states, "Leaders do not always lead, and followers do not always follow. Standing up to leaders when they are doing wrong is essential. Some followers enable bad leaders" (Allen, 2020–present). Moreover, if followers confront leaders, it should be done with care and compassion. It will also be a good idea to have a moderator present so the leader and followers can engage in multiple meaningful conversations to restore damage, heartbreak, and devastation. This kind of approach is restorative justice in higher education, which I have used several times as a practitioner in residence education and housing services, leading me to discuss unethical leadership further. Educational institutions and the greater society have not set anything in place that mandates leaders to have a specific credential to serve as a leader.

To put it another way, researchers are paying more attention to individuals in supervisory positions who perpetuate deceitful actions (Brown & Mitchell, 2010). In the same lines, unethical behavior is when individuals involve themselves in dishonorable behavior by getting involved in illegal situations. Unethical behavior usually involves the leader insulting, offending, and being rude to their followers. Similarly, research proves oppressive leaders are sarcastic, devious, and destructive. They engage in damaging behavior towards staff that may cause them legal ramifications (Brown & Mitchell, 2010). "Unethical leadership, however, transcends beyond the leaders' own behavior. In seeking to accomplish organizational goals, leaders can encourage corrupts and unethical acts within their organizations" (Brown & Mitchell, 2010, p. 588). As a result, the outcomes of unethical leadership are detrimental. Brown and Mitchell (2010) demonstrates that researchers discover unethical behavior costs American companies billions of dollars per year because of truancy, mental and physical health costs and concerns, and unproductivity due to leaders being unethical and mistreating employees. In other words (Brown & Mitchell, 2010) believes that some companies, such as Enron, caused the organization to go out of business due to unethical leadership practices, which leads me to my next argument concerning ineffective leadership.

Ineffective and Unethical Leadership

The combination of ineffective and unethical leadership is interchangeable. "Bad leadership falls into two categories: bad as in ineffective and bad as in unethical" (Kellerman, 2004, p. 32). Kellerman states, "Unethical leadership fails to distinguish between right and wrong. Because common codes of decency and good conduct are in some way violated, the leadership process is defiled" (Kellerman, 2004 p. 34). Therefore, often it is challenging for followers to see anything else outside of their tunnel vision of corruptness. "According to our definition, behaviors are destructive if they violate the legitimate, that is, the rightful and lawful interests of the organization" (Einarsen et al. 2007, p. 210). Additionally, Brown and Mitchell (2010) go on to say, "Unethical leadership, however, transcends beyond the leaders' behavior. In seeking to accomplish organizational goals, leaders can encourage corrupt and unethical acts within their organizations" (p. 588). For an example situated in higher education, the board of trustees at a college or university handles many of its decision-making and managerial concerns. Whatever they decide transcends to departments, faculty, students, and staff of the university community. Furthermore, if the board of trustees makes ineffective or unethical decisions, they will affect the entire institution.

Types of Bad Leadership

Kellerman (2004) offers seven types of bad leadership that connect to ineffective and unethical leadership. As discussed above, ineffective means a leader does not produce the ambition or aspirations as everyone else on the team or organization. Unethical means unlawful, improper, and unprofessional practices. Therefore, ineffective and unethical leadership are in alignment with the seven types of bad leadership. Table 5.1 further describes the meaning of the seven types of bad leadership which include incompetent, rigid, intemperate, callous, corrupt, insular, and evil. The first three types represent patterns of *ineffective* leadership, and the last four types represent *unethical* leadership.

Table 5.1

Seven Types of Bad Leadership

Types	Meaning of the Leadership Type
Incompetent	The leader and at least some followers lack the will or skill (or both) to sustain effective action. With regard at least one important leadership challenge, they do not create positive change.
Rigid	The leader and at least some followers are stiff and unyielding. Although they may be competent, they are unable or unwilling to adapt to new ideas, new information, or changing times.
Intemperate	The leader lacks self-control and is aided and abetted by followers who are unwilling or unable to intervene effectively.
Callous	The leader and at least some followers are uncaring or unkind. Ignored or discounted are the needs, wants, and wishes of most members of the group or organization, especially subordinates.
Corrupt	The leader and at least some followers lie, cheat, or steal. To a degree that exceeds the norm, they put self-interest ahead of the public interest.
Insular	The leader and at least some followers minimize or disregard the health and welfare of "the other"—that is, those outside the group or organization for which they are directly responsible.
Evil	The leader and at least some followers commit atrocities. They use pain as an instrument of power. The harm done to men, women, and children is severe rather than slight. The harm can be physical, psychological, or both.

BAD LEADERSHIP: A HIGHER EDUCATION EXAMPLE

The combination of ineffective and unethical leadership, and the seven bad leadership types reminds me of an example situated in higher education in which I read about approaching the fall 2020 semester. The complexities concerning college presidents trying to decide if they should open for the fall 2020 semester or not. The headlines reflected competing values and wide-reaching implications: *Colleges Worry They Will Be Sued if They Reopen Campuses* (Murakami, 2020) and *Here is What College Leaders Said in Their Covid-19 Call with the White House* (Ellis, 2020). Both articles mention 14 college presidents having a Zoom video call with the vice president of the United States and the U.S. Secretary of Education to see if they could create a liability protection plan to protect university presidents if they decide to open during the fall 2020 academic year. The liability protection plan would stop presidents from being sued by faculty, staff, students, and parents if they were to open their colleges and universities during a pandemic, although there was with no cure, treatment, or vaccine for coronavirus (COVID-19). The college presidents were concerned with the option of getting a liability protection plan. They were experiencing pressure from tensions of multiple stakeholders and their expectations.

Learning from the 14 college presidents and the federal government is essential because we do not want history to repeat itself. For instance, if another pandemic were to occur in the future, I would want the North American government officials and college presidents to be kinder and more considerate when thinking about the university community's humanity at large. I care about the various takeaway strategies that can be learned from this situation. One of the takeaway strategies that come to mind is following the safety measures set in place by the Centers for Disease Control and Prevention. The centers sent out statements, brochures, and literature on their website, which is now general knowledge to everyone in the United States to stay home, practice social distancing, wash hands regularly, and get tested for COVID-19 whenever possible. If the federal government and college presidents would have kept that in mind, there would have been no need to meet concerning strategies to open colleges and universities during a pandemic. Moreover, leaders must learn how to stay in their lane. For example, since the Centers for Disease Control and Prevention representatives are experts concerning public health and caring about the population, the federal government and college presidents should listen to the experts to be promptly taken care of by following the rules and guidelines.

LEARNING FROM THE BAD: CULTIVATING THE GOOD

Everyone can be a leader. The call for leaders extends to individuals from all socioeconomic statuses, ethnicities, gender, race, religious beliefs, sexual orientations, and age groups. Leadership is not linear, it happens in a dynamic fashion, and leaders need to lead diverse groups of individuals because we live in a globally diverse society. We need to be more conscious in our daily observations by recognizing when a leader engages in bad leadership behavior by confronting their actions. Leaders also need to be adaptive, meaning when leadership within an organization or institution changes, the organization's policies and procedures change as well (Hopen, 2010). In other words, diversity is here to stay, and it is not going anywhere. Therefore, leaders need to serve all ethnicities by being able to communicate and articulate clear directions. Leaders need to be approachable and compassionate concerning humanity and realize the experiences of the individuals sitting next to them in meetings. I have always believed everyone can be a phenomenal leader, and we expect all of our leaders to listen, lead with integrity, and treat everyone with respect by being open to different views, learning, and management styles of the individuals within their institution.

Acknowledging an Evil History

Today's leaders need to recognize the historical legacy of bad leaders and leadership. It can be difficult to confront and reflect on evil personal behaviors and national policies that shaped the culture of the United States: bigotry, brutal violence, separation of Black families sold into slavery, Black women raped by White slave masters, and Black people owned by White people. Though slavery is abolished, the legacy—and pain—of systemic racism continues to this day. The actions and inaction of leaders and followers across generations has resulted in relentless emotional and bodily abuse towards Black men, women, boys, and girls.

A Hope for the Future

I am optimistic about the future of our country as it relates to leadership. One day, I hope a change will come when all leaders always treat each person as a human being and with respect. Although this is a simple concept, it can go a long way in day-to-day interactions within various organizations. Leaders whose priorities align with supporting the unlearning of racism and rebuilding an America rooted in social justice, equality, social acceptance, and racial injustice can help bring this into fruition. "Success is less and less dependent on personal knowledge and skills and more dependent on the leader's ability to encourage and support other efforts. Acceptance, adaptability, and interpersonal abilities are the new keys to accomplishment" (Hopen, 2010, p. 9). When leaders learn how to support and accept others by centering the human experience and developing empathy, their leadership efforts will be more valuable and appreciated. Leaders will touch lives, and Black people will no longer feel marginalized. When thinking about bad leadership, I think about how sometimes leaders lose focus and stray away from what they were initially nominated or appointed to do when no one is around to hold them accountable. Another critical thing to remember is that leaders need to remind themselves of their values and morals when difficult and complex situations happen. Usually, what keeps leaders grounded are their beliefs.

Application and Accountability

When leaders find themselves in chaotic situations, they have to remain laser-focused and redefine why their work matters to them and rediscover what motivates them to develop their leadership capacity to be the most effective. Moreover, accountability is essential for significant positive change in leadership in the non-profit, for-profit, public, and private sectors. In closing, I offer a few questions that can prompt leaders and leadership educators to use the lens of bad leadership as a tool for application and accountability.

1. What morals and values guide me in difficult and complex situations? What do I believe about right and wrong?
2. How do I approach leaders who lead ineffectively?
3. What types of interventions can I implement when unethical leadership emerges?
4. How can we hold each other accountable as leaders to not pick-up bad habits concerning bad leadership traits or characteristics?
5. Since ineffective leadership brings about change and unethical leadership means having difficulties knowing the difference between right and wrong. How can we, as leaders, educate ourselves and our followers so that there is no confusion or a gray area in the future?

REFERENCES

Allen, S. J. (Host). (2020–present). *Phronesis: Practical wisdom for leaders* [Audio podcast]. NPR. https://podcasts.apple.com/us/podcast/phronesis-practical-wisdom-for-leaders/id1510441734?i=1000485602947

Brown, M. E., & Mitchell, M. S. (2010). Ethical and unethical leadership: Exploring new avenues for future research. *Business Ethics Quarterly, 20*(4), 583–616.

Blair, C. A., Helland, K., & Walton, B. (2017). Leaders behaving badly: The relationship between narcissism and unethical leadership. *Leadership & Organization Development Journal, 38*(2), 333–346.

Einarsen, S., Aasland, M. S., & Skogstad, A. (2007). Destructive leadership behavior: A definition and conceptual model. *The Leadership Quarterly, 18*(3), 207–216.

Ellis, L. (2020, May 15). COVID-19 call with the White House. *The Chronicle of Higher Education.* https://www.chronicle.com/article/heres-what-college-leaders-said-in-their-covid-19-call-with-the-white-house/

Hogan, R., & Kaiser, R. B. (2005). What we know about leadership. *Review of General Psychology, 9*(2), 169–180.

Hopen, D. (2010). The changing role and practices of successful leaders. *The Journal for Quality and Participation, 33*(1), 4–9.

Kellerman, B. (2004). *Bad leadership: What it is, how it happens, why it matters.* Harvard Business Press.

The King Center. (n.d). *About Mrs. King.* https://thekingcenter.org/about-mrs-king/

Murakami, K. (2020, May 15). Colleges worry they'll be sued if they reopen campuses. *Inside Higher Ed.* https://www.insidehighered.com/news/2020/05/15/colleges-seek-protection-lawsuits-if-they-reopen

Parker, K., Graf, N., & Igielnik, R. (2019). *Generation Z looks a lot like Millennials on key social and political issues* (Report). Pew Research Center. https://www.pewresearch.org/social-trends/2019/01/17/generation-z-looks-a-lot-like-millennials-on-key-social-and-political-issues/

CHAPTER 6

EXPANDING THE SCOPE OF SCHOLARSHIP IN LEADERSHIP EDUCATION

**Martinella Dryburgh, Elizabeth Goryunova,
Carol Clyde Gallagher, Trent Grundmeyer,
and Cristina de Mello e Souza Wildermuth**

Teaching, service, and scholarship: these are the primary roles for faculty at colleges and universities, including those working in leadership studies or related disciplines. While teaching and service are essential faculty activities, for many, conducting research and creating scholarly artifacts are often perceived as having higher importance for two critical reasons. First, institutional tenure and promotion decisions heavily emphasize scholarship output. Faculty may need to document a specific number of publications or other forms of scholarship to meet tenure and promotion requirements. This documentation provides an objective and distinct measure by which a committee can determine whether an individual has earned tenure and promotion. Second, scholarship output is a quantifiable way for faculty to show professional vitality, especially outside one's institution. Professional vitality is important for faculty members as they look for employment or other opportunities outside their institution, whether within higher education or other sectors of the economy. Indeed, publications can be considered the currency of academia. Publication in

Navigating Complexities in Leadership: Moving Toward Critical Hope, pp. 57–66
www.infoagepub.com
Copyright © 2022 by Information Age Publishing
All rights of reproduction in any form reserved.

peer-reviewed disciplinary academic journals is the current gold standard that supports promotion and tenure, as well as professional vitality.

However, the higher education landscape is experiencing seismic changes, such as digital restructuring, the dwindling of available resources, and the resulting pressure on faculty to do more with less. Such changes create internal and external tensions that undermine faculty members' capacity to conduct research, write and publish. These tensions prompt critical questions: Has the scaffolding offered by the existing long-running tradition of scholarship inadvertently become limiting to our ability to achieve our fullest capacity? Could it be that the traditional system no longer reflects specific circumstances and needs of higher education institutions? And how can we as leadership faculty help create an enduring scholarship process that is flexible enough to adjust to changes in the environment?

Given the evolving nature of the academic profession and its increasingly conflicting demands, we propose a reevaluation of traditional scholarship requirements. This chapter will explore emerging questions for faculty in leadership education and development: *What kind of scholarship is needed? And, how can faculty be supported in creating new forms of acceptable scholarship that will help them meet their tenure and promotion goals while also demonstrating professional vitality?* We utilize an adaptive action framework to challenge the status quo that fails to account for the multidimensionality of the rapidly evolving environment (Eoyang & Holladay, 2013). Following an inquiry cycle of: "What?, So What?, and Now What?", we describe and question scholarly processes as we experience them today, emerging patterns of a future system that could be enduring in its capacity to adjust to ongoing continual changes in our world and institutions as they occur (Eoyang & Holladay, 2013).

First, we build upon Boyer's framework of scholarship and our own experiences, illuminating current patterns and pressures in the field of higher education that affect faculty members and their scholarship performance. Then, we look to the future and propose questions to explore when creating more inclusive scholarship practices. We hope these questions encourage ongoing, robust conversations among leadership educators about developing new, positive, and equitable opportunities for faculty to create innovative scholarship.

WHAT KIND OF SCHOLARSHIP IS NEEDED?

When looking to untangle the tensions within a complex process, one must focus on its intrinsic meaning, which may lead to a paradigm shift. This approach was taken by Boyer (1990) who recognized the emerging tensions within the scholarship process, explored the meaning of scholarship, pointed out that the scholarship concept could be more inclusive, thus contributing to the legitimacy of engaged, interdisciplinary, and teaching scholarship in higher educational institutions (O'Meara et al., 2015). Boyer proposed multiple scholarship formats beyond the traditional "discovery" approach and challenged the belief that there was only a single kind of scholarship with only one way to assess its quality (O'Meara et al., 2015). Boyer brought awareness to the need to provide recognition and legitimacy to other scholar methods; he also challenged the existing reward system to allow faculty members to get credit for all their diverse hard work and meaningful contributions. Boyer's model includes the scholarship of discovery, integration, teaching, and application. The scholarship of discovery is advancing new knowledge, while the scholarship of integration is synthesizing knowledge in new ways. The scholarship of teaching is focused on advancing teaching methods, and the scholarship of application is applying knowledge in different contexts (Boyer, 1990).

Leadership education is multidisciplinary and welcomes a wide variety of activities and artifacts that are considered scholarly, including traditional journal articles, book reviews, podcasts, blogs, and the sharing of best practices through conference presentations and workshops (Priest & Jenkins, 2019). Additionally, leadership education is very open to research collaborations between leadership education scholars and practitioners and between students and faculty. These scholarly activities are meant to bridge theory and practice and enhance the field of leadership education. However, the lack of clarity on how to assess the rigor, intentionality, and impact of these efforts on the advancement of leadership education scholarship and practice is one of the tensions to resolve (Pierre et al., 2020)

OUR STORY OF SCHOLARSHIP

Our individual experiences reveal some of the tensions of existing scholarship processes and provide a foundation from which to compare our collective experience with those of the broader circle of our colleagues. Starting "where we are," we collectively define scholarship in a traditional sense: scholarship allows a faculty member to show excellence in their discipline by contributing to a body of knowledge. The creation of knowledge includes research, along with opportunities to integrate existing knowledge in new ways (making linkages, applying knowledge in new ways, or coming up with new methods). This knowledge must also be disseminated in the public domain; for many faculty members, this is accomplished by publication in peer-reviewed academic journals.

Two of us are tenured, two are on the tenure track, and one serves as an administrator with faculty status. Contextually, we are all situated in leadership-focused departments within our institutions with titles such as organizational leadership, educational leadership, or leadership and counseling. While we all actively participate in teaching, scholarship, and service (both institutionally and in our discipline), four of us serve as "single faculty" members, that is, as the only full-time faculty members in our disciplinary departments at our institutions. Because single faculty status comes with additional departmental administrative duties, we have found that scholarship is the most difficult requirement to fulfill. We often lack time to engage in the kinds of research projects that produce multiple journal articles and professional conference presentations each year. Additionally, the desire to build collaborative partnerships with others is in tension with the implied responsibility to carry a shared burden of creating scholarly artifacts. When there are many competing commitments, any additional time for meetings or cowriting feels like a heavy lift.

Along with differences in the scope of duties, the scholarship criteria at our institutions differ as well. This prompts the question: *What counts as scholarship?* A published article in a peer-reviewed academic journal is considered a standard form of scholarship at our institutions. Yet, our universities differ in the level of emphasis placed on a journal's impact factor (a measure reflecting the frequency of citations for the articles published in a particular journal). For some of us, publishing in the "right" academic journal (i.e., a journal with a high impact factor) weighs heavily on promotion and tenure decisions. Likewise, writing a book chapter counts toward the scholarship at two of our institutions but does not count at the remaining three, *so there is a bit of risk taking in tackling this very endeavor.* At the same time, we recognize that publishing a book chapter supports our professional vitality toward future opportunities outside our current organizations. Regardless, we hope that taking the step to produce this work will contribute to the expansion of scholarship requirements we want to see in the field.

Another area where scholarship requirements differ is in the area of student research. As previously mentioned, leadership education welcomes student research and collaborations between faculty and students. However, while several of us conduct research with undergraduate or graduate students, this is seen as "service" or "good teaching" at our institutions. Only one of our institutions actively encourages student scholarship, and counts it as scholarship when presented at the college's student scholarship conference.

The question of where to focus research energy is a common struggle among each of us. Our shared experiences prompted us to come together to explore ways to support faculty in creating new forms of acceptable scholarship for tenure/promotion and professional vitality. At the same time, we were curious: How did our experiences relate to others' experiences?

We conducted a pilot survey study during the height of the COVID-19 pandemic with volunteer members of the International Leadership Association. From this study, we found that other faculty are facing similar barriers to creating scholarship along with unique barriers driven by the pandemic. Data suggested that the gold standard scholarly artifact across all higher education institutions was a publication in a peer-reviewed disciplinary journal. However, universities also frequently created unique criteria regarding other forms of research and publication that may count as scholarship for tenure and promotion. Our survey illustrated the same tensions we were feeling. Data showed that faculty members often chose to engage only in the type of the scholarship that adhere to their institution's standards, foregoing the creation of innovative research that would not count toward tenure and promotion because it would be a "waste" of their limited time and resources. Other challenges mentioned by our colleagues included (a) heavy administrative and teaching loads that limit their ability to engage in research, (b) inconsistent and inflexible scholarship criteria, (c) inadequate resources, and (d) conflicting demands on time. These seem to point to systemic challenges within higher education as a whole. In the following section, we look at the unfolding dynamics of the environments in which faculty scholarship creation occurs.

HIGHER EDUCATION PANDEMIC-DRIVEN PRESSURES AND SCHOLARSHIP

Higher education has been facing complex pressures due to social, governmental, economic changes, and digital transformation. These pressures also affect leadership studies as it is a young field of study where faculty are still building a body of knowledge. Higher education costs are increasing, leading many to wonder if a college degree is a worthwhile investment (Tretina, 2021). Whether funded by public or private money, universities' available funding appears to be dwindling, and competition for resources is rising (Feller, 2016). Higher education institutions must demonstrate excellence to attract the resources necessary to provide high-quality educational opportunities for students. Thus, cutting-edge research typically overshadows teaching and service to local communities

(Paradeise, 2019). The competition for resources translates into a tense environment where faculty are asked to "do more with less" as they approach the challenge to meet their scholarship requirements.

The disruption caused by the COVID-19 pandemic has brought into stark reality the barriers that faculty must now face to engage in research and create a meaningful scholarship. In March 2020 when the world "shut down," faculty found themselves swiftly pivoting away from traditional face to face to remote only and hybrid (or flex) teaching formats. Educators devoted significant amounts of time to adapting course materials and learning to teach in this new online modality. There was a steep learning curve for many faculty members who integrated new technological tools into their instruction to mimic traditional face-to-face engagement. For example, small group discussions were now held in virtual breakout rooms, brainstorming was generated through word clouds on Poll Everywhere or PearDeck, and whiteboard interactions were facilitated through Google Jamboard.

The focus on learning and implementing new teaching methods meant taking time away from conducting research and writing scholarly publications. Interestingly, this is another tension in scholarship creation. Capturing best practices in using these teaching methods could have contributed to the knowledge within the body of work that makes up the scholarship of teaching and learning. Faculty could have shared their teaching methods through publication as well as other methods such as workshops. In leadership education, sharing teaching methods and best practices in pedagogy is a highly encouraged form of scholarship. However, if an institution does not value publication in the scholarship of teaching and learning arena, faculty may not allocate time sharing these insightful and valuable practices.

The pandemic impacted scholarship activities in multiple ways. First, scholarly research has been affected in terms of its focus (dominated by COVID-related publications), scarce resources available for the field- and/or experiment-based studies, restricted access to real-life interactions with and recruitment of subjects, as well as limited "pandemic-proof" (web-based) methodology. At the same time, reports indicate an increase in the number of manuscripts submitted for publication in scholarly journals, resulting in rapid reviews that may have led in some cases to inadequate quality and subsequent retractions by journals (Harper et al., 2020).

Second, as global lockdown orders began and travel ceased in March 2020, academic conferences had to adjust accordingly. Some professional organizations held interdisciplinary leadership education conferences in a virtual format (e.g., 2020 Association of Leadership Educators and International Leadership Association conferences). However, some other discipline-specific academic and professional organizations made decisions to cancel their events (e.g., 2020 Annual Conference of the Western Academy of Management). Without conferences, some leadership faculty lost forums to share research with colleagues, make new connections, and establish collaborations to engage in new research opportunities.

Third, as campuses across the country switched to virtual teaching formats, faculty who relied on community engagement and service learning projects as a foundation for their research lost this outlet. Government and nonprofit organizations focused on helping their community members no longer had time or resources to host students and their research projects. This loss affected faculty who used collaborative research with students to add to their scholarship output. While not every institution values faculty/student research, student collaborations are encouraged within the leadership studies discipline, as their reflections demonstrate the impact of leadership education and development.

Fourth, the pandemic emphasized gender inequality where female scholars working from home (compared to their male counterparts in the same position) increasingly negotiate multiple conflicting priorities of research and caring for children and families (Harper et al., 2020). Furthermore, as women take on the "invisible labor" of supporting students as they manage the stress of the pandemic, they find the time allotted for research dwindling (Shalaby et al., 2020). This disruption of research productivity for women, a well as Black, Indigenous, and people of color, can have long-term consequences for the professional vitality of these faculty both inside and outside their institutions (Shalaby et al., 2020).

As the pandemic progressed, higher education institutions demonstrated some flexibility by rethinking timelines regarding tenure and promotion for faculty members. Several survey respondents stated that faculty at their institutions were allowed to extend their tenure clocks by 1 or 2 academic years. Institutions recognized what we have previously mentioned: taking time to learn how to teach online took time away from focusing on research and writing and conference cancellations impacted faculty members' research productivity. It is critically important to note that while institutions have changed the *timeline* regarding scholarship activities, many have not changed the *criteria* and *requirements* needed to achieve tenure or be granted promotion.

The COVID-19 pandemic has ushered in a "new normal" for higher education generally, and leadership education specifically. We must question whether the traditional scholarship criteria and requirements are flexible enough to accurately reflect the evolving scope of faculty responsibilities or responsive enough to the critical emerging questions of our times. If not, where do we go from here? How can the structure of scholarship respond to the new realities facing colleges and universities as they grapple with smaller budgets, less departmental faculty, as well as competition or funds and students?

IMAGINING A NEW FUTURE

In light of the complexities facing leadership scholars in higher education, we return to our initial inquiry: how can faculty be supported in creating new forms of acceptable scholarship that will help them meet their tenure and promotion goals while demonstrating professional vitality? That is, what adaptive action should we collectively take? To help facilitate constructive and open conversation on this issue inclusive of viewpoints of faculty members, professional associations, tenure and promotion committee members, and institutions we propose the following questions and discussion:

Faculty Members

What leadership learning and development activities could be explored or considered as new avenues of scholarship? How should promotion and tenure and professional review guidelines be designed to provide actionable feedback related to (a) professional preparation and practice for leadership educators and (b) the rigor and intentionality of collaboration between leadership education scholars and practitioners? While we do not suggest doing away with the peer-review system, we encourage faculty to look for new and meaningful ways to create scholarship and identify existing activities that faculty engage in that could be redefined to demonstrate rigor that qualifies as scholarship.

Professional Associations

How can current technology be leveraged to bring together faculty for knowledge sharing and collaboration opportunities outside of the traditional annual professional conference venue? Some faculty may want to return to traditional annual professional conference events for face-to-face interactions and organic connections that lead to collaborative efforts. However, some faculty, especially those in far-away international locations, may be locked out of these opportunities due to inadequate funding resources. Creating opportunities to share research, generate ideas, and connect across institutions via communication technologies

(Zoom, WebEx, Microsoft Teams, etc.) would be extremely valuable to all faculty.

Tenure and Promotion Committee Members

What insights can members of current tenure and promotion committees share to shed light on evolving standards of scholarship? Faculty members who serve or have served on tenure and promotion committees could provide valuable mentorship to others in the field. They can share context on what activities could be considered scholarship and how individuals can tell the story of their scholarship in ways that align with tenure or promotion requirements. Furthermore, faculty members who have served on hiring committees can offer information on what determines professional vitality when individuals apply for jobs in their institutions.

Institutions

What can be done at the institutional level to create more inclusive practices around scholarship? Specifically, how can institutions reassess the heavy emphasis on peer-reviewed academic journals in favor of the inclusion of venues that not only demonstrate faculty member's expertise, but are disseminated to a wider audience? There needs to be conversation about how "public" academic journals really are when these same journals are limited to only individuals who have institutional access. Can scholarship include other ways to share knowledge, especially in venues where practitioners and scholars can come together? The notion of "public domain" and how accessible that domain actually is to the public is in question. Institutions need to honestly evaluate the purpose of knowledge creation and how it benefits society. The balance of faculty service outcomes for expertise and rigor in relation to scholarship needs to be reenvisioned

CONCLUSION

Increasing costs, dwindling funding, escalating stratification of higher education create an inequitable playing field for institutions and faculty. As universities resort to redistributing administrative and service duties to the faculty, they undermine their capacity to engage in scholarship as currently defined by the academic gold standard. COVID-19 further increased these internal and external tensions. It appears that the traditional scholarship system no longer reflects the contemporary realities, the evolving nature of the academic profession, and its increasingly conflicting demands, and the time may have come to reevaluate it and build an enduring and agile system for the future. With this chapter we call on the leadership scholars to play an active role in this systemic change, as we cannot advance overarching purposes and goals of the leadership education without exemplifying the values we are hoping to nurture.

REFERENCES

Boyer, E. (1990). *Scholarship reconsidered: Priorities for the professoriate.* The Carnegie Foundation for the Advancement of Teaching.

Eoyang, G., & Holladay, R. (2013). *Adaptive action: Leveraging uncertainty in your organization.* Stanford University Press.

Feller, I. (2016). This time it really may be different. In E. P. Berman & C. Paradeise (Eds.), *Research in the Sociology of Organizations: Vol. 46. The university under pressure* () (pp. 453–488). Emerald. https://doi.org/10.1108/S0733-558X20160000046015

Harper, L., Kalfa, N., Beckers, G., Kaefer, M., Nieuwhof-Leppink, A. J., Fossum, M., Herbst, K. W., Bagli, D., & ESPU Research Committee (2020). The impact of COVID-19 on research. *Journal of Pediatric Urology, 16*(5), 715–716. https://doi.org/10.1016/j.jpurol.2020.07.002

O'Meara, K., Eatman, T., & Petersen, S. (2015). Advancing engaged scholarship in promotion and tenure: A roadmap and call for reform. *Liberal Education, 101*(3), 52–57.

Paradeise, C. (2019). Stormy weather on higher education: Globalization and change. *Revista Brasileira de Ciencias Sociais, 34*(100). https://doi.org/10.1590/3410019/2019

Pierre, D., Dunn, A. L., Barnes, A. C., Moore, L. L., Seemiller, C., Jenkins, D. M., Priest, K. L., Guthrie, K. L., Beatty, C. C., Bitton, A. L., Duran, A., Bailey, K. J., & Odom, S. F. (2020). A critical look at leadership educator preparation: Developing an intentional and diverse approach to leadership learning and development: Priority 4 of the National Leadership Education Research Agenda 2020–2025. *Journal of Leadership Studies, 14*(3), 56–62. https://doi.org/10.1002/jls.21712

Priest, K. L., & Jenkins, D. M. (2019). Developing a vision of leadership educator professional practice. In K. L. Priest & D. M Jenkins (Eds.), *New Directions for Student Leadership: No. 164. Being and becoming a leadership educator* (pp. 9–22). Wiley. https://doi.org/10.1002/yd.20355

Shalaby, M., Allam, N., & Buttroff, G. (2020, December 18). Gender, COVID, and faculty service. *Inside Higher Ed.* https://www.insidehighered.com/advice/2020/12/18/increasingly-disproportionate-service-burden-female-faculty-bear-will-have#.YHn2KCbQ72s.link

Tretina, K. (2021). Is college worth the cost: Pros vs. cons. *Forbes Advisor.* https://www.forbes.com/advisor/student-loans/is-college-worth-it/

PART II

LEADERSHIP PRACTICE IN HIGHER EDUCATION

CHAPTER 7

EMERGENT STRATEGY

A Tool for Transforming Leadership in Higher Education

Ciera Fluker

Today we face a myriad of tensions and complexities in higher education. The COVID-19 pandemic has brought on unsurmountable challenges as many colleges and universities are rethinking their operations and programs to adapt to social distancing restrictions and other safety and health considerations. Higher education institutions have reacted to the global pandemic differently. Some institutions have closed their physical campuses and utilized virtual platforms to replace in-person interactions, while others have created hybrid educational offerings. Many students, faculty, and staff have experienced a sudden shift in leadership education as face-to-face advising, instruction, and student organization events have moved to virtual spaces. This transition to virtual spaces has required considerable time and resources not afforded to all institutions (Marshall et al., 2020).

The COVID-19 pandemic has also highlighted racial disparities in the United States and led to increasing political unrest. Citizens across the United States continue to demand changes to systems and structures that perpetuate racial inequality. Cries for racial equality and equity have been

Navigating Complexities in Leadership: Moving Toward Critical Hope, pp. 69–77
www.infoagepub.com

Copyright © 2022 by Information Age Publishing
All rights of reproduction in any form reserved.

exacerbated by political politicization as well as a reappearance of xeno-phobia in the United States (Anand & Hsu, 2020). The culmination of these factors has forced higher education institutions to address structures and systems that perpetuate racism and discrimination on college and university campuses. Some institutions have responded by removing con-federate flags and statues, reevaluating their campus climates, and imple-menting more equitable admission processes. However, research suggests there is still a great need for structural changes in higher education (Burke, 2020).

To face current complexities in higher education, institutions must implement strategies that allow them to remain adaptive and innovative (Yukl & Mahsud, 2010). This shift may require higher education institu-tions to rethink traditional approaches to leadership. Adrienne Brown's (2017) emergent strategy framework provides tools to navigate uncer-tainty and constant change. Emergence involves creating critical, deep human connections that together have the power to create innovative solutions. This chapter provides recommendations on how higher educa-tion institutions can utilize emergent strategy principles to improve lead-ership capacity and realize social change.

LEADERSHIP DEVELOPMENT

Leadership development involves growing the combined capacity of orga-nizational members to participate in leadership roles and activities (McCauley et al., 1998). Day (2000) makes an important distinction between leader development and leadership development. Leader devel-opment involves investing in human capital, focusing on the individual development of knowledge, skills, and abilities needed to carry out leader functions (Day, 2000). When developing leaders, the goal is to increase their intrapersonal competence, focusing on self-awareness, self-regula-tion, and self-motivation skills (Neck & Manz, 1996; Manz & Sims, 1989; McCauley, 2000; Stewart et al., 1996). On the contrary, leadership devel-opment involves investing in social capital in an organization. Building social capital requires a focus on building a network of relationships among members in an organization to improve the flow of resources and organizational value (Bouty, 2000; Day, 2000; Tsai & Ghosal, 1998). These relationships are created through interpersonal exchanges (Bourdieu, 1986). As the world continues to change and transform, there is great interest in developing both leader and leadership capacity in higher edu-cation.

Brown (2017) posits leaders must be adaptive and intentional—similar to birds migrating against a storm. Leaders should also use visionary exploration to better understand humanity by first using their imagination to rethink systems of oppression and ideologies that instill fear and division in our society. However, this ideation does not stop at the individual level; leadership development in emergent strategy involves diverse individuals connecting, collaborating, and reimagining a new society together. Applying emergent strategy requires a shift in the way institutions approach constant change and complexity in our world as institutions focus on realizing social change through deep connections and collective ideation.

APPLYING EMERGENT STRATEGY

Brown's (2017) framework defines emergence as the ways small compounded interactions lead to complex schemes and patterns. Examples of emergence in nature are how trees develop root systems to withstand harsh weather and cellular systems that form the bases of multifaceted organisms. Like these relationships found in nature, strong human relationships have the power to improve a system's strength. The ripple effect of human exchanges in higher education can create trailblazing solutions to some of our society's worst ills, such as racism and discrimination, and help institutions plan for and face uncertainty. Emergent strategy consists of six elements: (a) fractal, (b) adaptive, (c) interdependence and decentralization, (d) non-linear and integrative, (e) resilience and transformative justice, and (f) creating more possibilities (Brown, 2017). These elements offer a framework for leading change in higher education.

Fractal

Fractals describe how patterns at the micro level span out and scale up to larger patterns at the macro level. Brown (2017) argues organizations often perpetuate patterns that uphold the status quo and cycle upward to local, state, and international levels. To realize social change, individuals working in higher education must live adaptive and intentional lives. Brown suggests individuals should start by practicing justice and liberation in their own lives. Practices such as creating meaningful friendships, practicing meditation, generative somatic, and yoga can improve our emergent potential at the individual level.

Fractals can also inform leadership instructional practices. Guthrie (2016) offers four suggestions for leadership educators developing online service-learning courses and applied more broadly to implementing virtual leadership education: (a) construct virtual spaces that encourage continuous interaction, communication, and relationship building, (b) develop instructional practices that embrace autonomy and collaboration, (c) create, implement and necessitate spaces for critical reflection and investigation, and (d) support the development of secondary skills in addition to primary leadership learning goals. Developing students' adaptive leadership skills can prepare students for leadership opportunities on campus and in their careers.

Higher education institutions often have lofty mission statements. Breaking down the mission into simple principles and values helps departments develop and take obtainable actions to realize change at the institutional level. Every institution approaches their work through their own socially constructed beliefs. An institution's operating beliefs should integrate the beliefs of the individuals that make up the organization. These operating beliefs should then guide how individuals in the organization carry out their work. Higher education institutions should involve constituents across their institution in determining organizational mission, values, and strategic plans. Furthermore, who leads makes a difference (Brown, 2017). It is imperative to not only hire more diverse faculty and staff and recruit and retain diverse students, but also to give these individuals a voice in decision-making throughout the institution (Burke, 2020).

Intentional Adaption

Intentional adaptation is a strategy that realizes change is inevitable and persistent and requires an organization to remain adaptive to change in a purposeful manner (Brown, 2017). At the personal level, this involves increasing capacity for adaptation by moving with intention towards one's personal vision. Brown argues adaptation can reduce stress and fear in an institution. Those working in higher education can start at the individual level by ensuring they are open to and embrace change. Along with being adaptive, individuals should assess whether activities align with their visions and goals. Continual assessment allows opportunities for people to reroute their energy to activities that make a difference.

At the organizational level, adaptation requires organizations to create a shared vision and cultivate deeply connected relationships that build trust. Institutions can build trust by implementing facilitation strategies that create conditions for people to shape what is discussed and give voice to everyone involved. Some strategies include articulating the goal of a meeting, inviting people who are impacted by the issue of discussion, setting a flexible agenda, and articulating the next elegant step (Brown, 2017). These discussions should include students, staff, faculty, and stakeholders outside the institution to ensure those impacted by decisions have input.

As higher education institutions face increasing uncertainty, they can operate with intention by staying in touch with their identified guiding principles and organizing beliefs. For example, many institutions cite a commitment to diversity and inclusion in their mission and values. However, Black students, staff, and faculty continue to experience macro and microaggressions on university and college campuses (Corbin et al., 2018; Hotchkins, 2017; Husband, 2016; Minnett et al., 2019; Smith, 2004; Smith et al., 2011). Burke (2020) encourages institutions to couple their mission statements with structures and systems that support the safety and security of Black students. Some actions may include creating safe places for Black students to express themselves, offering culturally competent counselors, and comprehensively scrutinizing reported cases of racism and discrimination (Burke, 2020). Institutions can also offer cultural centers and Black professional organizations to provide counter spaces where Black people on campus can feel empowered (Husband, 2016). These strategies allow institutions to operate intentionally and proactively as opposed to reacting to racial tensions and incidents as they occur.

Interdependence and Decentralization

Organizations typically focus on independence and competition to survive and achieve success (Brown, 2017). Higher education institutions should instead focus on building "mutual reliance and shared leadership, and vision." (Brown, 2017, p. 87). This type of interdependence requires institutions to decentralize idea generation and focus on creating solutions and decisions together. When more people are involved in creating solutions, more people have a greater opportunity to have their concerns addressed. Creative ideation requires strong and deep relationships. Interdependence requires individuals to realize and accept complexity and be open to learning with and from others.

Brown (2017) suggests several strategies that institutions can implement to practice interdependence and decentralization: learning communities, assigning roles, agenda templates, and succession planning. Learning communities are spaces where people can come together to practice ideation through different socially constructed lenses and ways of knowing (Brown, 2017). Higher education learning communities can provide spaces for faculty, staff, and administration to come together to share their knowledge, experiences, and creativity and learn from one another.

Groups and departments in higher education can utilize the Decider/ Delegator, Accountable, Responsible, Consulted, and Informed (DARCI) tool to organize decisions in groups or networks across the institution (Brown, 2017). This tool helps to identify, assign, and clarify roles individuals play within the broader system. Assigning roles can eliminate confusion and conflict and help the group. Agenda templates are also helpful in ensuring meetings have purpose and intention behind them. Agenda templates can include space to discuss report outs, previous and future decisions, next steps or assignments, as well as relationship-building activities (e.g., games or ice breakers (Brown, 2017). Institutions should also consider succession planning to ease leadership transitions in case members leave or are unavailable so that the group's work can continue without disruption or lost focus (Brown, 2017).

Nonlinear and Iterative

Brown's (2017) emergent strategy framework recognizes transformation is not linear and instead occurs in cycles or bursts. Higher education institutions must embrace the iterative nature of transformation and change. Institutions should not be afraid to experiment, learn from their mistakes, adjust, and begin the cycle again. Brown suggests several tools for non-linear and iterative leadership: Post-it planning, circular agendas, and individual and collective reflection. Groups engaging in ideation and brainstorming can utilize reusable and movable Post-It notes to visually plan tasks, assign work, and recognize moving parts of processes and practices. Circular agendas provide space and opportunity for groups to engage in iterative and non-linear conversations and brainstorming. With circular agendas, groups collectively set clear goals and focus for meetings beforehand but avoid firm time-bound agenda articles that constrict creativity and innovation. Institutions operating in virtual spaces may use virtual whiteboards or sites such as Miro to mimic this activity online.

Transformation requires reflection and exploration of decisions and changes at the individual and group level. Institutions should create space for individuals to engage in constructive feedback that supports institutional learning and improvement. Change is difficult and often can result in feelings of grief (Brown, 2017). The COVID-19 pandemic brought on an unprecedented amount of loss and angst in our country. Institutions need to give space for faculty, staff, and students to process their feelings and grief. These safe spaces should allow communities on campus to come together and express themselves as well as comfort and support one another.

Resilience

Brown (2017) posits resilience is one of humanity's greatest traits as we can recover from hardship and pain we experience in our lives. This same resilience can be harnessed in higher education by using transformative justice, a strategy for resilience that seeks to transform conditions that perpetuate social injustices. One tool for practicing transformative justice is generative conflict relationship prompts (Brown, 2017). Generative conflict relationship prompts are a series of questions that allow individuals to explore how they make sense of and approach conflict. This activity recognizes the fact that conflict is inevitable and healthy. Higher education institutions can encourage faculty, staff, and students to answer prompts that explore how they as individuals handle conflict, how they were socialized in their families and in other spaces to handle conflict. The goal is to identify patterns and create the agency needed to transform the group's leadership development. From these exercises' groups can better understand how each other approaches conflict and determine group norms and practices to approach conflict in the future. These conversations can occur at staff or faculty meetings, in classrooms, or in student organizations.

Creating More Possibilities

The last element of emergent strategy builds on the previous elements as it requires individuals in a group or institution to engage in a collaborative process of ideation early and frequently (Brown, 2017). The COVID-19 pandemic has presented unprecedented obstacles as institutions must adjust and respond to health and safety restrictions. At the same time, institutions must address structures that perpetuate racial and gendered inequality in higher education. To face these obstacles and remain adaptive and innovative, institutions must create strong relationships and connections, remaining resilient, and moving with intentional adaptation to cultivate real change. The emergent strategy framework provides practical tools and strategies to help institutions create small changes that can amount to larger, structural changes in higher education.

REFERENCES

Anand, D., & Hsu, L. (2020). Think outside the book: Transformative justice using children's literature in educational settings. *Journal of Curriculum Studies Research*, 2(2), 122–143.

Bouty, I. (2000). Interpersonal and interaction influences on informal resource exchanges between R&D researchers across organizational boundaries. *Academy of Management Journal, 43*, 50–65.

Bourdieu, P. (1986). The forms of capital. In J. G. Richardson (Ed.), *Handbook of theory and research for the sociology of education* (pp. 241–258). Greenwood.

Brown, A. M. (2017). *Emergent strategy: Shaping change, changing worlds.* AK Press.

Burke, M. G. (2020). Moving beyond the statements: The need for action to address structural racism at predominately White institutions. *International Journal of Multidisciplinary Perspectives in Higher Education, 5*(1), 174–179.

Corbin, N. A., Smith, W. A., & Garcia, J. R. (2018). Trapped between justified anger and being the strong Black woman: Black college women coping with racial battle fatigue at historically and predominantly White institutions. *International Journal of Qualitative Studies in Education, 31*(7), 626–643.

Day, D. V. (2000). Leadership development: A review in context. *Leadership Quarterly, 11*(4), 581–613.

Guthrie, K. L. (2016). Expanding leadership education: Teaching service-learning online. *ILA Member Connector, 6*, 15–17. https://ilaglobalnetwork.org/wp-content/uploads/2020/11/PAUSE-for-Pedagogy-June2016.pdf

Hotchkins, B. (2017). Black women students at predominantly White universities: Narratives of identity politics, well-being, and leadership mobility. *NASPA Journal about Women in Higher Education, 10*(2), 144–155.

Husband, M. (2016). Racial battle fatigue and the Black student affairs professional in the era of #BlackLivesMatter. *Vermont Connection, 37*, 91–98. https://scholarworks.uvm.edu/tvc/vol37/iss1/10

Manz, C. C., & Sims, H. P. (1989). *SuperLeadership: Leading others to lead themselves.* Prentice-Hall.

Marshall, J., Roache, D., & Moody-Marshall, R. (2020). Crisis leadership: A critical examination of educational leadership in higher education in the midst of the COVID-19 pandemic. *International Studies in Educational Administration, 48*(3), 30–37.

McCauley, C. D. (2000). *A systemic approach to leadership development* [Paper presentation]. 15th Annual Conference of the Society for Industrial and Organizational Psychology, New Orleans, LA, United States.

McCauley, C. D., Moxley, R. S., & Van Velsor, E. (Eds.). (1998). *The Center for Creative Leadership handbook of leadership development.* Jossey-Bass.

Minnett, J. L., James-Gallaway, A., & Owens, D. R. (2019). Help a sista out: Black women doctoral students' use of peer mentorship as an act of resistance. *Mid-Western Educational Researcher, 31*(2), 210–238.

Neck, C., & Manz, C. C. (1996). Thought self-leadership. The impact of mental strategies training on employee cognition, behavior, and affect. *Journal of Organizational Behavior, 17*, 445–467.

Smith, W. A. (2004). Black faculty coping with racial battle fatigue: The campus racial climate in a post-civil rights era. In D. Cleveland (Ed.), *A long way to go: Conversations about race by African American faculty and graduate students* (pp. 171–190). Peter Lang.

Smith, W. A., Hung, M., & Franklin, J. D. (2011). Racial battle fatigue and the "mis" education of Black men: Racial microaggressions, societal problems, and environmental stress. *Journal of Negro Education, 80*(1), 63–82.

Stewart, G. L., Carson, K. P., & Cardy, R. L. (1996). The joint effects of conscientiousness and self-leadership training on employee self-directed behavior in a service setting. *Personnel Psychology, 49*, 143–164.

Tsai, W., & Ghosal, S. (1998). Social capital and value creation: The role of intrafirm networks. *Academy of Management Journal, 41*, 464–676.

Yukl, G., & Mahsud, R. (2010). Why flexible and adaptive leadership is essential. *Consulting Psychology Journal Practice and Research, 62*(2), 81–93.

CHAPTER 8

POWER OF THE PEOPLE

Higher Education and Followership in the Time of Mass Media

Cassandra R. Kepple

Between Facebook, Instagram, and Twitter, Harvard University has more than 8.5 million followers (Best Colleges, 2020). The top 10 schools with the most followers each have more than 1 million across their platforms, meaning each post these institutions make could reach over 1 million people. As higher education institutions amass social media followers, it opens up new avenues of communication and connection. Through this mass media lens, followership in higher education has taken take on a new meaning, which parallels the ever-increasing complexities of our world. This chapter focuses on how higher education can leverage social media to foster followership. I begin by describing current scholarship on followership and followership education. Next, I outline highlight cases examples of social media use in higher education. Finally, I frame followership in times of uncertainty, and share strategies in how social media can foster followership.

FOLLOWERSHIP AND FOLLOWERSHIP EDUCATION

What does it mean to be a follower? How does it feel to be called follower? Prior research alludes to negative perceptions of followership, perhaps

Navigating Complexities in Leadership: Moving Toward Critical Hope, pp. 79–88
www.infoagepub.com
Copyright © 2022 by Information Age Publishing
All rights of reproduction in any form reserved.

due to Western society's overemphasis on being a leader. However, scholars have operationalized leadership as a process which involves both leaders *and* followers (Murji, 2015; Riggio, 2020; Uhl-Bien et al., 2014), and there is a growing focus on theories, practice, and education related to followership. Responding to the scarcity of literature, scholars are increasingly advancing followership as critical to leadership learning and development (Hurwitz & Hurwitz, 2020; D. Jenkins & Spranger, 2020; Murji, 2015).

Uhl-Bien et al. (2014) define followership as "an investigation of the nature and impact of followers and following in the leadership process" (p. 89). Riggio (2020) suggests exchanging the word "followership" for "citizenship" to gain a wider perspective on what it means to be a follower in different contexts. Newer definitions emphasize the ways followers take action in their organization rather than being passive members who do whatever is mandated by a leader. As researchers develop ways to teach effective followership, this idea of being an active member is central. Chaleff (2015) speaks to the active role a follower takes in suggesting how to provide feedback to leaders without overstepping their role as a follower. Some traditional theories of leadership define followers as holding passive roles in the total process of leadership, creating a negative connotation (Hurwitz & Hurwitz, 2020). Thus, there has been little interest or buy-in for followership-focused education. However, integration of social media has changed the societal meaning of followers, generating curiosity and receptiveness to followership (Hurwitz & Hurwitz, 2020).

Followership education has become more present in leadership research (Hurwitz & Thompson, 2020). Scholars propose the lack of focus on effective followership may lead to toxic leadership (Chaleff, 2020). Hurwitz and Hurwitz (2020) suggest that educators incorporate followership into their programs by (a) showing students that effective organizations foster active followership, (b) enabling students to appreciate followership, and (c) being cognizant of how the theories used portray followers. When advocating for followership education to occur in higher education settings, it is vital to recognize how mass media is reshaping how followers engage in the leadership process.

EXAMPLES OF FOLLOWERSHIP
AND HIGHER EDUCATION USING MASS MEDIA

Riggio (2020) describes three main components to the leadership process: leaders, followers, and context. In the following case examples, the leaders are higher education institutions/administrators, the followers are students and staff, and the context is mass media. Higher education institutions have begun to embrace social media platforms to advertise themselves and recruit future students. Institutional leaders actively use social media to spread positive information about their institution. Yet, followers also actively engage with each other about institutional decision-making, and their response is not always positive. As social media enables more extensive networks, higher education institutions have been forced to embrace the unpredictable nature of situational responses, whether willingly or not.

Example 1: Work From Home Policy at Florida State University Gains National Attention

In summer 2020, Florida State University released a work from home policy. The policy statement seemed to imply that employees would be penalized if they were found to be taking care of dependents during work hours. Staff and students took to sites such as Twitter and Facebook to share their displeasure with the statement. These posts spread like wildfire, even to the extent of being featured in major news outlets such as *The New York Times*. The *Times* story focused on the backlash the university received because of the policy change and how it was communicated, showcasing how a problem escalated from an internal situation to a highly public one due to social media reactions and subsequent news outlets (Fortin & Bryson Taylor, 2020). Institutional leaders responded to this backlash by clarifying the official statement and saying employees would not be punished for taking care of their loved ones. This example of active followership gave necessary feedback to the leaders, and the followers got the change they demanded.

Example 2: President of the University of Notre Dame Does Not Heed His Own Policy

While the University of Notre Dame was encouraging students to social distance and wear masks to mitigate the spread of COVID-19, the institution's president attended an event at the White House where he followed neither of those guidelines. Afterward, it was discovered he had contracted the virus. The Notre Dame community activated on social media, calling out the president for his behaviors and questioning why they should be following the guidelines when he did not himself, going so far as to call for his resignation (Hughes, 2020). The president released a statement responding to the criticism, acknowledging he was wrong in his actions and needed to be a better model for the community (J. Jenkins,

2020). In this case, we again see followers actively engaged in holding their leader accountable for his actions. Social media provided a large audience by which to magnify their influence. While it does not excuse his behaviors, the president's swift apology statement showed how the institution and its networks actively worked to fix the situation. And, the lessons learned have prepared them to respond to future issues that arise.

Example 3: Social Justice Movements in Mass Media

In 2020, students, faculty, and staff spoke up about racial injustices on campus and how it has affected their postsecondary experiences. The #Black@ and #BlackInTheIvory movements provided students and academics with an opportunity to express their experiences with racism on campus and fostered a way to bring down these historically oppressive systems (Ruf, 2020). Along with the #MeToo movement, these movements have been ways for followers to get their voices heard when the formal reporting systems on campuses have not done their jobs (Ruf, 2020). Additionally, other media movements have emerged in response to the murders of Black citizens across the nation and advocate for removing the presence of entities celebrating racist individuals. One such example has been occurring on the Texas A&M University campus concerning a statue of Lawrence Sullivan Ross, a previous university president and Confederate general (Svrluga et al., 2020). The University of Nevada at Las Vegas and Washington and Lee University are two other universities at which online petitions through such sites as Change.org have called for changes in mascots, names of buildings, and even the names of the institutions themselves (Svrluga, 2020).

The landscape of higher education continues to change rapidly in light of local and global challenges. Higher education leaders are well served to employ a systems theory approach to anticipate and respond to the needs of their followers.

USING SYSTEMS AND COMPLEXITY THEORY TO FRAME FOLLOWERSHIP

If leaders make decisions without understanding their followers or getting their input, it may lead to conflict. There must be a process between leaders and followers to resolve conflict, or even to realize conflict is occurring in the first place. A theoretical framework using systems and complexity theory approaches would best fit organizations trying to prepare for times of uncertainty, such as possible online backlash from decisions. These the-

Figure 8.1

Flow of Influence Between Followers and Leaders

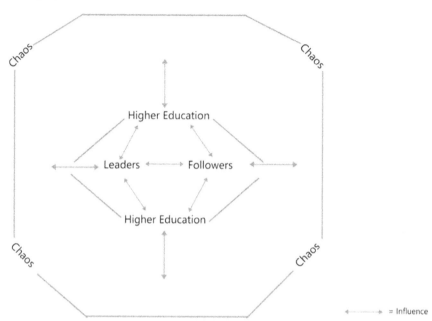

ories focus on the relationship between leaders and followers and recognize the importance of their network in remaining effective.

Two main components of systems and complexity theories help to frame engaged followership in higher education during times of uncertainty: (1) everything and everyone are connected; (2) prepare for the unexpected (Uhl-Bien & Arena, 2017, 2018; Uhl-Bien et al., 2020; Wheatley, 2006). Systems theory suggests effective organizations are effective because of the relationship networks between the people who make up the organization and their ability to remain adaptive in the face of change (Heifetz et al., 2009; Wheatley, 2006). Knowing followers influence leaders as much as leaders influence followers, and the environment influences everyone involved, a model was created to represent the flow of influence across each of these levels (as seen in Figure 8.1).

This model illustrates how influence can come from all directions, whether from individuals involved in the followership process, the higher education institution itself, and any of the chaos naturally existing in the world.

Leadership and leadership learning in higher education must involve active followers, and as our world becomes increasingly complex, part of this process is accepting the growing importance of social media. As mentioned previously, the word "follower" has historically had a negative connotation, but social media is helping to change this stereotype. Social media sites give the user a choice to "follow" whoever they want, and as followers, they have the option of whether or not they would like to actively engage with organizations. This change in narrative surrounding the term "follower" thanks to social media connects to followership theories. It supports actively engaged followers who are making real change happen by using their voices.

Social media is increasing the number of followers in higher education. More than ever before, people can see decisions being made, and voice their opinions on them. If leaders lean into the power of the organization's networks, they can move forward as an effective organization, even in times of uncertainty.

Followership education should also emphasize that chaos, or unpredictable occurrences, will always happen. A major aspect of systems and complexity theories is knowing chaos is going to happen, recognizing what will happen cannot be predicted, and embracing this knowledge so preparations can be made for anything to happen. Leaders can look to emerging perspectives in such fields as chemistry, physics, and biology to see that chaos occurs in nature regularly, and systems who embrace the idea of chaos and adapt are the ones who survive (Kilburg & Donohue, 2014; Marion & Uhl-Bien, 2014; Wheatley, 2006). A source of chaos in these complex times for higher education institutions is increased followership due to mass media. Decisions reach the public much faster than ever before, and higher education leaders must prepare for their followers to be active and be ready to respond. Otherwise, they may not be able to maintain the support of those followers.

USING MASS MEDIA TO EMBRACE AND NAVIGATE CHAOS

As leadership educators, we must teach about the entire leadership process, including the importance of followers and their engagement. Educators, students, and higher education administrators can actively use social media to engage in leadership and followership education, research, and practice.

Educators

To teach effective followership via mass media, educators should make it part of their curriculum. When creating this curriculum, educators can look to Ahlquist (2017), who covers how students are engaging in leadership on social media and provides instructors with pillars of digital leadership education. These pillars include both individual and global skills that educators should work on with their students to teach them how to properly engage in leadership online (Ahlquist, 2017). Educators can use these pillars and the provided reflection model for building their curriculum, as well as spend time dedicated to connecting leadership to followership.

As educators find ways to discuss the importance of followership and how students can engage in it effectively, they should provide practical ways for students to use the information, such as requiring social media engagement as part of the curriculum. Educators can also break down why real-life movements were successful by showing what strategies work, as well as those that do not. By making this pathway to followership an integral part of followership education, educators stand to embrace the ever-increasing presence of technology in students' lives, showcase the positive change students can make with active followership, and make sure they are sending out engaged and knowledgeable citizens once they leave their classroom.

Students

As history shows, students' voices have been vital in making sure education is an equitable environment for everyone. If students do not speak up when they see injustices, it will be assumed they agree with decisions being made. Students can make sure they are staying informed by following accounts on social media related to their institution, as well as following other actively engaged students. Not all decisions being made will be posted to social media, but if followers know of decisions that are made and they want to show their support or dissent of them, they can use social media as an avenue for their opinions. Students should actively engage in followership by giving feedback to higher education leaders, but they should make sure they are informed on the situation before speaking about it. Students could truly have an impact on decisions made by using their networks and engaging other interested parties.

Higher Education Administrators

Higher education administrators must be prepared for chaos and a wide array of responses from their decisions. Institutions are increasingly using social media platforms to recruit students and advertise their successes as they understand coming generations will be using these platforms more and more. They should also use this strategy when communicating decisions made by leaders, especially when those decisions may not be received well. Using systems theory, higher education institutions can embrace the knowledge that they are only as effective as the networks of people who make them. Institutions can use social media to gauge reactions to decisions made, poll followers about possible future decisions, and expand their networks of followers. Higher education leaders must be strategic with their social media use, be conscious not all followers will agree with every decision made, and recognize social media projects the opinions of their followers no matter if they are supporting or dissenting those decisions.

CONCLUSION

Leadership is a process that involves engagement by both leaders and followers. There may be more opportunities for us to be active followers than leaders in our lifetime. Emphasizing followership in leadership education is needed to support the development of informed and active followers (Murji, 2015; Riggio, 2020; Uhl-Bien et al., 2014). More practitioners are developing programs and coursework which aim to reframe followership in a positive light, get students to appreciate the importance of followership, and provide students with opportunities to be actively engaged followers (Hurwitz & Hurwitz, 2020; Jenkins & Spranger, 2020; Murji, 2015). Additionally, systems and complexity theories can help higher education leaders understand how leadership and followership occur as a process because of the relationships between the people in their organizations. As students and other followers are encouraged to engage via new and evolving communication platforms, educators and higher education leaders should be prepared to listen to and leverage followers' voices. Institutions will successfully grow throughout the chaos if leaders and followers know how to engage effectively and prepare for the unknown.

REFERENCES

Ahlquist, J. (2017). Digital student leadership development. In J. Ahlquist & L. Endersby (Eds.), *New Directions for Student Leadership: No. 153. Going digital in student leadership* (pp. 47–62). Wiley. https://doi.org/10.1002/yd.20229

Best Colleges. (2020). *The colleges dominating social media.* https://www.bestcolleges.com/features/best-college-social-media/

Chaleff, I. (2015). *Intelligent disobedience: Doing right when what you're told to do is wrong* (1st ed.). Berrett-Koehler.

Chaleff, I. (2020). Foreword. In M. Hurwitz & R. Thompson (Eds.), *New Directions for Student Leadership: No. 167. Followership education* (pp. 11–13). Wiley. https://doi.org/10.1002/yd.20394

Fortin, J., & Bryson Taylor, D. (2020, July 7). Florida State University child care policy draws backlash. *The New York Times*. https://www.nytimes.com/2020/07/02/us/fsu-telecommute-remote.html

Heifetz, R. A., Linsky, M., & Grashow, A. (2009). *The practice of adaptive leadership: Tools and tactics for changing your organization and the world*. Harvard Business Press.

Hughes, A. (2020, September 29). Notre Dame president apologizes for not wearing mask during White House announcement of Amy Coney Barrett's Supreme Court nomination. *Chicago Tribune*. https://www.chicagotribune.com/coronavirus/ct-nw-notre-dame-president-mask-apology-20200929-fa6ts6puindarjqwlfxzwbkj7e-story.html

Hurwitz, M., & Hurwitz, S. (2020). Integrating followership into leadership programs. In M. Hurwitz & R. Thompson (Eds.), *New Directions for Student Leadership: No. 167. Followership education* (pp. 23–35). Wiley. https://doi.org/10.1002/yd.20396

Hurwitz, M., & Thompson, R. (Eds.). (2020). *New Directions for Student Leadership: No. 167. Followership education*. Wiley. https://doi.org/10.1002/yd.20327

Jenkins, D. M., & Spranger, A. N. (2020). Followership education for postsecondary students. In M. Hurwitz & R. Thompson (Eds.), *New Directions for Student Leadership: No. 167. Followership education* (pp. 47–63). Wiley. https://doi.org/10.1002/yd.20398

Jenkins, J. (2020). A message from Rev. John I. Jenkins, C.S.C.: I regret my error of judgment in not wearing a mask. *University of Notre Dame*. https://president.nd.edu/homilies-writings-addresses/a-message-from-rev-john-i-jenkins-c-s-c-i-regret-my-error-of-judgment-in-not-wearing-a-mask/

Kilburg, R. R., & Donohue, M. D. (2014). Leadership and organizational behavior: A thermodynamic inquiry. *Consulting Psychology Journal: Practice and Research*, *66*(4), 261–287. https://doi.org/10.1037/cpb0000013

Marion, R., & Uhl-Bien, M. (2014). Beyond emotion: Broader lessons from the states of matter. *Consulting Psychology Journal: Practice and Research*, *66*(4), 306–309. https://doi.org/10.1037/cpb0000018

Murji, S. (2015). Taking followership education to the next level. *Journal of Leadership Education*, *14*(3), 168–177. https://doi.org/10.12806/V14/I3/I1

Riggio, R. E. (2020). Why followership? In M. Hurwitz & R. Thompson (Eds.), *New Directions for Student Leadership: No. 167. Followership education* (pp. 15–22). Wiley. https://doi.org/10.1002/yd.20395

Ruf, J. (2020, August 19). New media, new possibilities: How social media is shaping today's social movements. *Diverse Issues in Higher Education*. https://diverseeducation.com/article/188031/

Svrluga, S. (2020, June 19). As colleges grapple with racist legacies, a monument at Ole Miss will finally go. *The Washington Post*. https://www.washingtonpost.com/education/2020/06/19/colleges-grapple-with-racist-legacies-monument-ole-miss-will-finally-go/

Svrluga, S., Grant, M. L., & Martin, B. (2020, September 8). Debates over race, history and values roil Texas A&M as campus diversifies. *The Washington Post.* https://www.washingtonpost.com/education/2020/09/08/debates-over-race-history-values-challenge-texas-am-campuses-student-body-diversifies/

Uhl-Bien, M., & Arena, M. (2017). Complexity leadership: Enabling people and organizations for adaptability. *Organizational Dynamics, 46*(1), 9–20. https://doi.org/10.1016/j.orgdyn.2016.12.001

Uhl-Bien, M., & Arena, M. (2018). Leadership for organizational adaptability: A theoretical synthesis and integrative framework. *The Leadership Quarterly, 29*(1), 89–104. https://doi.org/10.1016/j.leaqua.2017.12.009

Uhl-Bien, M., Meyer, D., & Smith, J. (2020). Complexity leadership in the nursing context. *Nursing Administration Quarterly, 44*(2), 109–116. https://doi.org/10.1097/NAQ.0000000000000407

Uhl-Bien, M., Riggio, R. E., Lowe, K. B., & Carsten, M. K. (2014). Followership theory: A review and research agenda. *The Leadership Quarterly, 25*(1), 83–104. https://doi.org/10.1016/j.leaqua.2013.11.007

Wheatley, M. J. (2006). *Leadership and the new science: Discovering order in a chaotic world* (3rd ed.). Berrett-Koehler.

CHAPTER 9

EMERGING ENGAGEMENT AND LEADERSHIP DURING COMPLEX TIMES

Marissa Mainwood

Working with 25 Student Leadership Council members in a college of business for the past 3 years has been a unique experience. Traditionally the group dynamic develops based on each student's comfort level interacting within the group setting and their individual leadership style. However, during the COVID-19 pandemic, higher education learning shifted to primarily virtual spaces. I noticed a shift occurring within the Student Leadership Council as well. Many of the more outspoken students were not as vocal in meetings. In contrast, students who were typically more passive began finding their voices and redefining their engagement and position as a leader in the group.

Reflecting on the changing group dynamics, I wondered if the idea of students finding themselves in the middle of an unexpected crisis had changed the positionality of the members and caused a shift in their engagement with the leadership process. The student responses were similar to the findings of previous studies, for example, "groups in a crisis situation were more likely to be influenced by their leaders and were more likely to replace unsuccessful leaders than groups that were not in a crisis situation" (Hamblin, 1958, as cited in Halverson, Holladay, et al., 2004,

Navigating Complexities in Leadership: Moving Toward Critical Hope, pp. 89–97
www.infoagepub.com
Copyright © 2022 by Information Age Publishing
All rights of reproduction in any form reserved.

p. 264). Reflecting on my own experiences, I can recall situations where my engagement in leadership roles shifted when I least expected it. In the middle of particularly stressful situations–where I would normally step back or be unsure how to act—I found myself acting differently, decidedly. And this is what I noticed happening with students when environmental factors and crises began changing the educational landscape and creating personal struggles for so many.

Educators effectively facilitate learning when they utilize teaching methods that focus on students' recognition of their own ability to connect and lead within groups. This includes helping students realize the changing roles they play in leadership processes. Sometimes a person plays a leader role, and for various reasons, they may step into a follower role. This chapter focuses on the emergence of student leaders during times of stress and uncertainty resulting from significant campus or community events. The discussion will include possible explanations for why student leadership qualities emerge from stressful situations, some of the many influences on leadership development during trying times, and additional implications for educators to consider.

For the purpose of this chapter, I will frame the emergence of leader qualities and students' displays of leadership through a person-centered and role-based approach. Looking at leadership from this angle, I believe a few key considerations are likely to impact student leader development during complex times and in crisis situations. These include the unique personality types of students, basic needs fulfillment (or the lack thereof), and the burden of responsibility in a stressful environment.

STUDENT ENGAGEMENT DURING TURBULENT TIMES

The years leading up to and into the new decade have been characterized by disappointments, frustrations, and general anxiety. Arguably one of the most enduring and exhausting trials has been the COVID-19 pandemic. In addition to changing the landscape of higher education, the pandemic caused unemployment across the United States to skyrocket from 6.2 million to almost 20.5 million in only a few months during the spring of 2020 (Kochhar, 2020). Many students, particularly minority students, experienced increased hardships and stress that came with the shift in learning, including not having access to reliable technology to participate in coursework (Garcia et al., 2020). During this transitional time, the changing leadership dynamic became more apparent in many of our student leaders. Those who had previously been very vocal and active in campus organization organizations were not necessarily taking on the same responsibilities. Instead, they were on other students to more actively take a leading role in the group. Meanwhile, traditionally quieter students actively voiced their opinions and sought out added responsibilities; their leadership appeared to be emerging due to the pandemic crisis and changing environmental climate.

As the summer 2020 semester began, the killing of George Floyd, a Black man in Minnesota, triggered nationwide demonstrations and support for the Black Lives Matter movement in response to police brutality (Parker et al., 2020). According to the Pew Research Center (2020), "About 7-in-10 Americans," or 69% of those surveyed, were having conversations with "family and friends about racial equality" (Parker et al., 2020, para. 36). With important conversations happening in social circles and between loved ones, campuses across the nation, including Florida State University, also began engaging their communities in critical dialogue that was largely student driven. Generation Z's active engagement in social justice and demand for an institutional response led to the implementation of a variety of measures, such as creating task forces focused on equity and inclusion, providing additional support and platforms for minority students to voice their concerns, and ensuring training on diversity and inclusion for the campus community (Division of Student Affairs, 2020). Administrators, faculty, and staff began to listen more to student needs and concerns. More students exercised their voices and started leading their peers in dialogue and practices to help ensure the campus community understood the importance of the Black Lives Matter movement and displayed support for peers.

By the fall of 2020, the country was further divided politically by the looming presidential election. Friends and strangers alike became embroiled in debates regarding the candidates' responses to the COVID-19 pandemic, growing unemployment issues, police brutality, and racial injustices. By 6 months into the pandemic, most higher education courses continued to be offered remotely, and student leadership and overall motivation once again appeared to be shifting. "Zoom fatigue," or the mental exhaustion from the use of video-conferencing platforms (Sklar, 2020), further set in as students experienced mental exhaustion, withdrawal effects from the lack of real human connection, and disappointment at not getting a real campus experience.

INFLUENCES ON LEADERSHIP

The question of whether leaders are born or made has been a hotly debated issue for decades. While previous studies of twins have found that some traits and qualities encompassed in the societal definitions of a 'good leader' are inherited, studies have also indicated that the environment plays a role in shaping leaders (Boerma et al., 2017; Twito & Knafo-Noam, 2020). Environmental influence of leadership development aligns with my observations of the emergence of student leaders during unexpected crisis. Of note, however, is that previous research does not conclude whether leadership in stressful situations "changes leader behavior or changes follower perceptions of that behavior" (Halverson, Murphy, et al., 2004, p. 496). This could potentially be one of the spaces where students who may not be as outwardly inclined to take on leadership roles emerge and establish their position as a leader. There are many factors that could be at play in the emergence of student leaders during stressful times and crisis situations, including personality types, fulfill basic needs, and the influence of stressful environments.

Unique Personality Types

The approach to examining how personality relates to leadership, known as trait theory, characterizes an individual's "personality in terms of internal characteristics that are presumed to determine behavior" (American Psychological Association, n.d., para 1) which, in turn, influences leadership style. A popular psychometric assessment used in leadership development is the Myers-Briggs Type Indicator (The Myers & Briggs Foundation, n.d.). The Myers-Briggs Type Indicator offers insight into a person's unique preferences, or patterns of thinking and behavior in four domains: where you get energy (introversion or extroversion), how you take in information and make meaning (sensing or perception), how you make decisions (thinking or feeling), and how you order your world (judging or perceiving) (The Myers & Briggs Foundation, n.d.). Understanding one's own and others' preferences allows them to be more effective in leading others and working collaboratively with others.

For example, someone with a type profile of ISFJ (Introversion + Sensing + Feeling + Judging) may be more introverted and have a quieter personality. They may be more likely to excel in a remote situation, similar to what we have been in during the pandemic. Therefore, students who fit this personality type might be more apt to show emerging leadership development during a time of remote interaction, as the computer provides options for levels of engagement.

Basic Need Fulfillment

Another possible factor impacting students' emerging leadership is the ebb and flow of their basic need fulfillment during complex situations. With so many environmental and personal unknowns, students experience differing levels of having their basic needs fulfilled. For several months many did not have residence hall access, campus food options, or access to reliable technology and internet services to participate in online learning (Heitz et al., 2020). Employment became a concern for students who worked in service and hospitality industries which took a significant hit to business within the first few months of the COVID-19 pandemic. Nationwide, we experienced "one of the deepest economic downturns in our history," with over 30 million unemployment claims filed within about a month (Bernstein & Jones, 2020, para. 1). Additionally, many students feared for their personal safety following the killing of George Floyd and ongoing instances of police brutality and protesting.

The crises facing the nation and world had a direct impact on the basic needs of our students. According to Maslow's (1943) needs theory of development, people move through different need stages in which "the appearance of one need usually rests on the prior satisfaction of another" (Maslow, 1943, p. 370). The first two needs levels include physiological needs (e.g., food, water) and safety needs (e.g., health, personal safety). If students cannot meet their basic needs, it would be difficult for them to advance their thinking and focus on developing a stronger sense of self.

Along with uncertainty regarding basic physiological needs and safety needs, many students have likely been experiencing a shift in their need for love and belong (Maslow, 1943). Social distancing, masking guidelines, school and business closures, and travel restrictions were implemented to protect the health and safety of communities across the country and globe. However, these measures isolated students from their support systems, including family, friends, and social connections. According to Maslow (1943), without fulfilling this level of belonging, it is highly unlikely that students would have the capacity to focus on their esteem needs, the level at which more significant leadership development would potentially occur.

However, for some students the shift to remote learning was an opportunity to return home to their families and environments. Students in this situation would be far more likely to have their basic physiological, safety, and love needs fulfilled, allowing them to focus more on their esteem needs and personal self-development. In this case, these students may have been ready for leadership emergence.

Leading Under Stress

There are understood structures of organization, leadership hierarchy, and role assignments among team members in many businesses and educational institutions. The same is true with many on-campus student organizations where officers are typically elected every year to lead the group. Setting defined roles tends to place the expectation of group leadership primarily on designated officers, which can cause students holding those roles added stress, particularly in crisis situations. The authors of a study on charismatic leadership hypothesized that "crisis can be detrimental to leader behavior" in certain situations and that it could "push leaders beyond an optimal level of stress (eustress) into distress, resulting in poor leader behavior" (Halverson, Murphy, et al., 2004, pp. 496–497).

This idea aligns with the basic need fulfillment theory and why some students may display emerging leadership in times of crisis, while others temporarily step back in their organizations and take on more of a follower role. Faced with the pandemic, political uncertainty, and period of unrest from social justice issues, many of the student leaders I work with expressed feelings of being overwhelmed and burnt out with all that was going on in their lives. As a result, many were apologizing for stepping back from their usual activities and obligations. Meanwhile, other students in less stressful situations with more support from family and loved ones were coming forward, asking for additional opportunities to take on projects and roles that allowed them to support their campus and the greater community.

IMPLICATIONS FOR LEADERSHIP TEACHING AND LEARNING

As a best practice, faculty and staff at higher education institutions should continuously encourage the development of leadership qualities and capacity in all students. When faculty and staff notice students' emerging leadership behaviors in stressful situations, or other instances where they step outside of their normal patterns of behavior, educators should make an additional point of encouraging the student to reflect on their actions and emerging leadership.

Acknowledging Leadership Behaviors

In certain situations, students might not recognize their ability to lead or see the opportunity for leadership behaviors to emerge. A student may display leadership behaviors but not see how their contribution is an act of leadership based on a limited frame of the term. For example, a few years ago I advised a student in the Student Leadership Council who was incredibly shy. The student would often sit away from the rest of the group and not interact with other members. However, the student noticed an opportunity that would benefit the group and mentioned it to me, unsure about sharing it with peers. I encouraged the student to share the idea and used the experience as a coaching moment to point out how I saw their leadership behaviors and role within the group emerging. At the next meeting, the student shared the idea with the group, which was positively received, and from then on, the student became more actively engaging with the rest of the group. The student later became an officer in the council and, more importantly, a peer mentor for other younger members to help encourage them to explore their emerging leadership. They became an executive officer for the organization and, more importantly, leader role model for younger members.

Educators acknowledging and encouraging emerging leadership behaviors in students when they see them occurring can positively impact the students' development. By reaffirming the behaviors, students are more likely to have boosted self-confidence and continue to explore their leadership behaviors as they are receiving praise from a trusted leader.

Modeling Desired Leadership Behaviors

Another best practice for educators is modeling leadership behaviors. While this seems obvious and intuitive to most educators, it can be easy for us to forget that students continually observe our behaviors as a leader and look to us for advice. Too often, we can become comfortable in our positions and more casual roles of working with our students. Educators must continually self-evaluate their attitudes and actions, striving to model positive leadership behaviors.

Additionally, educators should help students recognize how they model behaviors for peers. Students who interact with younger peers, in the form of being a teaching assistant or officer of a student organization, should be especially aware of how their modeled leader behaviors can impact the emerging leadership of other students.

Intentional Peer-to-Peer Reflection

Educators should not only encourage students to reflect on their own emerging leadership but share their leadership journey with fellow peers as well, creating a peer-to-peer leadership development model. One great way to encourage peer-to-peer connection is through small-group activities and follow-up discussions that can help students better recognize and acknowledge their personal leadership behaviors in relation to their fellow peers.

Additionally, peer discussions allow students to explore their feelings related to experiences, share best practices in leading with their peers, and commit the process to memory as they continue developing their individual and group leadership skills. Small group discussions regarding potentially stressful or unexpected leadership situations are an opportunity for students to examine how they feel they would respond before possibly finding themselves in similar situations. In a future situation where they unexpectedly find their leadership emerging, the students will be more likely to recognize their own potential as a leader and broaden their understanding of how their leadership fits within the frame of the situation.

CONCLUDING THOUGHTS

Overall, educators need to keep in mind play a pivotal role in how student leadership develops and emerges. Through modeling positive leader behaviors, coaching students through stressful experiences, and making a point to discuss the various aspects of leadership, we have the potential to help our students find their self-confidence and emerge as strong leaders—now and in the future. Student leadership emerges at various times and can look very different for each student during times of crisis. However, there is no time like the present to support our students and help them recognize their capabilities and limitations in pursuit of leadership growth and development.

REFERENCES

American Psychological Association. (n.d.). *APA dictionary of psychology*. https://dictionary.apa.org/trait-theory

Bernstein, J., & Jones, J. (2020, June). *The impact of the COVID 19 recession on the jobs and incomes of persons of color*. Center on Budget and Policy Priorities. https://www.cbpp.org/research/full-employment/the-impact-of-the-covid19-recession-on-the-jobs-and-incomes-of-persons-of

Boerma, M., Coyle, E. A., Dietrich, M. A., Dintzner, M. R., Drayton, S. J., Early, J. L., Edginton, A. N., Horlen, C. K., Kirkwood, C. K., Lin, A. Y., Rager, M. L., Shah-Manek, B., Welch, A. C., & Williams, N. T. (2017). Point/counterpoint: Are outstanding leaders born or made? *American Journal of Pharmaceutical Education*, *81*(3), 1–5. https://doi.org/10.5688/ajpe81358

Division of Student Affairs. (2020). *Black Lives Matter statement*. Florida State University. https://studentaffairs.fsu.edu/statements/black_lives_matter

Garcia, L. L., Bohlig, M., & Adkins, C. (2020, July 10). *The early impacts of COVID-19 on the community college student experience - higher education*. Diverse Issues in Higher Education. https://diverseeducation.com/article/183750/

Halverson, S. K., Holladay, C. L., Kazama, S. M., & Quiñones, M. A. (2004). Self-sacrificial behavior in crisis situations: The competing roles of behavioral and situational factors. *The Leadership Quarterly*, *15*(2), 263–275. https://doi.org/10.1016/j.leaqua.2004.02.001

Halverson, S. K., Murphy, S. E., & Riggio, R. E. (2004). Charismatic leadership in crisis situations. *Small Group Research*, *35*(5), 495–514. https://doi.org/10.1177/1046496404264178

Heitz, C., Laboissiere, M., Sanghvi, S., & Sarakatsannis, J. (2020, April 23). *Getting the next phase of remote learning right in higher education*. McKinsey & Company. https://www.mckinsey.com/industries/public-and-social-sector/our-insights/getting-the-next-phase-of-remote-learning-right-in-higher-education

Kochhar, R. (2020, June 11). *Unemployment rose higher in three months of COVID-19 than it did in two years of the Great Recession*. Pew Research Center. https://www.pewresearch.org/fact-tank/2020/06/11/unemployment-rose-higher-in-three-months-of-covid-19-than-it-did-in-two-years-of-the-great-recession/

Maslow, A. H. (1943). A theory of human motivation. *Psychological Review*, *50*(4), 370–396. https://doi.org/10.1037/h0054346

The Myers & Briggs Foundation. (n.d.). *MBTI® Basics*. https://www.myers-briggs.org/my-mbti-personality-type/mbti-basics/

Parker, K., Horowitz, J. M., & Anderson, M. (2020, June 12). *Amid protests, majorities across racial and ethnic groups express support for the Black Lives Matter movement*. Pew Research Center. https://www.pewresearch.org/social-trends/2020/06/12/amid-protests-majorities-across-racial-and-ethnic-groups-express-support-for-the-black-lives-matter-movement/

Sklar, J. (2020, April 24). *'Zoom fatigue' is taxing the brain. Here's why that happens*. National Geographic. https://www.nationalgeographic.com/science/article/coronavirus-zoom-fatigue-is-taxing-the-brain-here-is-why-that-happens#close

Twito, L., & Knafo-Noam, A. (2020). Beyond culture and the family: Evidence from twin studies on the genetic and environmental contribution to values. *Neuroscience & Biobehavioral Reviews*, *112*, 135–143. https://doi.org/10.1016/j.neubiorev.2019.12.029

CHAPTER 10

MAKING THE WORLD YOUR CLASSROOM

Observation as a Pedagogical Tool for Leadership Learning

Brittany Devies

The start of the new decade has been marked by historic, life-altering events that required courageous leadership. In the midst of a global pandemic, the news cycles report stories of increased presence of grassroots organizing for Black Lives Matter, voter turnout and awareness, global climate change awareness in response to a number of natural disasters in North America, increased violence within immigration detention centers, and more. All represent complex and interconnected challenges that require leadership. Now more than ever, opportunities for leadership learning are needed. Conversations about leadership are needed. Leadership educators are needed. Our responsibility as leadership educators is to acknowledge what is happening and work collectively to create positive social change. It is time for leadership educators to adapt to our current climate and respond with new and innovative pedagogies for leadership learning, including leadership observation.

Navigating Complexities in Leadership: Moving Toward Critical Hope, pp. 99–108
www.infoagepub.com
Copyright © 2022 by Information Age Publishing
All rights of reproduction in any form reserved.

FRAMING LEADERSHIP LEARNING

For this chapter, I define leadership as a "purposeful, collaborative, values-based process that results in positive social change" (Komives & Wagner, 2009, p. xii). Leadership should work to promote "equity, social justice, self-knowledge, personal empowerment, collaborating, citizenship, and change" (Higher Education Research Institute, 1996, p. 18). Bruce et al. (2019) propose that transformative leadership for social change should be grounded in the skills to "confront the pressing issues of justice, equity, and liberation" (p. 537). Further, they suggest that leadership learning can support individuals' ever-increasing active and visible identities across a continuum of development, from *learner* to *ally*, to *advocate*, to *activist* (Bruce et al., 2019).

These are conceptualizations of leadership foundational to this chapter; however, they are socially constructed within Western understandings of what the leadership process looks like (Grint, 1997, 2005). Grounded in a constructivist paradigm, a socially constructed understanding of leadership focuses on the person, the situation, and people's perceptions (Grint, 1997). My socially constructed understanding of leadership assumes that learning and development are critical components of the process of leadership. Therefore, the leadership learning framework is one way to explore the complexities of this moment, develop new understanding, and shape patterns in leadership learning (Guthrie & Jenkins, 2018).

LEADERSHIP LEARNING FRAMEWORK

The leadership learning framework pulls together six elements of leadership learning: knowledge, development, training, observation, engagement, and metacognition (Guthrie & Jenkins, 2018). Metaphorically illustrated in Figure 10.1 as a steering wheel, the outer wheel is leadership knowledge, defined as "interdisciplinary, academic and applied field of study that focuses on the fluid process and components of the interaction between leaders and followers in a particular context" (Sowcik, 2012, p. 193). The internal spokes of the framework include leadership development, which focuses on preparing the person and the intrapersonal aspects of leadership learning (Guthrie & Jenkins, 2018). Leadership training focuses on scaffolding learning and practice to reach mastery and behavioral change (Guthrie & Jenkins, 2018). Leadership observation is a constructivist process focused on the cultural and social aspects of leadership learning (Guthrie & Jenkins, 2018). Leadership engagement requires active involvement in the "experiential, relational, interactional,

Figure 10.1

Leadership Learning Framework

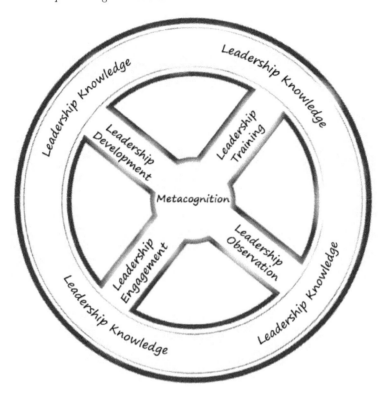

Source: Guthrie and Jenkins (2018, p. 58).

and interpersonal aspects of leadership learning" (Guthrie & Jenkins, 2018, p. 67). Finally, leadership metacognition centers on the "reflective, systemic, organizational, analytical, evaluative, adaptive, processual, mindful, and complex aspects of leadership learning" (Guthrie & Jenkins, 2018).

In traditional face-to-face curricular and cocurricular leadership learning, many options for leadership engagement, development, and training have been offered (Roberts & Ullom, 1989). But one spoke of the wheel often overlooked as a pedagogical tool and method of meaning making is leadership observation. In these pivotal moments of complexity, in our institutions and around the globe, it is time to pause and intentionally observe what is happening around us. Leadership observation is a critical tool for meaning making in complexity and uncertainty. Leadership educators have an opportunity to integrate the world and current climate into leadership learning spaces. We must pull in relevant examples, learn from personal leadership experiences, and help students make meaning of the world around them in these moments of historical significance.

WHY LEADERSHIP OBSERVATION?

Leadership observation "refers to the social, cultural, and observational aspects of leadership learning" (Guthrie & Jenkins, 2018, p. 65). It is a constructivist approach to leadership learning as the learner evaluating and making meaning of the effectiveness of the leadership process they are observing within the sociocultural context (Guthrie & Jenkins, 2018). While it is passive, observation is not simply looking at leadership but also evaluating and making meaning of the process as it unfolds (Guthrie & Jenkins, 2018). Through observation, the learner evaluates power, privilege, inequity, inclusion, engagement, and other dynamics between participants in the leadership process. It is critical to understand the cultural bounds of this particular medium of leadership learning as the sociocultural context undergirds the observation itself and the meaning making that comes from it (Guthrie & Jenkins, 2018; Merriam & Caffarella, 1999). Leadership learning models like the culturally relevant leadership learning model further emphasize the importance of culture in leadership learning, including campus culture (Bertrand Jones et al., 2016).

Mitra et al. (2010) used "the art of observation" as a tool to connect medical students to art to increase their observational skills in their medical practice. The students noticed increased observational skills and felt a significant sense of personal development (Mitra et al., 2010). "The ways of observing (or looking with intentionality) require us to go another step (or two) and to use our judgment and inference-making abilities to arrive at something resembling knowledge" (Mitra, 2011, p. 185). Looking with intention, or leadership observation, can be done through inductive looking (making sense of the world) or deductive looking (drawing inferences from previous experiences) (Mitra, 2011). Inductive looking often involves examining new ideas and concepts, where deductive looking is centered more on conclusions we draw from our previous experiences and universal principles (Mitra, 2011).

The first stage of the leadership identity development (LID) model is awareness. The model suggests that college students first learn leadership by observing others, illustrating how leadership identity development is grounded in leadership observation (Komives et al., 2005). "The first stage was the early recognition that leaders existed. As children, participants were particularly aware of parent figures and of national, historic, or charismatic leaders" (Komives et al., 2005, p. 606). In the awareness stage, a person holds a view of leadership that is external to oneself (Komives et al., 2005). As a learning strategy, observation asks students to look to leadership external to themselves. Connecting the leadership identity development model to the leadership learning framework, it is easy to conclude that leadership observation is a pedagogical approach to leadership learning that students are doing from a young age, whether it is intentionally or unintentionally. Society offers unending examples of leadership in action. Leadership educators need to utilize leadership observation as a pedagogical tool to help learners intentionally make meaning of the leadership they see daily on their campuses, on their Twitter feeds, in news cycles, and more.

THE RELEVANCE OF LEADERSHIP OBSERVATION

Rarely do real-life situations follow any leadership theory, model, or process perfectly. Leadership observation can be a challenging pedagogy to use in the classroom because of all the complexities real-life examples can add. It is easier to offer examples that neatly fit the theories or models we are teaching or have less additional noise and complex layers. There will always be space in leadership learning for instructor-created or book-provided simulations, case studies, or examples, as they often support scaffolded learning within curriculum. At the same time, students will be absorbing real-time examples of leadership whether or not we bring them into leadership learning spaces. They will still be looking at their Twitter timelines, YouTube channels, and news apps on their phones. Suppose the students are just absorbing these culturally relevant examples without the explicit connection to leadership learning. In that case, we are missing beautiful learning moments that students can deeply relate to their daily lives.

Pulling relevant, timely examples into our teaching gives students space to critically analyze and make meaning of the leadership processes they see happening in front of them every day. Observation opens the door to rich conversations about the social construction of leadership. Observation challenges students to consider multiple paradigms and how their worldviews have shaped their current constructions of leadership and identity. Actively using leadership observation as a pedagogical tool can also promote civic engagement and ground leadership education within higher education's purpose of benefiting the public good (Chunoo & Osteen, 2016; LeBlanc & Guthrie, 2021; Guthrie & Jenkins, 2018).

PUTTING LEADERSHIP OBSERVATION INTO PRACTICE

The study and practice of leadership are complex because it is interdisciplinary, not fitting into a box and following a formula. It is a focus of research for scholars across the world. Leadership educators utilize the leadership learning framework components daily while also navigating their own social identities, development, context, and communities (Priest & Jenkins, 2019). While leaning into complex contemporary issues as a pedagogical strategy can be intimidating and make facilitating leadership learning more complex, it is increasingly worth it if our aim is truly to develop and prepare the next generation of leaders and change agents.

Observations of Power

Leadership observation can open the door for conversations on power. We "see" what is going on around us daily, but "looking is an activity that involves a greater sense of purpose and direction.... Looking involves learning to interpret and like other practices, looking involves relationships of power" (Sturken & Cartwright, 2001, p. 10). Barnes et al. (2018) state, "A central focus of critical leadership development involves identifying and understanding how power flows through society" (p. 77). Dugan (2017) states, "power and authority are often presumed, unnamed, and left open to interpretation" (p. 20). Leadership development that omits conversations about power's role in the complexity of change paints an incomplete picture (Dugan, 2017). French and Raven's (1968) five types of power (legitimate, coercive, reward, referent, expert) are critical concepts when using leadership observation, allowing power to be identified, named, and critiqued. It is imperative leadership educators get comfortable talking openly with students about the role power plays in leader identity, capacity, and efficacy (Barnes et al., 2018). Observation in practice, and the meaning making that comes alongside it, can also be used to surface examples of power in action within groups, systems, institutions, communities. Using observation as a tool for assessing and understanding power in action helps learners wrestle with the human dimension of the leadership process.

Observations Grounded in Course Content

Operationalizing leadership observation begins with grounding the pedagogical tool within course content. For example, when teaching culturally relevant leadership learning, the model's domains can guide critical reflection questions (Bertrand Jones et al., 2016; Owen et al., 2021). For example, Owen et al. (2021) model exploration of the behavioral domain of CRLL by offering questions examining feminist leadership on campus. The question, "How do political happenings and current events affect understandings of gender and leadership?" challenges students to make meaning and critically reflect on events they see on and off campus that they observe every day (Owen et al., 2021, p. 93).

Another example could be when teaching Kouzes and Posners's (2012) five practices of exemplary leadership. Ask students how they see the leadership practice of "inspiring a shared vision" communicated on their Twitter timelines. This strategy is a way to practice leadership observation in the moment as students can use their phones or other devices to gather real-time evidence. If technology is not easily accessible, the facilitator could preselect examples to share for analysis. Pearson (2020) describes a facilitation activity using observation through social media platforms ("Digital Leadership Is Going to Go Viral"). And Kakim and Priest's (2020) description of visual thinking strategies utilizes art and mediated dialogue to practice observation and meaning making.

Observations to Amplify Student Experiences

Another consideration for practice is using leadership observation to amplify student interests and voices. Educators should give students agency to pull in relevant and contemporary examples from their lives, their observations of leadership. Students can more deeply connect leadership knowledge when they relate it to the content they already see in their day-to-day lives. For example, these connections may look like Kamala Harris embodying the social change value of *controversy with civility* in the vice-presidential debate, the STEM community coming together for the *common purpose* of creating a vaccine and slowing the spread of COVID-19, and consumers practicing *leadership ethics* in deciding where to spend their money and what businesses to support. In 2020, these examples were topical online, in conversations, in our email in–boxes, on our televisions, and more.

Observations as a Method of Accountability and Engagement

When students provide their own examples and observations, it increases agency, accountability, and engagement and allows their voices and lived experiences to be at the center of the collective community learning of leadership. This is also a way to increase the application of course material in day-to-day life. For example, Dr. Paige Haber-Curran uses an environmental scan in a curricular course to challenge students to notice and engage with mediums around them like social media, jokes, and advertisements (Guthrie & Jenkins, 2018). When conducting a media observation assignment in my own classrooms, I noticed in the weeks that followed how many students continued to bring up new pieces of media they observed, on their own, that reminded them of course learning. No longer requiring an instructor prompt, daily observation and critical reflection of leadership messaging became a natural and ongoing practice.

Observation Paired With Other Pedagogies

Leadership observation and experiences can be enhanced when paired when paired with other pedagogical approaches such as discussion, case study, reflection, team-based learning, service-learning, self- and peer assessments, role-play, simulation, games, and arts-based learning (Guthrie & Jenkins, 2018, 2020). Meaning making through observation is an integral component within experiential learning processes and other forms of group dynamics.

CONCLUSION

Observation can help us notice and evaluate events that cause pain, discomfort, and showcase bad leadership (Kellerman, 2004). However, observation can and should be used to illuminate inclusive leadership examples that give us hope for what is to come. This tension often requires us to analyze painfully complex moments with critical hope and empowerment to create positive social change. While this book and chapter are focused on the complexity of our current moment in time, we also need to find space for critical hope. "Critical hope is derived from the realistic appraisal of conditions, a sense of personal and collective resilience, and the ability to envision a better future" (Dugan, 2017, p. 51). Cultivating critical hope offers "a powerful sense of direction and purpose for using critical perspectives while simultaneously acknowledging that the struggle is real" (Dugan, 2017, p. 51). There must be space for both in the complexity of this moment. Simply observing the leadership around us is not enough; leadership educators must facilitate the meaning-making process to move from observation to leadership learning. I hope that using leadership observation can help intentionally move all of us leadership learners closer to critical hope at what is yet to come.

REFERENCES

Barnes, A. C., Olson, T. H., & Reynolds, D. J. (2018). Teaching power as an inconvenient but imperative dimension of critical leadership development. In J. P. Dugan (Ed.), *New Directions for Student Leadership: No. 159. Integrating critical perspectives into leadership development* (pp. 77–90). Wiley. https://doi.org/ 10.1002/yd.20299

Bertrand Jones, T., Guthrie, K. L., & Osteen, L. (2016). Critical domains of culturally relevant leadership learning: A call to transform leadership programs. In K. L. Guthrie, T. Bertrand Jones, & L. Osteen (Eds.), *New Directions for Student Leadership: No. 152. Developing culturally relevant leadership learning* (pp. 23–34). Wiley. https://doi.org/ 10.1002/yd.20205

Bruce, J., McKee, K., Morgan-Fleming, J., & Warner, W. (2019). The Oaks leadership scholars program: Transformative leadership in action. *International Journal of Teaching and Learning in Higher Education, 31*(3), 536–546.

Chunoo, V., & Osteen, L. (2016). Purpose, mission, and context: The call for educating future leaders. In K. L. Guthrie & L. Osteen (Eds.), *New Directions for Higher Education: No. 174. Reclaiming higher education's purpose in leadership development* (pp. 9–20). Wiley. https://doi.org/10.1002/he.20185

Dugan, J. P. (2017). *Leadership theory: Cultivating critical perspectives.* Jossey-Bass.

French, J. R. P., Jr., & Raven, B. H. (1968). The bases of social power. In D. Cartwright & A. F. Zander (Eds.), *Group dynamics* (3rd ed, pp. 259–269). Harper & Row.

Grint, K. (1997). *Leadership: Classical, contemporary, and critical approaches.* Oxford University Press.

Grint, K. (2005). *Leadership: Limits and possibilities.* Palgrave Macmillan.

Guthrie, K. L., & Jenkins, D. M. (2018). *The role of leadership educators: Transforming learning.* Information Age.

Guthrie, K. L., & Jenkins, D. M. (2020). *Transforming learning: Instructional and assessment strategies for leadership education.* Information Age.

Higher Education Research Institute. (1996). *A social change model of leadership development: Guidebook Version III.* National Clearinghouse for Leadership Programs.

Kakim, S., & Priest, K. L. (2020). Developing leadership capacity using visual thinking strategies. *Journal of Leadership Education, 19*(3), 83–86. https:// doi.org/10.12806/V19/I3/A4

Kellerman, B. (2004). *Bad leadership.* Harvard Business Review Press.

Komives, S. R., Owen, J. E., Longerbeam, S. D., Mainella, F. C., & Osteen, L. (2005). Developing a leadership identity: A grounded theory. *Journal of College Student Development, 46*(6), 593–611. https://doi.org/10.1353/ csd.2005.0061

Komives, S. R., & Wagner, W. (2009). *Leadership for a better world: Understanding the social change model of leadership development.* Jossey-Bass.

LeBlanc, J. B., & Guthrie, K. L. (2021). Community-university partnerships as socially just leadership education. In K. L. Guthrie & V. Chunoo (Eds.), *Shifting the mindset: Socially just leadership education* (pp. 219–228). Information Age.

Merriam, S. B., & Caffarella, R. S. (1999). *Learning in adulthood: A comprehensive guide.* Jossey-Bass.

Mitra, A. M. (2011). Learning how to look: The art of observation and leadership development. In M. Harvey & R. E. Riggio (Eds.), *Leadership studies: The dialogue of disciplines* (pp. 184–196). Edward Elgar.

Mitra, A. M., Hsieh, Y., & Buswick, T. (2010). Learning how to look: Developing leadership through intentional observation. *Journal of Business Strategy, 31.* 77–84. https://doi.org/10.1108/02756661011055212

Owen, J. E., Devies, B., & Reynolds, D. J. (2021). Going beyond 'add women then stir': Fostering feminist leadership. In K. L. Guthrie & V. S. Chunoo (Eds.), *Shifting the mindset: Socially just leadership education* (pp. 89–99). Information Age.

Pearson, C. (2020). Digital leadership is going to go viral. In J. M. Volpe White, K. L. Guthrie, & M. Torres (Eds.), *Thinking to transform: Facilitating reflection in leadership learning* (pp. 49–50). Information Age.

Priest, K. L., & Jenkins, D. M. (2019). Developing a vision of leadership educator professional practice. In K. L. Priest & D. M. Jenkins (Eds.), *New Directions for Student Leadership: No. 164. Becoming and being a leadership educator* (pp. 9–22). Wiley. https://doi.org/10.1002/yd.20355

Roberts, D., & Ullom, C. (1989). Student leadership program model. *NASPA Journal, 27*(1), 67–74.

Sowcik, M. (2012). Legitimacy, maturity, and accountability of leadership studies programs: A movement towards "good" practices. *Journal of Leadership Studies, 6*(3), 47–48. https://doi.org/10.1002/jls.21255

Sturken, M., & Cartwright, L. (2001). *Practices of looking: An introduction to visual culture.* Oxford University Press.

PART III

HIGHER EDUCATION
AS A PARTNER IN LEADERSHIP PRACTICE

CHAPTER 11

CONSIDERATIONS FOR COMMUNITY ENGAGEMENT IN COMPLEX TIMES

Julie B. LeBlanc

Community engagement is widely known as a pedagogical tool to develop students' leadership capacity (Dugan, 2006; Wagner & Pigza, 2016). The Carnegie Foundation's Classification for Community Engagement defines community engagement as "collaboration between institutions of higher education and their larger communities (local, regional/state, national, global) for the mutually beneficial exchange of knowledge and resources in a context of partnership and reciprocity" (Public Purpose Institute, 2021, para. 7). Explicit within this definition are the concepts of mutual benefit and reciprocity, meaning community engagement should benefit communities *and* students (Mitchell, 2008). Community engagement experiences are not immune to the historical, political, or current events relevant in a particular community at any given time. As an instrument of leadership learning pedagogy, leadership educators must structure community engagement with current events in mind; students' experiences do not occur devoid of what is happening in their home communities nor the communities in which community engagement occurs. Emerging attention on community engagement situates community conditions, tensions, and opportunities at the forefront of its development and practice.

Navigating Complexities in Leadership: Moving Toward Critical Hope, pp. 111–119
www.infoagepub.com
Copyright © 2022 by Information Age Publishing
All rights of reproduction in any form reserved.

This chapter frames community engagement in higher education through the lens of complex adaptive systems. I describe tensions and considerations among common forms of community engagement: 1-day events, short-term programs, and long-term programs; and offers insight and tools for educators who are navigating the complexities of each format. The chapter concludes with considerations for educators as we continue to grapple with the complexities surrounding community engagement in development and practice.

UNIVERSITIES AS COMPLEX ADAPTIVE SYSTEMS

Higher education institutions and their connected communities can be viewed as complex adaptive systems: networks of interconnected agents, whose interactions produce patterns that shape cultural norms and ongoing behaviors (Human Systems Dynamics Institute, 2021). In the context of a college or university campus, the complex adaptive system emerges from networks of faculty, administrators, staff, students, alumni, and external stakeholders and their interacting behaviors, thoughts, and patterns, which shape the institution's culture. A local community can also be a complex adaptive system given the interdependent nature of its residents and the corresponding patterns of interaction that shape the community's culture. The concept of complex adaptive systems is nested within broader theories of complexity leadership, adaptive leadership, and human systems dynamics. Since community engagement is a form of interaction that either replicates or influences patterns in a system, the dynamics of complex adaptive systems offer a lens for leadership educators to consider shaping conditions for community engagement to address inequity and injustice in communities. The lens of complex adaptive systems also reaffirms the connectivity between a community engagement experience focused on youth education and the interconnected nature of food insecurity in a given community; the influences and connection between injustices cannot—and should not—be underestimated.

POWER DYNAMICS

Traditional paradigms of community engagement situate "the community as the domain of the problem and the college as the domain of the solution" (Yapa, 1996, p. 19). This perspective reinforces deficit-based approaches to community engagement, positions the college as the producer of knowledge and resources, and reaffirms inequitable power dynamics between colleges and their students versus communities served.

Similarly, Kliewer and Priest (2017) argue the same inequity is true in terms of leadership and power; conventional leadership paradigms focus on the differentiation between those with power and those without power. Critical perspectives of leadership study and practice dissolve the distinction between knowledge producer and receiver and thus establishes a "coinquirer approach to leadership practice [which] requires a community-engaged approach" (Kliewer & Priest, 2017, p. 41). Therefore, evolving approaches to community engagement—when positioned as leadership practice—should acknowledge how power plays out in systems while also aiming to disrupt systems of power through collaboration and shared knowledge among community, campus, and students. Likewise, Mitchell's (2008) critical service-learning model advances understanding of how campus-community partnerships can reduce inequitable power dynamics between colleges, students, and the community.

Community Inequities

Community engagement provides the opportunity for students to confront systemic injustice on the ground, on issues ranging from environmental injustice, healthcare, racial injustice, hunger and food insecurity, LGBTQ+ rights, voting rights, and education; although for many students, such exposure may begin long before their higher education journey (Mitchell et al., 2012).

There is a historical legacy of racial injustice in our nation. The murders of Black people from police brutality—George Floyd, Breonna Taylor, Rayshard Brooks, Ahmaud Arbery, Atatiana Jefferson, Botham Jean, and many others—illuminate the significant racial injustices that permeate education, criminal justice, employment, and legal systems and spark calls for action within local communities. According to the Pew Research Center, 58% of Americans acknowledge the United States' race relations are bad (Menasce Horowitz et al., 2019). The urgency to address inequities fuels the need for community engagement to be responsive to racial injustice.

COVID-19 Pandemic

The emergence of the COVID-19 global pandemic in 2020 changed life as we knew it: mask mandates and social distancing, closed schools and businesses, and travel restrictions forced individuals to reconsider approaches to work, family, and most familiar aspects of daily life. Although individuals were affected in various ways and developed diverse coping mechanisms, the macrolevel impact of the pandemic on community engagement practices and nonprofit organizations' subsequent operational adaptations cannot be underestimated. Given the restructured operations of nonprofit organizations and community entities, colleges and universities reconsidered how traditional community engagement could be carried out in virtual ways. Purcell (2017) credits the expansion of online leadership education as a catalyst for virtual community engagement. Accordingly, the COVID-19 pandemic has accelerated the ways in which educators must envision and develop virtual community engagement as a means of leadership learning for students. This shift requires an expanded understanding of community engagement, including "research, advocacy, or social entrepreneurship" (Purcell, 2017, p. 67), in addition to more common practices of direct service. Although the pandemic has led to temporary virtual education, virtual community engagement will likely continue in leadership learning's future.

The following sections will explore common community engagement structures in higher education, offer insights on the complexities related to these structures, and outline considerations for educators to navigate these complexities.

One-Day Community Engagement Events

It is common for colleges and universities to host 1-day community service events for students to engage in direct service at various local nonprofit organizations. These types of events are frequently offered in conjunction with new student orientation, student activities, student organizations, or cocurricular leadership programs in the spirit of 'giving back' to the surrounding community. Although these types of events can be beneficial for students to learn about the service opportunities in their community, they have the potential to result in community harm if educators fail to approach 1-day community engagement events from a lens of mutual benefit and reciprocity.

Short-Term Community Engagement Programs

Short-term community engagement programs often take the form of alternative break experiences, in which students travel to another community for a designated time (typically a few days up to a week) to learn about that community and a focused social issue while engaging in direct service and reflection. These programs often have a significant focus on group development and relationship-building among students and their host community.

Long-Term Community Engagement Programs

Long-term community engagement programs take many forms, including semester-long service-learning experiences or internships with nonprofit organizations. Long-term community engagement provides the unique opportunity for sustained work and relationship building in a specific site, allowing students to have deeper, more immersive experiences. Hence, students have a more complex, nuanced, and accurate picture of communities and social issues, leading to a holistic understanding of community complexities.

ADDRESSING POWER DYNAMICS AND HEGEMONIC NORMS OF WHITENESS

There is a fine line between activity-based community service and intentional community engagement—whether in the context of a 1-day event, 1-week trip, or 3-month internship. Leadership educators must consider the *impact* versus the *intention* of the engagement. Regardless of if the event is intended to introduce students to the surrounding community or to inspire their ethos of community engagement, educators should embed historical context and education about the current status of the community. Otherwise, they risk students engaging as well-intentioned yet ill-informed, potentially reinforcing students' unconscious biases or stereotypes they may hold about low-income or BIPOC (Black, Indigenous, and people of color) communities (Mitchell et al., 2012). Higher education and leadership educators must take care not to use low-income or BIPOC communities as learning laboratories for their students without considering the associated complexities and risk of harm.

Mitchell et al. (2012) assert that Whiteness permeates many aspects of service-learning and community engagement, including the use of coded language when referring to race (e.g., using the terms "at risk" and "low-income" rather than explicitly naming "communities of color"), which may cause harm for BIPOC students. Leadership educators facilitating community engagement may be complicit in perpetuating Whiteness by adhering to traditional instructor and student power dynamics and expecting non-White students to carry the burden of conversations about race throughout the community engagement experiences and subsequent reflective discussions.

Further, leadership educators should consider if service projects are being developed based on assumed needs or the organization and community's actual needs. For example, a well-intentioned student organization might organize a sock drive for a local homeless coalition and plan to deliver a truckload of socks for their residents during the holiday season. Yet, this homeless coalition recently received a huge delivery of socks and is instead in more significant need of toiletry items for its residents. Communication with the community organization is of the utmost importance so that the community's needs are not assumed based on goodwill rather than factual insight. It is worth connecting with campus community engagement departments which could aid in the effective development of community engagement partnerships. The establishment of community needs assessments is beneficial to ameliorate the power dynamics between campus and community to ensure community engagement is conducted based on mutually established community needs and expectations.

Finally, reflection is central to leadership learning as a mechanism that catalyzes meaning making and stimulates continued action for social change (Volpe White et al., 2019). More specifically, critical reflection "shifts learners beyond their own experiences to analysis that is grounded in context and acknowledges the significant impact of social and political context" (p. 84). Therefore, critical reflection is central to students' understanding of complexities embedded within their community engagement experiences.

ADDRESSING COVID-19 AND THE VIRTUAL WORLD

Although traditional ideologies of community engagement center direct service, the COVID-19 pandemic has contributed to the shift in our approaches to what constitutes community engagement. Iowa and Minnesota Campus Compact's social change wheel 2.0 demonstrates the multitude of ways individuals can contribute to social change.

Figure 11.1, the Social Change Wheel 2.0 (2020), expands how we might think about community engagement activities, including opportunities that lend themselves to virtual platforms, including: advocacy and raising awareness, fundraising, voting and political activities, and socially responsible daily behavior.

Additionally, the toolkit supports the idea that students have different starting places and comfort levels with community engagement. A broader spectrum of activities facilitates the diversity of experiences and exposure that collectively contribute to social change and enhanced community capacity.

Figure 11.1

Social Change Wheel 2.0 (2020)

CC BY NC SA

Source: Campus Compact Iowa & Minnesota (2020).

FUTURE DIRECTIONS

Current complex times have brought a sense of urgency for leadership educators to examine the tensions between campus and community in facilitating community engagement experiences. The world continues to change rapidly; so too should our leadership education and community engagement curricula reflect these current and future complexities. Our responsibility is to design leadership learning experiences for students that provide them with tools to navigate constantly changing conditions.

In agreement with Chunoo et al. (2019), leadership educators must be proactive in confronting their own complicity in upholding Whiteness and the White supremacist culture of higher education. There is an urgent need for students to be aware of their own social and racialized identities before entering any communities, especially low-income or BIPOC communities. Based on dimensions of complex adaptive systems, leadership educators must consider how conditions shape patterns and patterns shape culture. In other words, aims to transform community engagement as a system must first change how agents within the system interact. Therefore, the following list of critical questions can aid leadership educators in interrogating their opportunities for confronting these tensions and complexities.

Leadership Educator Critical Questions

- How do I show up in my own racial and social identities?
- How do my identities inform my perspectives of the community and my behaviors within the community?
- What is my current practice of reflection, and how can I expand my practice to enhance my own self-awareness?
- How may I be unintentionally perpetuating systems of oppression, and what can I do to change it?
- How can I embody a human-centered approach to community engagement, with respect to both my students and my communities?
- What conditions do we aim to replicate or alter through community engagement?
- What new assets can I leverage through virtual community engagement?
- How can I center equity and justice as core foci of my work with community engagement programs?

Using complex adaptive systems and human systems dynamics as frameworks to design community engagement experiences, leadership educators can position community engagement within the complex systems in which they occur. As we push the needle toward a future in which all university-sponsored community engagement is facilitated in a way that advances equity and justice, let us not lose sight of the critical hope and possibilities that exist for our communities, our students, our campuses, and ourselves as leadership educators.

REFERENCES

Chunoo, V. S., Beatty, C. C., & Gruver, M. D. (2019). Leadership educator as social justice educator. In K. L. Priest, & D. Jenkins (Eds.), *New Directions for Student Leadership: No. 164. Becoming and being a leadership educator* (pp. 87–103). Wiley. https://doi.org/10.1002/yd.20360

Dugan, J. P. (2006). Involvement and leadership: A descriptive analysis of socially responsible leadership. *Journal of College Student Development, 47*, 335–343.

Human Systems Dynamics Institute. (2021). *Complex adaptive system.* https://www.hsdinstitute.org/resources/complex-adaptive-system.html

Kliewer, B. W., & Priest, K. L. (2017). Normative foundations of community-engaged scholarship as a method of leadership inquiry. *Journal of Leadership Studies, 11*(1), 40–44.

Menasce Horowitz, J., Brown, A., & Cox, K. (2019, April 9). *Race in America 2019.* Pew Research Center Social & Demographic Trends. https://www.pewsocial-trends.org/2019/04/09/race-in-america-2019/

Mitchell, T. D. (2008). Traditional vs. critical service-learning: Engaging the literature to differentiate two models. *Michigan Journal of Community Service Learning, 14*(2). https://files.eric.ed.gov/fulltext/EJ831374.pdf

Mitchell, T. D., Donahue, D. M., & Young-Law, C. (2012). Service learning as a pedagogy of whiteness. *Equity & Excellence in Education, 45*(4), 612–629. https://doi.org/10.1080/10665684.2012.715534

Public Purpose Institute. (2021). *Community engagement classification (U.S.).* https://public-purpose.org/initiatives/carnegie-elective-classifications/community-engagement-classification-u-s/

Purcell, J. W. (2017). Community-engaged pedagogy in the virtual classroom: Integrating eservice-learning into online leadership education. *Journal of Leadership Studies, 11*(1), 65–70.

Social Change Wheel 2.0 Toolkit. (2020, June 16). Minnesota Campus Compact. https://mncampuscompact.org/resource-posts/social-change-wheel-2-0-tool-kit/

Volpe White, J. M., Guthrie, K. L., & Torres, M. (2019). *Thinking to transform: Reflection in leadership learning.* Information Age.

Wagner, W., & Pigza, J. M. (2016). The intersectionality of leadership and service-learning: A 21st-century perspective. In W. Wagner & J. M. Pigza (Eds.), *New Directions for Student Leadership: No. 150. Leadership development through service-learning* (pp. 11–22). Wiley. https://doi.org/10.1002/yd.20167

Yapa, L. (1996). What causes poverty? A postmodern view. *Annals of the Association of American Geographers, 86*, 707–728.

CHAPTER 12

AGRICULTURE AND RURAL COMMUNITIES

Leadership Learning and Implications for Higher Education

Susan Metzger and Russell Plaschka

The development of agriculture and rural communities has played an important role in the advancement of the American economy, higher education, and leadership education. The agricultural industry grew alongside the innovation of American farmers, developing infrastructure that enabled transport and distribution of raw products to population centers. The 1862 Morrill Act established land-grant institutions that focused on agriculture and engineering, extending affordable higher education to rural and working-class people who previously had been excluded from such opportunities. Land-grant institutions like Kansas State University deliver teaching, research, and outreach services with a commitment to discovering knowledge and improving the quality of life of citizens locally and globally.

A key component of outreach and service is the Cooperative Extension System, a partnership between land-grant institutions and the U.S. Department of Agriculture, as well as local and state governments. Exten-

Navigating Complexities in Leadership: Moving Toward Critical Hope, pp. 121–130
www.infoagepub.com
Copyright © 2022 by Information Age Publishing
All rights of reproduction in any form reserved.

121

sion professionals and programs serve as a bridge between research and practice, translating research into action in the areas of agriculture-related, health, and human sciences. University faculty members and county-based educators engage with communities to respond to local needs, evaluate learning tools, and prioritize future areas of research (National Institute of Food and Agriculture, n.d.). For example, K-State Research and Extension (n.d.) sought grassroots feedback to identify five grand challenges facing every Kansan: global food systems, water, health, community vitality, and developing tomorrow's leaders.

These topics inform the focus of our work as practitioners and community-engaged researchers. Through our professional roles in state government (Russell, Kansas Department of Agriculture) and higher education (Susan, Kansas State University's College of Agriculture), we engage and serve rural communities, agricultural producers, and industry in Kansas. This chapter explores the tensions rural communities experience in pursuit of sustainability and growth. Specifically, we highlight the perceived rural/urban divide, the role of natural resources, and trends in rural economic development. While our experiences and perspectives may be rooted in Kansas, the dimensions of complexity we see also reflect broader conditions and cultural patterns across the United States. There are no easy solutions to grand challenges; making progress will require reimagining the role of higher education and the government in supporting the future of rural communities. We offer insight on how higher education, through engaged scholarship, research, and leadership development, can assist rural communities in solving their own issues.

REDEFINING RURAL

Events of 2020 and beyond—a contentious presidential race, the global health pandemic, racial tensions inflamed by the murder of George Floyd, insurrection at the Capitol, environmental crisis—have only exacerbated a political and social divide between rural communities and urban America. We paint this picture as a growing chasm between rural and urban communities because, in our experience, that is how those in rural communities describe the relationship. Love and Hadden Loh (2020) describe how polarization is reinforced through political narratives and myths that presents these two communities as fundamentally opposed factions, "barely belong to the same world, framing urban America as diverse, educated, and economically productive and rural America as White, dependent on dying industries, and characterized by stagnation, decline, and despair" (para. 2). Next, we describe how system forces defining "rural" contribute to this perceived divide, and offer an alternative lens for analysis.

More Than "What's Left"

For some, the term "rural" generates nostalgic images of scenic landscapes dotted with iconic farmsteads, small-town businesses, and friendly faces with a smile and wave ever at the ready. For others, the term conjures a bleaker picture, such as the opioid crisis, failing economies, and population declines (Bennett et al., 2019). Technical definitions of "rural" consider population thresholds, density, land use, and distance from urban areas. The U.S. Census Bureau defines rural as "what is not urban—that is, after defining individual urban areas, rural is what is left" (Ratcliffe et al., 2016, p. 1). It is not surprising that this definition, *what is left*, leaves some rural residents feeling undervalued and creates a rift between rural and urban communities.

Population Trends

Population trends in Kansas serve as an example of shifts occurring throughout the United States. According to the Center for Economic Development and Business Research (2016), out of 105 counties in Kansas, 19 Kansas "urban" counties are home to nearly 70 percent of the state's population. The remaining 86 counties considered "rural" represent only one third of the state's population. Projections show that, by 2044, just two counties will together account for almost half of the state's population (Center for Economic Development and Business Research, 2016). These geographic and population divides have implications for higher education institutions. The perceived urban/rural divide must be considered when working with communities, perhaps more so now than ever. In describing higher education for the public good, Gee et al. (2019) suggest that "Land-grant institutions must transcend the urban-rural divide by focusing on what is good and right for all of our nation's communities, regardless of their geographic location" (para. 9).

Rural/Urban as Interdependent Pairs

In a technical sense, urban and rural represent a polarity: two extreme sides of a continuum by which to identify and make sense of place, people, and policy. However, the issues and challenges facing humanity and the planet are too complex to reduce to either/or. In reality, urban and rural communities are an interdependent pair, with common challenges that lie along a continuum. Shifting from a polarity to an interdependent pair model is an opportunity to consider the dynamics and patterns that shape significant challenges, identify the factors at play and how they influence each other (Human Systems Dynamic Institute, 2016). In doing so, we redefine rural not only by geography, population, or political views; but as a lens for understanding implications of broader challenges facing humanity and the planet: social, environmental, and economic. The decisions for and by rural communities are inextricably linked to the greater good of all.

COMPLEXITIES IN AGRICULTURE AND RURAL COMMUNITIES

This section highlights complex challenges of natural resources, community economic development, and political representation through the lens of agriculture and rural communities.

Care and Use of Natural Resources

Wide open spaces, clean air, and access to natural resources are often features that attract visitors and residents to rural areas. Those same natural assets are the resources that sustain crop and livestock production and challenge rural opportunities when they become impaired or overused. Competition for water and other natural resources is a growing tension both locally in our rural communities and across the nation. The responsibility to care for natural assets often becomes too distributed and individualistic, making shared action challenging but not impossible. Conserving and extending the useful life of the natural resources that serve as the lifeblood of agriculture and rural communities will require the long-term collective and shared commitment of local leaders. Higher education institutions can be essential partners in providing adaptive and responsive research and outreach to identify innovative, workable solutions to sustain local natural assets.

Community Economic Development (CED)

In our experience working directly with rural communities, sustainability is a top priority. There are several tensions at play in community economic development. Externally, programs and incentives that favor more populated areas of the state have unintendedly set up conditions for economic instability in rural communities through reduced access to funding. Many of the incentive programs designed for CED cater to larger entities that might employ hundreds of people. Some rural communities cannot support such growth due to limited workforce or capital investments. As a result, they are left out as a possible site location for new or expanding businesses.

Internally, the desire for growth is in tension with a fear of uncontrolled expansion; thus, communities may correspondingly resist any change to the quality of small-town life (Clark, 1990). Many rural communities still follow traditional economic development programs and business development practices congruent with their traditional thinking. They rely on the same industries that were supporting their communities, 20, 40, or even 60 years ago.

Engaging in discussions of what is and is not community development is futile; instead, organizations need to be clear about how political and organizational processes impact their renderings of community development, both theoretically and practically (Hudson, 2004). Every community is different, with its unique discourses, practices, and contexts. The bureaucratic response to citizen demands is often complicated by special interests and a dynamic environment, and limited time and information to make policy decisions (Handley & Howell-Moromey, 2010). It is not enough to just say the right thing; for change to occur, communication is needed to form and transform new discourses and actions. Positive CED requires continued involvement, discussion, and action on the part of the community members.

Higher education and CED professionals need skills to work with and in rural communities. Exercising leadership with and in communities requires being a steward of place—absorbing the essence and distinct characteristics of its surrounding communities, both to enrich those communities and to become enriched *by* them (Terenzio, 2019). In our experience, relationships are key to gaining entry, trust, and commitment from the community members. Effective leadership processes occur when leaders and followers can develop mature leadership relationships (partnerships) and thus gain access to the many benefits these relationships bring (Graen & Uhl-Bien, 1995).

Shifting Political Capital and Representation

Programs and resources focused on housing, economic development, and technology infrastructure have historically come in the form of top-down governmental initiatives, with little input from those on the grassroots level. Communities often do not have the resources to accomplish these tasks alone, so they look to the state for assistance (Clark, 1990). Though some policymakers may be eager to tackle the challenges facing rural areas, discussions on this topic tend to make sweeping generalizations about the dynamics at work in these communities, leaving many Americans out of the conversation (Ajilore & Willingham, 2019).

Incentive and community development programs, in most cases, are a political issue, with a focus on those areas of the state that can provide the greatest return on investment. As the rural population declines and urban area population increases, political district boundaries are redrawn, leaving rural communities struggling to feel adequately represented at the state level. As described by the president and chief executive officer of a western Kansas economic development corporation, "the real challenge is that you know all of the votes belong to a part of the state that does not understand us in any way ... we literally don't fit on either side of the aisle." She summed up the impact of this challenge as "we don't have enough of a voice" (L. Duvall, personal communication, September 16, 2020). This example highlights a tension of competing values, not just gaps in representation. And these divides are not unique to rural communities; they represent broader challenges that are playing out in our families, in our communities, and across the country, not just on the Senate floor.

IMPLICATIONS FOR LEADERSHIP PRACTICE AND HIGHER EDUCATION

Tackling issues such as the long-term reliability of the natural resources, economic development, and political representation and decisions that sustain rural communities will require diverse perspectives and participation. No one individual or organization holds the knowledge or resources to make meaningful change. As a partner in progress, higher education institutions can leverage teaching, research, outreach, and service in pursuit of the public good. More specifically, Priest and Kliewer (2017) suggest that leadership researchers and educators can inform and intersect the public good "through community partnership, collaboration, community organizing, and structures of learning that develop our critical capacity to make progress toward social change" (p. 38).

As part of a leadership communication doctoral program, we take a community-engaged scholarship approach to our work with rural communities. Community-engaged scholarship is an integrated approach where learning reaches across disciplines and communities—and between faculty, students, and community members—to create reciprocal and mutually beneficial partnerships. In the following section, we share our perspectives and critical insight into what it means for those who practice and seek to develop leadership in and through higher education.

Building Trust:
The Perception and Role of Outside "Experts"

In our experience, many rural communities function as a close-knit network of families, churches, schools, and businesses—with histories of relationships and spoken and unspoken ways of doing things. When consultants, extension specialists, researchers, or educators engage a community in CED or other forms of leadership development, it is critical to understand the culture and context. There is often a tension between a distrust of outside help and the recognition that help is needed.

For rural communities, engagement and leadership work is not an assignment or research project, the outcomes can have life and death consequences. As Deetz (2008) wrote, "Like it or not, as scholars we carry moral responsibilities, we are part of what people will become and choices that will get made." That is a heavy responsibility we carry each time we "show up" to help solve problems. As invited consultants or educators, we must be mindfully reflective of our own positionality: our intersecting identities, beliefs, and bias that can influence our perceptions, actions, and interactions. And we must be able to recognize and hold space for others' perceptions of us. Understanding the Foucauldian big "D" discourse (our historical way of knowing) and knowing how their little "d" discourses (current language use) (Gee, 2015) continue to shape their understanding of their world is paramount in gaining acceptance within the community.

For example, I (Russell) was once introduced to a community gathering as "the man from the state department of agriculture is here to tell us what to do." The immediate response from a lifelong resident was, "You know, we are a long way from Topeka" (state Capitol). I used my own story of experience as rural Kansan who worked with rural Kansans to build a connection. They needed to know that I understood their environment in order for me to facilitate the discussion from a place of mutual trust. Some questions for practitioners and developers can use to learn more about a community include: What is the goal of this program/meeting/workshop? What are this community's previous experiences with outside "experts"? Who makes up this community network, and where do influence and power reside?

Making Progress on Grand Challenges

As previously mentioned, water is a "grand challenge" facing our state. Ensuring availability and sustainable management of water is also a global development goal (United Nations, n.d.). Engaged scholarship that addresses this challenge locally contributes to a broader global impact. The community of Finney County, located in western Kansas, serves as a case study to highlight tensions with natural resources with which many communities throughout the United States are grappling. In Finney County, groundwater from the Ogallala Aquifer is the primary source of water supporting the county's economy and communities, with some additional water provided by the Arkansas River. In the past ten years, some county areas have seen declines of more than 70 feet in the water table, impacting farmers' ability to irrigate (Whittemore et al., 2018). Several local water rights owners, including those reported to be the highest water users across the aquifer in Kansas, are seeking ways to reduce the rate of decline in the Ogallala Aquifer in this region (Dillon, 2018).

In 2019, members of the Finney County community, including an irrigation cooperative, local electric company, two cattle feedyards, a dairy heifer development company, large meat processor, and the local municipality began meeting to identify opportunities for collective conservation action, with the vision to make the county a model for natural resource conservation and sustainable food production. They were committed to collaborative but locally defined, solutions to the declines in groundwater, and partnered with industries, nonprofits like The Nature Conservancy, and university researchers and extension professionals. Not only is the Finney County community collaboration exemplary of the type of diverse participation and cooperation necessary to tackle tough natural resource concerns, they are a flagship for effective community-engaged scholarship. In partnership with researchers and outreach professionals from Kansas State University and Colorado State University, the locals are defining the resources needed, from skilled facilitators to irrigation technology research, to improve local water conservation. Members of the community team also represented young farmers, the dean of workforce development at the local community college, and a sustainable food system intern to help address local workforce development needs specialized in the natural resources field. Rather than the top-down approach, expertise-driven approach, the Finney County partnership illustrates the leveling effect called for in engaged scholarship. The relationship between researchers and participants is equal (Ellingson, 2009). Together, the community and the university partners identify opportunities and implement actions to reduce water use and collectively commit to a sustainable and resilient Finney County.

Leading Change

We invite leadership researchers, developers, and educators to see themselves as "scholar-practitioners," integrating "teaching, research, and civic engagement to produce new knowledge for social, political, economic, and moral change" (Priest & Kliewer, 2017, p. 37). Land grant institutions and rural-serving universities have a distinct opportunity and obligation to support sustainability efforts in their communities (Terenzio, 2019). Rural communities already possess the power to create meaningful change and reverse the trends of population loss, economic declines, and depletion of their natural resources. Community-engaged scholarship approaches can connect community innovators with like-minded leaders in other rural communities and support collaboration with university and industry experts to bring those concepts to life. In doing so, they improve the future for rural communities, demonstrating these communities are much more than "what is left." Progress at the local level on global challenges contributes to a better future for all.

REFERENCES

Ajilore, O., & Willingham, Z. (2019, July 17). *Redefining rural America.* Center for American Progress. https://www.americanprogress.org/issues/economy/reports/2019/07/17/471877/edefining-rural-america/

Bennett, K. J., Borders, T. F., Holmes, G. M., Kozhimannil, K. B., & Ziller, E. (2019). What is rural? Challenges and implications of definitions that inadequately encompass rural people and places. *Health Affairs, 38*(12), 1985–1992. http://dx.doi.org.er.lib.k-state.edu/10.1377/hlthaff.2019.00910

Center for Economic Development and Business Research. (2016). *Kansas population forecast.* Wichita State University. https://www.cedbr.org/population-projections-2

Clark, H. J. (1990). Successful community economic development through community leadership: Elements of some state-sponsored programs which have proven effective. *Economic Development Review, 8*(3), 7–11.

Deetz, S. (2008). Engagement as co-generative theorizing. *Journal of Applied Communication Research, 36*(3), 289–297. https://doi.org/10.1080/00909880802172301

Dillon, K. (2018). Running out of water and time: Dealing with the Ogallala aquifer in western Kansas. *The Journal: Inspirations for the Common Good, 10*(2), 10–41.

Ellingson, L. L. (2009). Ethnography in applied communication research. In L. R. Frey & K. N. Cissna (Eds.), *Handbook of applied communication research* (pp. 129–152). Routledge.

Gee, E. G., Gavazzi, S. M., Shirangelo, J., & Pittman, K. J. (2019, May 13). *Placing 4-H within the 21st century land-grant mission.* The EvoLLLution. https://evolllution.com/revenue-streams/extending_lifelong_learning/placing-4-h-within-the-21st-century-land-grant-mission/

Gee, J. P. (2015), Discourse, small d, big d. In K. Tracy, C. Ilie, & T. Sandel (Eds.), *International Encyclopedia of Language and Social Interaction.* Wiley-Blackwell. https://doi.org/10.1002/9781118611463.wbielsi016

Graen, G. B., & Uhl-Bien, M. (1995). Relationship-based approach to leadership: Development of leader-member exchange (LMX) theory of leadership over 25 years: Applying a multi-level multi-domain perspective. *The Leadership Quarterly, 6*(2), 219–247.

Handley, D. M., & Howell-Moroney, M. (2010). Ordering stakeholder relationships and citizen participation: Evidence from the community development block grant program. *Public Administration Review, 70*(4), 601–609.

Hudson, K. (2004). Behind the rhetoric of community development: How is it perceived and practiced? *Australian Journal of Social Issues, 39*(3).

Human Systems Dynamics Institute. (2016). *Interdependent pairs.* https://www.hsdinstitute.org/assets/documents/5.1.1.9.interdependent-pairs-03may16.pdf

K-State Research and Extension. (n.d.). *Grand challenges.* https://www.ksre.k-state.edu/reports/grandchallenges.html#:~:text=During%20a%20strategic%20planning%20process,vitality%20and%20developing%20tomorrow's%20leaders.

Love, H., & Hadden Loh, T. (2020, December 8). *The 'rural-urban divide' furths myths about race and poverty – concealing effective policy solutions.* https://www.brookings.edu/blog/the-avenue/2020/12/08/the-rural-urban-divide-furthers-myths-about-race-and-poverty-concealing-effective-policy-solutions/

National Institute of Food and Agriculture. (n.d.). Cooperative extension system. https://nifa.usda.gov/cooperative-extension-system

Priest, K. L., & Kliewer, B. W. (2017). Introduction: Advancing leadership education through community engagement. *Journal of Leadership Studies, 11*(1), 36–39. https://doi.org/10.1002/jls.21510

Ratcliffe, M., Burd, C., Holder, K., & Fields, A. (2016). Defining rural at the U.S. Census Bureau: American community survey and geography brief. https://www2.census.gov/geo/pdfs/reference/ua/Defining_Rural.pdf

Terenzio, M. (2019, November 21). *Dismantling the last acceptable prejudice.* Inside Higher Ed. https://www.insidehighered.com/views/2019/11/21/rural-serving-institutions-play-vital-role-their-regions-opinion

United Nations. (n.d.). *The 17 [Sustainable Development] Goals.* https://sdgs.un.org/goals

Whittemore, D., Butler, J., & Wilson, B. (2018). *Status of the High Plains Aquifer in Kansas.* Kansas Geological Survey Technical Series 22. http://www.kgs.ku.edu/Publications/Bulletins/TS22/HPA_tech_series22.pdf

CHAPTER 13

INTEGRATING LEADERSHIP FRAMEWORKS TO DIAGNOSE AND ADDRESS THE CHALLENGE OF HEALTH EQUITY

Mac T. Benavides, Saya Kakim, and Jurdene Coleman

The novel coronavirus (COVID-19) pandemic swept the world and surfaced significant ethnoracial and class inequities within our societies (Laurencin & McClinton, 2020). In the United States, Fortuna et al. (2020) suggested that "COVID-19 has highlighted existing disparities and risks for children, families, and communities of color and those living in poverty" (p. 445). These disparities are likely related to how the U.S. healthcare system (1) has not fully addressed a legacy of medical oppression (Brandon et al., 2005), (2) perpetuates Western modes of efficiency that do not align well with other cultural frameworks (Machado, 2014), and (3) operates within a system of racial capitalism (McClure et al., 2020). Racial capitalism "refers to the centrality of race in structuring social and labor hierarchies in capitalist economies" (McClure et al., 2020, p. 2), offering a systemic lens by which to recognize how oppression creates strong ties between minoritized ethnoracial groups and poverty.

Navigating Complexities in Leadership: Moving Toward Critical Hope, pp. 131–139
www.infoagepub.com
Copyright © 2022 by Information Age Publishing
All rights of reproduction in any form reserved.

Addressing health inequities magnified by the current global pandemic will require significant structural and procedural changes that recognize the living legacy of historical racial hierarchies (Cooper & Williams, 2020) within the healthcare system and beyond. We recognize the complexity of this issue and acknowledge the need for a long-term systemic overhaul of the health community. For the purpose of this chapter, we focus our discussion on short-term, actionable strategies communities can take toward health equity.

Furthermore, we also recognize that broader systemic challenges test the permeable boundaries of systems. In other words, the challenges we identify here are not bound within the walls of healthcare institutions. They trickle into the lives of all members of our societies, creating and exposing additional challenges that need to be addressed. For example, in higher education worldwide, students' experiences within and outside of the classroom continue to be affected by the pandemic (Aristovnik et al., 2020). Within the study of leadership, the global health crisis exemplifies an adaptive challenge that requires diagnosis, interpretation, and intervention. Integrating work on real-life and close-to-home challenges into leadership education curriculum or programming is one strategy to (a) make progress locally and (b) contribute to efforts more globally.

This adaptive problem calls for a collaborative effort among all impacted and urges practitioners and scholars to conceptualize and practice leadership differently. This chapter will examine health inequity from the lens of adaptive and collective leadership theory, discuss how integrated leadership frameworks can offer new insights into pathways toward progress, and explore implications for leadership educators.

VIEWING THE PROBLEM FROM A LEADERSHIP THEORY LENS

Healthcare trends created and exacerbated by the arrival of the novel coronavirus in the United States represent an adaptive challenge, which Heifetz et al. (2009) explain can only be addressed through changes in systemic ways of operating. This involves engaging with and building consensus around people's differing priorities, beliefs, habits, and loyalties. The complexity of the adaptive challenge requires a collaborative effort of local healthcare professionals, local officials, and community members. Heifetz (1994) explains that the real work of leadership involves challenging group members to face adaptive problems—problems with no simple solutions that require learning new ways of engaging in shared leadership activities. As such, issues like healthcare inequity require scholars to conceptualize adaptive leadership through collective lenses (Drath et al., 2008; Heifetz et al., 2009; Uhl-Bien & Ospina, 2012).

Adaptive Leadership

The adaptive leadership model can be understood as a process for observing social stresses and identifying within these stresses the work that must be done (Safer et al., 2010). Rather than trying to remove this stress, adaptive work must begin by coming to terms with clarifying value conflicts, narrowing the gap between our current value beliefs and those created by the current operating environment (Flower, 1995). In moments of crisis or discord, Heifetz (1994) contends that people tend to expect leadership (authority) will provide solutions, decisions, and strength and ultimately chart a path forward. In other words, we look for someone who knows where we ought to be going and who can make hard problems simple. Yet, an adaptive perspective of leadership recognizes that adaptive issues cannot and will not be solved by heroes. The issues are more complex, and the solutions "reside in the heart" (Safer et al., 2010, para. 8). Global pandemic solutions will require healthcare leadership to renegotiate their priorities, loyalties, and practices in order to redesign a system that does not continue to promote inequity. An adaptive lens of leadership allows leadership educators and practitioners to diagnose tensions within the complex issue and begin to dream of a path forward. We contend that this opens the door to a collective and relational process of leadership-as-practice to then address these adaptive challenges.

Adaptive challenges require an organization to go beyond any authoritative expertise to mobilize discovery. This mobilization involves building capacity for productively working through the tension that is inherent in adaptive challenges. Differing, even competing, worldviews can shed light on the issue from many different angles and are necessary to make progress. Being able to navigate these tensions requires that, to some extent, we shed deeply entrenched ways of being, knowing, and doing in order to truly consider other perspectives. In doing so, we organizations can collectively imagine pathways forward.

Collective Leadership

Drawing on Ospina et al. (2020), we address the complexity of the issue through the blended locus of leadership and an integrative collective leadership framework, which includes relational and practice perspectives. This framework assumes that social reality lies in the context of relationships (Bradbury & Lichtenstein, 2000). Additionally, taking a relational perspective, the collective leadership framework focuses on "coordination" of people's actions and language in relation to each other and the dynamic socioeconomic environment (Abell & Simons, 2000). Moreover, leadership emerges when certain social practices and ways of understanding and knowing establish social order (Raelin, 2016; Reckwitz, 2002). In this regard, working toward alignment of thinking and actions through interpretation with others (Edwards, 2005; Raelin 2016) promotes leadership, which Ospina and Schall (2001) explain emerges out of a context-specific meaning-making process.

By applying a collective leadership framework, we believe that public issues can be addressed through cocreation between participants with different world views. By using dialogue and collaborative learning, leadership actors are able "to create spaces where a shared common purpose can be achieved while the diversity of perspectives is preserved and valued." (Ospina & Schall, 2001, p. 16). To accomplish this requires intentionality around the relational nature of public problem solving and practices that lead to positive changes in local communities. Through intentional design emphasizing process over agency, individuals can enact collective leadership by which marginalized voices become powerful and produce collective achievement in a specific context.

POSSIBILITIES FOR ACTION AND PATHWAYS FORWARD

In the case of health inequity, the United States seems to be unable to adequately address needs of diverse communities due in part to a disconnect between mainstream healthcare practices and the racially minoritized communities that providers seek to serve. As we discussed earlier, there are three adaptive challenges we have identified as contributing to this issue: (a) the legacy of medical oppression, (b) the normative practices that perpetuate Western modes of efficiency, and (c) the healthcare system operates within a system of racial capitalism. An adaptive lens of leadership allows us to diagnose these complex structural issues and bring attention to the need for systemic and cultural change. Next, we will describe how applying practices associated with integrative collective frameworks can provide tangible avenues for making progress on each of these adaptive challenges.

Legacy of Medical Oppression

Social distancing mandates have been prevalent throughout the United States during the COVID-19 pandemic. It is important to recognize how telehealth services fit into broader patterns of the oppressive relationship between medicine and racially minoritized communities. Early in the pandemic, scholars noted that racially and ethnically minoritized people were less likely to use telehealth services for various reasons (Nouri et al., 2020; Reed et al., 2020). Whether the underutilization of telehealth services by minoritized communities is related to lower usage of digital health tools specifically or to lack of consistent access to primary healthcare in general, this trend speaks to lack of trust and buy-in regarding the healthcare system.

Collective leadership frameworks encourage leadership actors to recognize minoritized communities as experts in their own health and well-being and to urge community healthcare providers to work with their communities to identify solutions unique to their consumers' needs. Building mutually beneficial relationships and partnerships between health providers and local communities require that health professionals look beyond the assumed benefit of medical care. While it may seem logical that providing health services to patients is an added value to their lives, due to the oppressive and exploitative history of the U.S. healthcare system, communities of color often lack faith in this value. Healthcare providers must reestablish trust and build meaningful connections to their local communities. When providers demonstrate a commitment to the community, they can improve access to and engagement with healthcare systems during the COVID-19 pandemic. This intentionality around the relational nature of equity cannot and should not end postpandemic. Continuing to expand infrastructure to support telehealth services and strengthening connections with racially and ethnically minoritized communities can be a powerful driver for equity (Kaplan, 2021).

Western Modes of Efficiency

Western and Eurocentric value systems have traditionally been the foundation of mainstream healthcare practices (Brown & Campelia, 2021). To continue making progress on the issue of cultural disconnect, community conversations (Born, 2010) between community members and local health providers could serve as powerful avenues through which providers can better understand local needs and inclusive ways to address those needs. Within Indigenous communities, for example, Leader (2020) argued that "Indigenous communities should be at the forefront of the conversation, especially while adopting Western telehealth frameworks in Indigenous contexts" (p. 43). Because traditionally, white people have served as the control group within medical knowledge production, experiences and needs of communities of color have largely been overlooked (Yearby, 2021). Centering the experiences and needs of racially and ethnically minoritized communities through interventions like community conversations is necessary to address the healthcare equity gap. Conversations create the conditions for leadership-as-practice activities such as weaving, inviting, and reflecting (Raelin, 2016). As previously noted, establishing meaningful relationships within their communities is essential for local healthcare professionals and officials to ensure equitable and collaborative processes.

One strategy for starting dialogic engagement is through convening small segments of their community to discuss their overall impressions of the area's healthcare system. Dialogue should be conducted by trained facilitators hosting small group discussions focused on specific needs and possible actions to address those needs. The goal at this early stage is to take the temperature of the community. This data should be shared with both the healthcare community and local citizens, increasing transparency. Providing all documents and instructions in multiple languages and offering interpreter services to ensure all are welcome and contribute to the dialogue. By bringing community members' voices to the table, acknowledging differences, respecting and being responsive to differences, local healthcare professionals and officials, along with community members, will engage in weaving practices and create a sense of shared purpose. This way, coconstructed solutions can be unique to community members' needs.

Racial Capitalism

Engaging communities in programs like community conversations is one way to make progress on local issues amplified by racial capitalism. Approaching health equity from a collective lens inherently addresses the issue of racial capitalism by listening to and centering the perspectives and experiences of communities of color who have historically been ignored or silenced. Community conversations should be intentionally designed to promote equitable decision making and recognize multiple ways of knowing and understanding. Relational perspectives ask all group members to respect the dignity and knowledge of all other members. Additionally, by fostering collaborative learning, parties can cocreate a shared understanding of possible pathways and solutions centered around experiences of communities of color. It is important for leadership practitioners and educators to intentionally consider context and community-centered design while forming partnerships and collaborative processes with community members.

CONCLUSION

Higher education institutions are often sites of health services, and they are situated within networks of knowledge, resources, and influence within and across communities. Higher education administrators, faculty, staff, and students are therefore stakeholders in the adaptive challenge of health equity. There is a developmental process involved in building capacity to address adaptive problems. Through work in the classroom or with community partnerships and programs, leadership educators have an opportunity to develop learners' ability to examine issues from a systemic lens and generate tangible pathways moving forward.

To make progress on issues of inequity, leadership educators must have a critical understanding of the current reality, as well as a willingness to believe that a better future is possible. By building critical hope, we are able to work together to generate adaptive solutions to create real and lasting change. Yet, adaptive solutions come at a cost. Leadership educators, practitioners, and learners will be required to let go of past structures and processes and risk failure when attempting new solutions. While there is a sense of urgency around issues like health inequity, time is also a vital resource when seeking adaptive solutions. These types of problems require intensive diagnosis and collaborative brainstorming of interventions. Leading amid the complexity of these issues involves developing the capacity to hold the tension between the challenges of today and hope for a better tomorrow. The focus shifts from the "who" and "where" to the "how" and "what" of leadership; in other words, how individuals together produce collective outcomes through collaborative efforts (Ospina & Foldy, 2010). Adaptive leadership provides an excellent perspective to help leadership learners and practitioners recognize and diagnose adaptive challenges. Collective leadership lenses allow them to break down these issues and identify tangible pathways forward to make progress on these issues.

REFERENCES

Abell, E., & Simons, S. (2000). How much can you bend before you break: An experience of using constructionist consulting as a tool for organizational learning in the corporate world. *European Journal of Work and Organizational Psychology 9*(2), 159–175.

Aristovnik, A., Keržič, D., Ravšelj, D., Tomaževič, N., & Umek, L. (2020). Impacts of the COVID-19 pandemic on life of higher education students: A global perspective. *Sustainability, 12*(20), 8438. https://doi.org/10.3390/su12208438

Born, P. (2010). *Community conversations: Mobilizing the ideas, skills, and passion of community organizations, governments, businesses, and people.* BPS Books.

Bradbury, H., & Lichtenstein, B. (2000) Relationality in organizational research: Exploring the "space between." *Organization Science, 11*(5), 551–564.

Brandon, D. T., Isaac, L. A., & LaVeist, T. A. (2005). The legacy of Tuskegee and trust in medical care: Is Tuskegee responsible for race differences in mistrust of medical care? *Journal of the National Medical Association, 97*(7), 951–956. https://www.ncbi.nlm.nih.gov/pmc/articles/PMC2569322/

Brown, C. E., & Campelia, G. D. (2021). Counteracting COVID-19 healthcare inequity: Supporting antiracist practices at bedside. *The American Journal of Bioethics, 21*(2). https://doi.org/10.1080/15265161.2020.1861370

Cooper L. A., & Williams, D. R. (2020). Excess deaths from COVID-19, community bereavement, and restorative justice for communities of color. *JAMA.* https://doi.org/10.1001/jama.2020.19567

Drath, W. H., McCauley, C. D., Palus, C. J., Van Velsor, E., O'Connor, P. M. G., & McGuire, J. B. (2008). Direction, alignment, commitment: Toward a more integrative ontology of leadership. *Leadership Quarterly, 19*(6), 635–653. https://doi.org/10.1016/j.leaqua.2008.09.003

Edwards, A. (2005). Relational agency: Learning to be a resourceful practitioner. *International Journal of Educational Research, 43*(3), 168–182. https://doi.org/10.1016/j.ijer.2006.06.010

Flower, J. (1995). A conversation with Ronald Heifetz: Leadership without easy answers. *The Healthcare Forum Journal, 38*(4), 30–36.

Fortuna, L. R., Tolou-Shams, M., Robles-Ramamurthy, B., & Porche, M. V. (2020). Inequity and the disproportionate impact of COVID-19 on communities of color in the United States: The need for a trauma-informed social justice response. *Psychological Trauma: Theory, Research, Practice, and Policy, 12*(5), 443–445. http://dx.doi.org/10.1037/tra0000889

Heifetz, R. A. (1994). *Leadership without easy answers.* Harvard University Press.

Heifetz, R., Grashow, A., & Linsky, M. (2009). *The practice of adaptive leadership.* Harvard Business Press.

Kaplan, B. (2021). Access, equity, and neutral space: Telehealth beyond the pandemic. *Annals of Family Medicine, 19*(1), 75–78. https://doi.org/10.1370/afm.2633

Laurencin, C. T., & McClinton, A. (2020). The COVID-19 pandemic: A call to action to identify and address racial and ethnic disparities. *Journal of Racial and Ethnic Health Disparities, 7*, 398–402. https://doi.org/10.1007/s40615-020-00756-0

Leader, J. S. (2020). *Mutual shaping of tele-healthcare practice: Exploring community perspectives on telehealth technologies in northern and Indigenous contexts* [Unpublished doctoral dissertation, University of Saskatchewan]. http://hdl.handle.net/10388/12889

Machado, A. (2014, May 7). Why many Latinos dread going to the doctor: How cultural barriers can be more important than income. *The Atlantic.* https://www.theatlantic.com/health/archive/2014/05/why-many-latinos-dread-going-to-the-doctor/361547/

McClure, E. S., Vasudevan, P., Bailey, Z., Patel, S., & Robinson, W. R. (2020). Racial capitalism within public health: How occupational settings drive COVID-19 disparities. *American Journal of Epidemiology, 189*(11), 1244–1253. https://doi.org/10.1093/aje/kwaa126

Muñoz-Price, L. S., Nattinger, A. B., Rivera, F., Hanson, R., Gmehlin, C. G., Perez, A., Singh, S., Buchan, B. W., Ledeboer, N. A., & Pezzin, L. E. (2020). Racial disparities in incidence and outcomes among patients with COVID-19. *JAMA*, *3*(9). https://doi.org/10.1001/jamanetworkopen.2020.21892

Nouri, S., Khoong, E. C., Lyles, C. R., & Karliner, L. (2020). Addressing equity in telemedicine for chronic disease management during the COVID-19 pandemic. *NEJM Catalyst*. https://doi.org/10.1056/CAT.20.0123

Ospina, S., & Foldy, E. (2010). Building bridges from the margins: The work of leadership in social change organizations. *Leadership Quarterly*, *21*(2), 292–307.

Ospina, S., & Schall, E. (2001). *Leadership (re)constructed: How lens matters.* [Paper presentation]. APPAM Research Conference, Washington, DC, United States. https://wagner.nyu.edu/files/faculty/publications/Leader.pdf

Ospina, S. M., Foldy, E. G., Fairhurst, G. T., & Jackson, B. (2020). Collective dimensions of leadership: Connecting theory and method. *Human Relations*, *73*(4), 441–463. https://doi.org/10.1177/0018726719899714

Raelin, J. (2016). *Leadership-as-practice: Theory and application.* Taylor & Francis.

Reckwitz, A. (2002). Toward a theory of social practices: A development in culturalist theorizing. *European Journal of Social Theory*, *5*(2), 243–263. https://doi.org/10.1177%2F13684310222225432

Reed, M. E., Huang, J., Graetz, I., Lee, C., Muelly, E., Kennedy, C., & Kim, E. (2020). Patient characteristics associated with choosing a telemedicine visit vs office visit with the same primary care clinicians. *JAMA Network Open*, *3*(6). https://doi.org/10.1001/jamanetworkopen.2020.5873

Safer, L., Wilhite, R., & Mann, S. (2010). Applying adaptive leadership to sustain K-12 district initiatives and challenges. *International Journal of Educational Leadership Preparation*, *5*(3). http://cnx.org/content/m34765/latest/

Uhl-Bien, M., & Ospina, S. M. (Eds.). (2012). *Advancing relational leadership research: A dialogue among perspectives.* Information Age.

Yearby, R. (2021). Race based medicine, colorblind disease: How racism in medicine harms us all. *The American Journal of Bioethics*, *21*(2), 19–27. https://doi.org/10.1080/15265161.2020.1851811

PART IV

IDENTITY

CHAPTER 14

FROM #BLACKLIVESMATTER TO CRITICAL HOPE

Reflecting on Socially Just Leadership in Higher Education

Jesse R. Ford and Brandy S. Propst

Jesse's positionality: I anchor my thoughts as a new assistant professor in the work of Meyerson (2001), who calls attention to tempered radicals. Meyerson (2001) states,

> tempered radicals are people who want to succeed in their organizations yet want to live by their values or identities, even if they are somehow at odds with the dominant culture of their organization. Tempered radicals want to fit in, and they want to retain what makes them different. They want to rock the boat, and they want to stay in it. (p. xi)

As a Black man navigating historically White racialized environments, my intellectual ontology positions my Blackness at the epicenter of how I understand education. As such, my views are often in a state of flux as I am trying to make meaning of how my Blackness influences my logic, epistemology, and axiology. As a scholar, I am always trying to push my thinking to "rock the boat" while wanting "to stay in it" as I believe

Navigating Complexities in Leadership: Moving Toward Critical Hope, pp. 143–151
www.infoagepub.com
Copyright © 2022 by Information Age Publishing
All rights of reproduction in any form reserved.

leadership educators must push change to happen from within. More-over, the change I am pushing for calls for my students and peers to rethink and retool as they develop leadership identities leading to a more just society, despite the injustices that plague our country.

In conjunction, recent trends call me to reflect on how there is no greater barrier to simply thriving in our American society than the pos-session of Black skin. The murders of Eric Garner, Trayvon Martin, Philando Castile, Freddie Gray, Tamir Rice, Michael Brown, and others have proven that race is the apex of America's struggles. The higher edu-cation system has historically been hostile to Black bodies; but, I find myself teaching and inspiring students with whom I work to have a sense of vital optimism in addressing the problems of higher education and our ever-changing global society.

Brandy's positionality: I come to this work as a student affairs profes-sional of 15 years whose double-bind identities as a Black woman have shaped my experiences and interactions within higher education. How I choose to show up and engage with my colleagues and students in histori-cally White spaces is a testament to my will as a Black woman, as my mere existence is a form of resistance. In doing so, I work to disrupt oppressive structures and practices within higher education that were created for myself and others who look like me not to succeed. Lorde (1988) pro-fessed that "sometimes we are blessed with being able to choose the time, and the arena, and the manner of our revolution, but more usually we must do battle where we are standing" (p. 120). In the current socio-polit-ical climate within our country, I battle daily from where I stand as a Black woman, scholar-practitioner. I believe that leadership educators must make the same decision to create socially just environments and develop socially just leaders on college campuses. Black and Brown students depend on it for their survival.

Our critical hope is that leadership educators learn how to support, develop and cultivate Black student leaders on college campuses. This chapter is a call to action for all leadership educators to be bold, authen-tic, and transformative in their efforts to equip Black students with critical hope in a time when Black students are existing with racial injustices amplified by the COVID-19 pandemic.

BLACK STUDENT EXPERIENCES IN HIGHER EDUCATION

Historically, the exclusion of Black people in educational settings mirrors the greater American societal challenges in our country. Majors and Gordon (1994) state, "Blacks have been miseducated by the educational system, mishandled by the criminal justice system, mislabeled by the mental health system, and mistreated by the social welfare system" (p. 31). Collectively, these social-cultural generational injustices have been highlighted as challenges facing Black people in the United States and subsequently, Black students in higher education (Ford, 2020). Sedlacek (1987) positioned, "because of racism, Blacks have been excluded historically from being full participants in many of the White-oriented communities that have been developed in the United States and in the education system" (p. 542). Contemporary research reinforces these historical, social barriers and reveals that much has not improved for Black students in the last three decades (Ford, 2020; Smith et al., 2007).

More recently, the systematic historical challenges of Black students are highlighted by racial battle fatigue (Smith et al., 2007), financial challenges (Perez-Felkner et al., 2020), and a lack of role models and mentors (Ford, 2020) in academic spaces. These challenges, which often are multifaceted and complex, are ingrained into the fabric in higher education campus environments and the academic success of Black students (Ford, 2020). As a result, hostile racial campus environments have been documented as causing endemic systemic racism which is occurring in Black student experiences (Hotchkins & Dancy, 2017).

In addition to facing challenges due to race and racism in higher education, Black students must often determine how to navigate racial microaggressions in their collegiate experience. Sue (2010) positions racial microaggressions as "everyday verbal, nonverbal, and environmental slights, snubs, or insults, whether intentional or unintentional, that communicate hostile, derogatory, or negative messages to target persons based solely upon their marginalized group membership" (p. 3). This is further compounded by the negotiation of racially hostile environments. For all students, the negotiation of the campus culture is closely related to their success; but for Black students, their treatment when they navigate institutional spaces is often dependent on their racial identification (Ford, 2020), which has been further complicated by the COVID-19 pandemic.

COVID-19 COMPLICATIONS OF BLACK STUDENT EXPERIENCE

Following a mass exodus from college campuses, many Black students returned home to communities that had been deeply affected by the COVID-19 pandemic. COVID-19 has become a racialized epidemic that has disproportionately affected the Black community due to the persistence of institutional inequality ingrained in American structures (Poteat et al., 2020). Despite accounting for 12.4% of the U.S. population, Blacks have accounted for 15.7% of COVID-19 deaths as of February 2021 (American Public Media Research Lab, 2021). Historically, Blacks have higher rates of underlying health conditions, higher unemployment rates, and lack of access to health care (Majors & Gordon, 1994). The deaths of Ahmaud Arbery, Breonna Taylor, and George Floyd in 2020 have also created elevated levels of racial trauma and racial battle fatigue within the Black community, affecting Black students' and their pursuit of a higher education as they were simultaneously uprooted from college campuses.

According to Soria and team (2020), "the COVID-19 pandemic has disproportionately impacted students who identify as Black, Indigenous, People of Color (BIPOC)" (p. 1). Moreover, research shows that due to the COVID-19 pandemic, "BIPOC students were more than likely to experience symptoms of generalized anxiety disorder and major depressive disorder" (Soria et al., 2020, p. 1). BIPOC students are also more likely than White students to experience obstacles while transitioning to remote instruction, struggle with financial hardships, and have higher rates of food and housing insecurity (Harper, 2020; Soria et al., 2020). Moreover, lack of access to student employment, technology, and adequate academic spaces has created increasing racialized challenges for Black students.

As campuses made the decision to reopen in fall 2020, Black students faced more challenges with marginalization and finding belonging and support. "A May 2020 Gates Foundation analysis found that…59% of Black parents of high school seniors reported that their child's postsecondary plans had been disrupted due to COVID-19, compared to 43% of White parents" (The Steve Fund Crisis Response Task Force, 2020, p. 3). As a result of the upheaval, the number of Black students who arrived on college campuses in fall 2020 decreased dramatically, resulting in less diverse campuses. Furthermore, there are insufficient support systems and safe spaces for Black students on college campuses due to lower numbers of Black students on campuses and higher numbers of Black faculty and staff working from home due to underlying health problems and lack of access to childcare. Social distancing policies and restrictions have heavily influenced student engagement programs for Black students that fill the void of familial and cultural norms when away from home. The impacts of COVID-19 and the fight for racial justice require that leadership educators and practitioners create environments where Black students feel they can survive and thrive in academic spaces.

Fostering Critical Hope: Being a Leadership Educator in Contemporary Times

Education has changed drastically in the past 20 years. Political, societal, and systematic changes have played a significant role in how we see and understand the role education plays in the ever-changing American society. With increased documentation of racialized incidents on college campuses, the role of leadership educators in educational systems must continue to evolve. In addition, contemporary challenges call for leadership educators to meet the needs of transforming educational demographics (Khan, 2017), diverse faculty and staff (Smith, 2015), and the leadership, financial, and socialization experiences of students of color (Ford, 2020; Perez-Felkner et al., 2020). Fullan (2006) posits we must develop a new kind of leadership—"system thinkers in action" or "the new theoreticians" (p. 114), and this approach also applies to how higher education institutions should adjust to the changing times.

We position Tupac Shakur's (1999) popular term "a rose that grew from concrete" as a direct response to Fullan's (2006) call for new theoreticians. Before his death in the late 1990s, Shakur's phrase "a rose that grew from concrete" became well-known. This term denotes the development of Black American youth from the struggles, hazardous conditions, and ghettos of the 1980s and 1990s. The phrase suggests that a rose will emerge from concrete in spite of the material considered to be almost impenetrable. Shakur uses this phrase to illustrate how Black people have traditionally risen above the barriers of poverty, drugs, racial inequality, and insufficient educational opportunities, which he defines as almost impossible (Shakur, 1999). Duncan-Andrade (2009) adds that "it is almost difficult to manage the litany of social stressors that arise from growing up in concrete" (p. 186).

Although this concept, "a rose that grows from concrete," was used to describe the almost impossible circumstances for Black youth, it also illustrates the recurring barriers that Black students have encountered in education environments. To combat these challenges or existing in the trenches (Ford, 2020), we suggest that leadership educators and student affairs practitioners should cultivate critical hope in the worlds they are creating or fostering for Black students. West (2004) contends critical hope is a committed and active struggle "against the evidence in order to change the deadly tides of wealth inequality, group xenophobia, and personal despair" (pp. 296–297).

RECOMMENDATIONS TO FOSTER CRITICAL HOPE FOR LEADERSHIP EDUCATORS

Leadership educators are a part of, not apart from, student experiences on college campuses. The very presence of being a leadership educator in an academic space bounds our actions to the invisible fabric of the institution. Moreover, since leadership educators are part of the lacework of the community, we must remember our interactions with students create snapshots of isolated parts of their experiences. Leadership educators are interconnected to the influences of COVID-19 and racial injustices presented earlier in this chapter. As practitioners and scholars of the Black student experience in higher education, we offer the following suggestions for fostering leadership environments that will motivate and cultivate Black student leaders at a time when critical hope is essential for Black students navigating our ever-changing global society. As such, we offer the following recommendations for fostering a community of critical hope for Black students in unprecedented times in higher education.

Acknowledging and Establishing a Community of Care

Tatum (1997) highlights "one of the consequences of racism in our society is that those who oppose racism are often marginalized and as a result their stories are not readily accessed" (p. 109). Furthermore, she cites James Baldwin by adding, "not everything that is faced can be changed. But nothing can be changed until it is faced" (p. xix). Collectively, their quotes position that racism is inevitable in our educational system. However, this reality prompts the questions: Whose responsibility is it to ignite change? And who is responsible for fostering hope?

These are questions we ask ourselves and other leadership educators as we position a new set of challenges for Black students and a call to action for leadership and higher education. As history cannot be erased, moving forward starts by acknowledging that we need to foster a culture of care. Critical hope, which has been under assault in our country (Duncan-Andrade, 2009), must be used to generate social and political change in higher education. Unlike Freire, who believes critical hope is innate, we agree with Duncan-Andrade (2009), who suggests that critical hope can be cultivated through our attitudes, beliefs, views, and perceptions. We are inextricably linked to COVID-19's influences and racial injustices; thus, critical hope is essential for achieving a supportive culture of care and understanding student identities.

Acknowledging Student Identities in Educational Spaces

Before college, students have experiences that have often leave an indelible mark on their lives. These imprints, or life stories, follow students to college campuses. The cultural, historical, and racialized experiences that Black students bring to college campuses aid in the knowledge acquisition of all students. Thus the need and significance of socially just leadership (Guthrie & Rodriguez, 2016), by which leadership educators approach leadership development with student identities in mind. According to Guthrie and Rodriguez (2016), socially just leadership educators as those who "empower and encourage leader's identity, capacity and efficacy. It is the role of educators and advisors to invest in the development of all students and validate their knowledge and lived experiences as strengths rather than weaknesses" (p. 250).

As leadership educators, it is our responsibility to encourage students to see the world through different lenses, to reflect on and assess what they're seeing and learning, and to formulate their own critical hope as a result. We must allow students to affirm their identities, cultures, and values in order to be successful. In addition, we call for leadership educators to acknowledge students' identities. The navigation of assisting students with developing their own level of understanding around identities often calls for us to do internal work and reflection as educators. Furthermore, we urge leadership educators to recognize their own identities in academic settings.

Acknowledging Self Care for Leadership Educators

Bertrand Jones et al. (2016) emphasize that "understanding how students with different identities define and learn about leadership helps educators appreciate the critical connections of leadership and diversity" (p. 9). Moreover, to do leadership education well, social justice education and identity acknowledgment must be a key component in creating socially just spaces for leadership educators. With the impacts of COVID-19 and racial injustices as highlighted earlier in this chapter, while leadership educators work to use socially just leadership, they meet constant battles "educating a campus populace that can be resistant to social justice content" (Miller Dyce et al., 2021, p. 168). These battles lead to what Miller Dyce and team (2021) call "social justice battle fatigue," which consists of "intersectional challenges, systemic and institutional constraints, emotions, and identity related factors that create the conditions for the many battles they navigate" (p.167). This phenomenon requires leadership educators to reflect and evaluate their self-care practices to sustain their well-being.

As leadership educators focus on socially just and culturally relevant practices that build a community of care for Black students, institutions must also build a community of care for educators. Institutions must create a culture of self-care to maintain and support educators who do social justice work (Miller Dyce et al., 2021). This requires institutions to examine how their campus climate supports both students and leadership educators who are tasked with creating socially just spaces for Black student leaders. Institutional commitments focused on the well-being of students *and* educators are necessary for creating pathways to fostering a community of critical hope within higher education.

CONCLUDING THOUGHTS

This chapter explored the experiences of Black students navigating racial injustice in the midst of COVID-19. Through their racialized identities, as a result, their never-ending struggle to exist in our global society, Black students' experiences are seen, explored, and understood. As such, the significance of developing Black students is critical for the continued upward mobility for this population. Higher education must do more to engage, support, and retain Black students in navigating the myriad of challenges and inequalities in our society.

REFERENCES

American Public Media Research Lab. (2021). *The color of coronavirus: COVID-19 deaths by race and ethnicity in the U.S.* [Data Set]. https://www.apmre-searchlab.org/covid/deaths-by-race

Bertrand Jones, T., Guthrie, K. L., & Osteen, L. (2016). Critical domains of culturally relevant leadership learning: A call to transform leadership programs. In K. L. Guthrie, T. Bertrand Jones, & L. Osteen (Eds.), *New Directions for Student Leadership: No. 152. Developing culturally relevant leadership learning* (pp. 9–21). Wiley. https://doi.org/10.1002/yd.20205

Duncan-Andrade, J. (2009). Note to educators: Hope required when growing roses in concrete. *Harvard Educational Review, 79*(2), 181–194.

Ford, J. (2020). *In the trenches: Black men in the academy navigating racialized encounters* [Doctoral dissertation, The Florida State University]. ProQuest Dissertations and Theses Global.

Fullan, M. (2006). The future of educational change: System thinkers in action. *Journal of Educational Change, 7*(3), 113–122. https://doi.org/10.1007/s10833-006-9003-9

Guthrie, K. L., & Rodriguez, J. (2016). Creating cocurricular socially just leadership learning environments. In K. L. Guthrie & V. S. Chunoo (Eds.), *Changing the narrative: Socially just leadership education* (pp. 245–258). Information Age.

Harper, S. (2020). Covid-19 and the racial equity implications of reopening college and university campuses. *American Journal of Education, 127*(1), 153–162.

Hotchkins, B. K., & Dancy, T. (2017). A house is not a home: Black students' responses to racism in university residential halls. *Journal of College & University Student Housing, 43*(3), 42–52.

Khan, N. (2017). Adaptive or transactional leadership in current higher education: A brief comparison. *International Review of Research in Open and Distributed Learning, 18*(3), 178–183.

Lorde, A. (1988). *A burst of light: Essays by Audre Lorde.* Firebrand Books.

Majors, R. G., & Gordon, J. U. (1994). *The American Black male: His present status and his future.* Nelson-Hall.

Meyerson, D. E. (2001). *Tempered radicals: How people use difference to inspire change at work.* Harvard Business School Press.

Miller Dyce, C., Propst, B. S., & Balady, B. (2021). Can I get a witness? A case study of self care practices as an act of radical social justice for social justice and diversity professionals in higher education. In A. L. Palmadessa (Ed.), *Education in America: Perspectives, challenges, and opportunities* (pp. 143–200). Nova Science.

Perez-Felkner, L., Ford, J. R., Zhao, T., Anthony, M., Jr., Harrison, J. A., & Rahming, S. G. (2020). Basic needs insecurity among doctoral students: What it looks like and how to address it. *About Campus, 24*(6), 18–24.

Poteat, T., Millett, G. A., Nelson, L. E., & Beyrer, C. (2020). Understanding COVID-19 risks and vulnerabilities among Black communities in America: The lethal force of syndemics. *Annals of Epidemiology, 47*, 1–3. https://doi.org/10.1016/j.annepidem.2020.05.004

Sedlacek, W. E. (1987). Black students on White campuses: 20 years of research. *Journal of College Student Personnel, 28*(6), 484–495.

Shakur, T. (1999). *The rose that grew from concrete.* Simon and Schuster.

Smith, D. G. (2015). *Diversity's promise for higher education: Making it work.* JHU Press.

Smith, W. A., Allen, W. R., & Danley, L. L. (2007). "Assume the position … you fit the description" psychosocial experiences and racial battle fatigue among African American male college students. *American Behavioral Scientist, 51*(4), 551–578. https://doi.org/10.1177/0002764207307742

Soria, K. M., Roberts, B. J., Horgos, B., & Hallahan, K. (2020). *The experiences of undergraduate students during the COVID-19 pandemic: Disparities by race and ethnicity* [Policy Brief]. SERU Consortium, University of California-Berkeley and University of Minnesota. https://cshe.berkeley.edu/seru-covid-survey-reports

Sue, D. W. (2010). *Microaggressions and marginality: Manifestation, dynamics, and impact.* Wiley.

Tatum, B. D. (2017). *Why are all the Black kids sitting together in the cafeteria?: And other conversations about race.* Basic Books.

The Steve Fund Crisis Response Taskforce. (2020). *Adapting and innovating to promote mental health and emotional well-being of young people of color: COVID-19 and beyond.* The Steve Fund. https://www.stevefund.org/crisis-response-task-force

West, C. (2004). The impossible will take a little while. In P. Rogat (Ed.), *The impossible will take a little while: A citizen's guide to hope in a time of fear* (pp. 293–297). Basic Books.

CHAPTER 15

UNPACKING THE INFLUENCE OF LEADERSHIP TAX ON BLACK WOMEN

Brittany Brewster

Hope. Fear. Triumph. Concern. Pride. Throughout my life, the everyday achievements of Black women continuously spark a range of emotions. From our advocacy of fair and just living and working conditions to the startup of local businesses or the joy-filled pivot into a new career, Black women's bridge-building leadership is expansive. In these realizations, I see glimpses of familiar moments of Black womanhood. Then my mind begins to race. The weight associated with leadership, of being first or creating room alongside and for others, is often underpinned by a hidden tax. This tax demands an even higher cost for people pushed to the margins of society, particularly for Black women.

WHY DO WE NEED TO TALK ABOUT LEADERSHIP TAX?

Modern-day intricacies lean heavily on leadership to confront, advance, and liberate our ever-evolving world. The post-2020 U.S. presidential election reminded us of the gift of Black women's leadership. Our foresight, power, and resilience. Through Black women's world views, new

Navigating Complexities in Leadership: Moving Toward Critical Hope, pp. 153–162
www.infoagepub.com
Copyright © 2022 by Information Age Publishing
All rights of reproduction in any form reserved.

possibilities are imagined. Contemporary celebrations of our ideas and labor are well deserved; yet, they can also overshadow the challenges and sacrifices made when we engage in leadership. Leadership as a "multicultural initiative" brings together a wide array of world views and social locations (Watt, 2016, p. 41).

As individuals from varying facets of organizations and broader systems are called to navigate mishandled trials and unaddressed sufferings, challenges within the leadership process become increasingly more complex. The critical nature of working across differences in identities, beliefs, norms, and values is increasingly evident. Globally, public health and climate crises continue to strain all facets of life. In the United States and beyond, calls for racial justice and the erosion of White supremacy continues in response to ever-present police brutality and systemic violence. Our world must be radically reimagined.

Our communities need people to exercise leadership collectively to address these adaptive challenges. Leadership processes demand critical and courageous voices and perspectives to dismantle and reconstruct systems. Those of us engaged in leadership education and practice must also consider how our participation impacts our well-being. Despite the depth and interdisciplinary nature of leadership scholarship exploration, few have investigated the costs of leadership: the exchange of emotional, mental, and physical labor and its taxing influence on minoritized leadership experiences. More specifically, to fully live in possibility, we must name and unpack the taxing effects of leadership for Black women.

BLACK WOMEN'S BRIDGE BUILDING LEADERSHIP

The influence and shared collective mobility of Black women's leadership is a global phenomenon that spans movements, sectors, and approaches. The advancement of feminist waves often occurred as a result of the development of social movements led and supported by Black women (Rosser-Mims, 2010). Resistance stories capture the dynamic nature of Black women's leadership and followership through abolitionist movements catalyzed by Harriet Tubman and Sojourner Truth. Activist foremothers, including Fannie Barrier Williams and Mary Church Terrell, organized Black feminist movements to generate social, political, and economic access to inequitable structures (Cooper, 2017). Likewise, their leadership created inroads for Septima Clarke, Ella Baker, and Daisy Bates' contributions that progressed the modern civil rights movement (Horsford, 2012). In conjunction with these social movements, Anna Julia Cooper, Ida B. Wells, and Pauli Murray's intellectual activism amplified the experiences of Black women and expanded our understanding of their perspectives. Their labor paved the way for Brittany Cooper's *Eloquent Rage,* Issa Rae's *Awkward Black Girl,* Raquel Willis' organizing for trans rights, and countless other Black women's leadership that continues to advance our communities forward.

Literature on Black women's leadership remains scant despite our powerful narratives and contributions (Rosser-Mims, 2010). Like other culturally rooted scholarship, a central framework for Black women's leadership does not exist. Broad framing of leadership often illustrates themes to capture shared consciousness while honoring the multiplicity within social groups. With this knowledge, Black women's leadership evolved as a "survival technique" in response to familial, spiritual, and communal needs (Collins, 2002). Slavery forced new norms of labor on Black women as they "managed homes; nursed babies; tended the fields; traded goods' raised their own children, those of others, and children of slave owners" (Meriwether, 2018, p. 95). In many ways, Black women's leadership reared a country.

The collectivist nature of Black women's leadership emphasizes community empowerment (Rosser-Mims, 2010). Networks of Black women create a cyclical development of leaders who engage in the pursuit of Black social upliftment (Allen, 1997). King and Ferguson (2011) observed this norm via the motherline in their conceptualization of Black womanist leadership. Central to its function, motherline is the transmission of leadership knowledge, rooted in the disruption of systems, passed down from mother-daughter relationships. As a process, Black women engage in leadership through a lens that centers our perspectives, countering oppressive norms and resisting authoritative models (Collins, 2002).

BLACK WOMEN'S SOCIAL LOCATIONS AND LEADERSHIP EXPERIENCES

The culturally relevant leadership learning model highlights the influence of individual identity, capacity, and efficacy within leadership (Bertrand Jones et al., 2016). The model also signals the influence of five environmental dimensions which heavily shape the leadership learning including: the historical legacy of inclusion/exclusion, compositional diversity, psychological, behavioral, and organizational, and structural dimensions. With this knowledge, we recognize Black women's engagement in leadership is heavily influenced by who they are, their skill competence, and belief in self. Furthermore, these aspects of self are contextualized by broader domains shaped by sociopolitical and sociohistorical truths. The lens of culturally relevant leadership learning model illuminates our awareness of the taxing effects of Black women's leadership engagement.

A distinct form of gendered racism forces Black women to weather the harmful dual effects of anti-Blackness and sexism known as *misogynoir* (Essed,1991). Existence at the intersections of race, gender, and class oppression equips Black women with a unique standpoint of our global society (Crenshaw, 1991). This view arms Black women with an "outsider within" status which historically situates them on the outskirts of dominant feminist and Black social movements (Collins, 1986). Nevertheless, these efforts failed to derail Black women's change-making capacity and efficacy in their everyday lives, communities, and broader spheres.

Within leadership practice, Black women's advocacy continues to serve as a gateway for transformation and liberation for many who suffer at the hands of inequitable systems. Horsford (2012) notes the intersectional existence of Black women generates leadership which serves "as a bridge for others, to others, and between others" (p.12). This metaphorical yet experienced bridge places Black women at the center of complex social issues, and subsequent leadership efforts sought to create social change (Collins, 2002). Furthermore, these practices position them to be overworked yet devalued within the leadership process. In pursuit of understanding the tax placed on marginalized individuals and others existing within leadership processes, Black women's experiences serve as a natural starting point.

THE TAX OF LEADERSHIP ON BLACK WOMEN

Black women continue to navigate the effects of controlling images of the mammy, matriarch, welfare queen, and jezebel crafted by gendered racism (Collins, 2002). Collectively, they contribute to prejudicial and discriminatory practices which support our exploitation and strengthen our social stratification. These narratives construct self-schemas generated from Black women's perceptions and ideas of ourselves influenced by social beliefs. Strong Black Woman schema is characterized by the enduring strength Black women must possess to negotiate multiple roles within their communities and broader society. Abrams et al. (2014) note the influence of "sociohistorical antecedents specific to Black women have contributed to the development, endorsement, internalization, and maintenance of the Strong Black Woman phenomenon" (p. 1). In response, scholars developed a variety of constructs to understand strong Black woman schema, including the sisteralla complex (Jones & Shorter-Gooden, 2009), Sojourner Truth Syndrome (Mullings, 2002), and the Superwoman Schema (Woods-Giscombé, 2010). Black women exist in expansive and vibrant ways, yet, experiences steeped in misogynoir create collective understanding and fatigue.

Black women's standpoints remain foundational to the progression of communities. Consequently, social position, along with preexisting barriers within leadership, yields a distinctive experience for Black women. Joy and pride in Black womanhood are central to our existence and shapes our worldviews. Within leadership, Black womanhood emphasizes the importance of culturally relevant leadership experiences to nurture our development and increase participation. Individuals may disengage or resent leadership in environments where culturally responsive practices are absent or devalued. In response, Black women may find themselves volunteered or inherently called to cultivate spaces where they can authentically and safely engage in leadership. For example, Black women on college campuses may find themselves creating formal student organizations exploring the experiences of Black women. In business settings, establishing affinity spaces or creating professional development experiences targeting Black women can create opportunities for self-definition and meaningful engagement.

Where empowering and vital for Black women's leadership success, attempts to center the needs of Black women are met with resistance from broader structures due to bias, ignorance or the inability to "surveil" and subsequently control these interactions (Collins, 2002). Navigating these interactions often results in emotional labor expelled by way of code-switching and self-silencing. Code-switching is the act of making specific linguistic choices in response to different audiences, often as a form of assimilation (Koch et al., 2001). Consequently, these added responsibilities further contribute to our leadership strain. The suppression of emotions and subsequent outward amiability occurs as a result of self-silencing, commonly as a survival strategy (Abrams et al., 2014). Negotiating both can contribute to higher levels of stress and depression among Black women. Despite the need to advocate and create culturally responsive practices, the sacrifices made to foster change further point to exhaustion for Black women.

Suffering by Way of Leadership Tax

At what cost does engaging in leadership influence those who opt in to the process? For Black women, the literature highlights the negative effects of stress on their health and well-being by way of the Strong Black Women Schema (Woods-Giscombé, 2010). Subsequently, disruptions within the leadership process can exacerbate and create real health implications. Challenges within and beyond the leadership process can create dangerous responses for individuals. Marginalization may result in the erasure or silencing of people within the process. Situating Black women at the peripheral of change-making processes hinders the ability to disrupt oppressive power structures and stagnates radical transformation. Additionally, it contributes to people's tokenization and cultural tax by empowering them only when their perspectives or expertise aligns with temporal agendas.

Diversion by way of distraction from the goal or focus of the change further dilutes progress. Similarly, attacking an individual's character or leadership style displaces attention away from important issues. Diversion away from critical tasks further upholds the status quo. These responses may signal to Black women that their perspectives are not valued or supported. Understanding Black women's leadership highlights their deep connection between beliefs, identities, and worldviews (Rosser-Mims, 2010). Dismissal might result in further disengagement within the process, stagnating the dismantling of dangerous practices and oppressive systems.

DISRUPTING LEADERSHIP TAX

Toni Morrison (2020) reminds us that the purpose of freedom is to free others. From my purview, one also of a Black woman, this function is central to leadership, which seeks to positively transform and liberate in large and small ways. The permanent and ordinary nature of racism and the effects of misogynoir make leadership tax an unavoidable reality for Black women (Moya Bailey & Trudy, 2018). Morrison's statement also reminds us of the shared responsibility we have to dismantle roadblocks for all people. These barriers task us to understand this tax by way of study and theorization and integrate this learning into new teachings and practices. Opportunities to disrupt harmful practices within leadership learning experiences can occur within and beyond the classroom. The following strategies are offered as starting points for readers to consider implementing within their leadership journey or practice as leadership educators.

Center Black Women's Experiences

Critical to disrupting leadership tax is unpacking and addressing the interlocking nature of oppression that supports the exploitation of Black women and normalizes their exhaustion within and beyond leadership (Collins, 1986). Shifting these norms call for us to interrogate broader stereotypes which discourage Black women's leadership engagement. Individuals can commit to educating themselves on the historical and political experiences of Black women within and beyond the United States. Engaging in music, literature, movies, dance, and other forms of expression produced by Black women in a wide array of social locations provide counternarratives that further challenge our knowledge. Counternarratives or "talking back" for Black women, as described by hooks (1989), disrupts dominant discourse by focusing on experiences of resistance by individuals and communities strained by oppressive structures. Stories of resistance illustrate systems of oppression, their enduring function within the lives of Black women, and the negotiations we must make to survive and thrive. For Black women, leaning on literature produced by and centered on our many truths can further affirm internal feelings and strengthen our shared consciousness.

Celebrate the Contributions of Black Women's Leadership

Progress by way of Black women's leadership is often minimized, colonized, or erased. Creating intentional space to acknowledge Black women's leadership contributions and achievements further supports the disruption of leadership tax. Leaning on the knowledge developed through the immersion of Black women's perspectives, leadership educators can utilize their curriculum to showcase historical and contemporary examples of Black women's leadership. Simple adjustments in readings, guest lectures, and visuals elevating Black women showcase an appreciation for their viewpoints while broadening leadership learning.

Additionally, championing the achievements of Black women's leadership can occur in everyday interactions. Expressing gratitude for the contributions that Black women bring into cocurricular, professional, and or personal spaces should occur, while being mindful *not* to tokenize their existence. Personally, while writing this chapter, my community of scholar-peers celebrated this project's potential and uplifted not only me but the stories of other Black women in the process. Recognition, where seemingly simple, can further interrupt attempts to overlook the leadership efforts of Black women.

Normalize Challenge, Failure, and Support in Leadership

Engagement in leadership rarely exists without complication. For Black women, environments should promote a fail-forward culture that normalizes challenge and the need for support when leading. The pressure to personify strength via Strong Black Women schema impacts Black women's leadership engagement and subsequently contributes to our tax. This inherent call or external expectation to be resilient can establish an unwavering commitment to the process and provide little room for negotiation. Black women may find themselves committed to causes or entrenched in projects that lack alignment with our interests and contradict our politic. Additionally, deep alignment with the strength schema fosters a need for self-efficacy and independent thinking. These traits can positively contribute to leadership efforts; likewise, they can be detrimental to well-being and the overall process.

Normalizing disruption and failure within leadership learning can signal to Black women that overexertion often fails to minimize the everyday challenges that exist within the process. As a relationship-based experience, asking for assistance from others may be critical not only to our development but also essential to the progression of the collective cause. Leadership establishes distinct challenges for individuals to navigate that may be difficult to unpack and understand alone. The pressure to be independent and self-efficacious can prevent Black women from exploring feelings of being overwhelmed, overcommitted, and exhausted. It is essential to cultivate culturally responsive spaces for Black women to process their emotions without the need to assume additional responsibilities in exchange.

Make Self-Care a Core Leadership Practice

The call to exhibit strength may result in Black women managing too many responsibilities due to overcommitment. Within the leadership learning environment, individuals should be mindful of this natural attraction to engage in transformative experiences, which may result in overloading and subsequent self-sacrifice. Introducing self-care as a foundational element of leadership learning can combat exhaustion and positively redefine Strong Black Women schema. The strengthening of one's internal voice is a valuable element of self-care. Leadership learning should integrate self-care practices by way of curriculum, norms, and practices to encourage individual reflection centered on their values, beliefs, and connections to their engagement experiences.

Iterative reflection and grounding activities performed in meetings or developed as assignments should help clarify individuals' guiding values within leadership, serving as a roadmap and constant guide on its purpose. This practice can help uncover if participation is in service to Black women's interests, self-care, and well-being. Additionally, policies and practices to support the maintenance of healthy leadership loads should be implemented. For Black women, shifting the narrative to include self-care as a central leadership tenet can be a liberatory practice and support the resistance of leadership tax.

As leadership considerations shift in response to Black women's knowledge and practices, leadership learning must also change in its approach. It is no longer enough to speak value into Black women's lives and subsequent perspectives without disrupting systemic violence. Understanding and restructuring broader structures of power within the leadership process and beyond to center the needs of Black women demands a new tax from others as a necessary step towards our shared liberation. Without these changes, the pervasive nature of White supremacy wins and leadership as a values-based experience rooted in transformation has again, failed.

REFERENCES

Abrams, J. A., Maxwell, M., Pope, M., & Belgrave, F. Z. (2014). Carrying the world with the grace of a lady and the grit of a warrior: Deepening our understanding of the "strong Black woman" schema. *Psychology of Women Quarterly*, *38*(4), 503–518.

Allen, B. L. (1997). A re-articulation of Black female community leadership: Processes, networks and a culture of resistance. *African American Research Perspectives*, *3*(2), 61–67.

Bertrand Jones, T., Guthrie, K. L., & Osteen, L. (2016). Critical domains of culturally relevant leadership learning: A call to transform leadership programs. In K. L. Guthrie, T. Bertrand Jones, & L. Osteen (Eds.), *New Directions for Student Leadership: No. 152. Developing culturally relevant leadership learning* (pp. 9–21). Wiley. https://doi.org/10.1002/yd.20205

Cooper, B. C. (2017). *Beyond respectability: The intellectual thought of race women*. University of Illinois Press.

Collins, P. H. (1986). Learning from the outsider within: The sociological significance of Black feminist thought. *Social Problems*, *33*(6), s14–s32.

Collins, P. H. (2002). *Black feminist thought: Knowledge, consciousness, and the politics of empowerment*. Routledge.

Crenshaw, K. (1991). Mapping the margins: Intersectionality, identity politics, and violence against women of color. *Stanford Law Review*, *43*, 1241–1299.

Essed, P. (1991). *Understanding everyday racism: An interdisciplinary theory* (Vol. 2). SAGE.

Horsford, S. D. (2012). This bridge called my leadership: An essay on Black women as bridge leaders in education. *International Journal of Qualitative Studies in Education*, *25*(1), 11–22.

hooks, b. (1989). *Talking back: Thinking feminist, thinking Black* (Vol. 10). South End Press.

Jones, M. C., & Shorter-Gooden, K. (2009). *Shifting: The double lives of Black women in America*. Harper Collins.

King, T. C., & Ferguson, S. A. (Eds.). (2011). *Black womanist leadership: Tracing the motherline*. SUNY Press.

Koch, L. M., Gross, A. M., & Kolts, R. (2001). Attitudes toward Black English and code switching. *Journal of Black Psychology, 27*, 29–42.

Meriwether, L. R. (2018). Getting in formation to lead: Black female student leadership development. In K. L. Guthrie & V. S Chunoo (Eds.), *Changing the narrative: Socially just leadership education* (pp. 93–108). Information Age.

Morrison, T. (2020). *The source of self-regard: Selected essays, speeches, and meditations*. Vintage.

Mullings, L. (2002). The sojourner syndrome: Race, class, and gender in health and illness. *Voices, 6*(1), 32–36.

Rosser-Mims, D. (2010). Black feminism: An epistemological framework for exploring how race and gender impact Black women's leadership development. *Advancing Women in Leadership Journal, 30*(15), 2–10.

Watt, S. K. (2016). The practice of freedom: Leading through controversy. In K. L. Guthrie, T. Bertrand Jones, & L. Osteen (Eds.), *New Directions for Student Leadership: No. 152. Developing culturally relevant leadership learning* (pp. 35–46). Wiley. https://doi.org/10.1002/yd.20207

Woods-Giscombé, C. L. (2010). Superwoman schema: African American women's views on stress, strength, and health. *Qualitative Health Research, 20*(5), 668–683.

CHAPTER 16

THE RISKS OF BEING
A STUDENT-ATHLETE LEADER
IN THE MIDST
OF SOCIAL UNREST

Sherrina S. Lofton

When the topic of leadership arises, most people tend to consider leaders in politics, professional organizations, and community activist organizations. Less often are athletes, let alone collegiate athletes, considered in conversations about leadership. However, when athletes speak out on topics many deem as outside of the realm of sports such as racism, war, discrimination, police brutality, and other social issues based on socially constructed norms of society; they often face harsh realities of the division that permeates through the country. Within the start of the 21st century, we have witnessed an outpouring of professional and collegiate athlete leaders leveraging their engagement in sport as an opportunity to voice their concerns about social injustice as a strategy to promote social change (Kluch, 2020). For some that process has been a successful display of leadership and activism, whereas for others the process has been risky.

Scholars have often focused on "how" athletes from minoritized groups use their platforms—celebrity and global identity—to discuss social injustice, deconstruct stereotypes, and abate discrimination. However, in this

Navigating Complexities in Leadership: Moving Toward Critical Hope, pp. 163–173
www.infoagepub.com
Copyright © 2022 by Information Age Publishing
All rights of reproduction in any form reserved.

chapter, I will discuss the process and the risks of being a collegiate athlete leader and taking a brave stand against "the powers that be" within the sports realm. This chapter will first define leader, leadership, and athlete activists (i.e., athlete leaders), as activists are commonly considered leaders within their respective communities, societies, and interests groups. Then, I will provide examples of athlete activism, followed by responses to modern displays of athlete activism regarding social issues. Lastly, I will discuss the implications of those responses, which have either motivated or hindered the civic development of athlete activists and provide some questions for consideration.

STUDENT-ATHLETE LEADERS AS ATHLETE ACTIVISTS

The words leader and leadership have taken many forms over the years and have been used to describe why any person should be admired, revered, or bestowed with the power of total control over a people or movement. "Leadership is somewhat like describing the taste of water. We all know the taste, but trying to articulate a specific description of that taste is almost impossible" (O'Boyle et al., 2015, p. 10). Scholars have advanced understandings of leaders and leadership through many facets of consideration and fields of study (Bertrand Jones et al., 2016; Guthrie et al., 2013; Rost, 1993). However, there has been less holistic or global conversation about all aspects of leader(ship). Current literature on athlete leadership, also known as athlete activism, suggests that a leader tends to advocate for or those who are oppressed, taken advantage of, manipulated, or mistreated (Cooper et al., 2019; Edwards, 2016b). Leaders have followers whom they influence and collaborate to create necessary social change (Rost, 1993). Leadership involves how a leader behaves, and consequently, influences followers to behave in new ways (Guthrie et al., 2013). Leaders often seek to achieve beneficial social change that results in improving the human rights of all people. Therefore, being a leader who possesses the ability to exercise leadership requires developing relationships and garnering followers who acknowledge, legitimize, and support the leader's cause (O'Boyle et al., 2015).

Collegiate athletes have a unique opportunity to operate as leaders in many levels of society—from their college campus community to the larger national community to address issues from educational disparities to gender discrimination. A leader needs the support and buy-in of the people around them to create change. Athletes can develop celebrity status as a result of their athleticism, which allows them to garner global support when change is needed; from this perspective, athletes can be leaders inside and outside of sports.

Unfortunately, some critics have suggested that athletes need to stay out of social and political issues. For example, Laura Ingraham is a Fox News host known for her criticism of National Basketball Association superstars LeBron James and Kevin Durant. When James and Durant spoke out against former President Trump's hate speech, Ingraham suggested they "shut up and dribble." It would seem that athletes are expected to operate both within and outside the lanes of sports as role models, idols, humanitarians, and volunteers—but not leaders. However, athletes can garner followers and develop relationships of support, which allows them to influence the behaviors of said followers. Therefore, we must also acknowledge athletes and their contributions to society as leaders.

Many collegiate student-athletes, particularly African Black athletes, have spoken out during moments of social unrest when they felt an issue had detrimental impacts on themselves or others. I use the term African Black to refer to unmixed Blacks descended from African populations (Davis, 1991). In accordance with the actions of their predecessors, modern-day athlete activists have made some significant rifts in the power dynamic that exists within the sports realm and society (Beachy et al., 2018; Kaufman, 2008; Kluch, 2020; Pope et al., 2019). Athlete activists often disrupt hegemonic social norms and are rejected and criticized for doing so. Understanding and supporting the actions of athlete activists requires consideration of how power dynamics in sport and society, particularly on college campuses, influence those actions.

Activism on college campuses has been viewed as a strategy to be managed rather than cultivated, even though it fosters the political engagement, social responsibility, civic-mindedness, and social change understandings that college students should develop (Martin et al., 2019). These challenges can be exacerbated when collegiate athletes lend their support to activism and social movements. When student-athletes engage in activism, they have the potential to develop leadership skills, empower themselves and their peers, and positively impact the campus environment (Kezar et al., 2017). The majority of research on athlete activism has centered efforts of professional athletes; however, collegiate athletes are now becoming a group of interests as more of them (particularly African Black athletes) are engaging in social issues (Kluch, 2020).

Historical Legacy of Athlete Activism

Athlete activism is not a new concept, as professional and collegiate athletes have been engaging in activism throughout the 20th century.

Athlete activists were involved in various sociopolitical issues, from anti-apartheid, war, and Civil Rights to racism and discrimination on college campuses (Edwards, 2016a). These early athlete activists stuck to their beliefs and protested, boycotted, and issued demands for resolutions. When Muhammad Ali, considered the "godfather" of the African Black athlete activism movement, refused the 1967 draft, the path and trajectory of African Black athlete activism influenced by the broader community and societal issues were irreversibly joined (Edwards, 2016a). In 1970, the African Black football players from Syracuse University boycotted the entire season due to a lack of equality and diversity among the coaching staff. The era of activism of African Black student-athletes in the 1960s and 1970s has become known as "the revolt of the Black athlete" (Ruffin, 2014, p. 260).

However, their efforts did not always end in victory. The negative repercussions of their actions also serve as a warning for contemporary athletes engaging in sociopolitical issues. Yet, the strength of the activist movement continues to inspire many student-athlete activist agendas of recent times (Ruffin, 2014). Cooper et al. (2019) suggest that contemporary athlete activist (2005 to present) are using their activism for "securing and transferring power via economic and technological capital" (p. 161). Athletes find that disrupting the sacred institution of sport can be an effective strategy to draw attention to inequalities. Social media empowers today's student-athletes to drive the national conversation on social issues in ways their predecessors may not have been afforded (Tracy, 2020).

Contemporary Examples of Athlete Activism

Contemporary athlete activists are still fighting the battles of their predecessors, namely issues of race and gender (Edwards, 2016b). Over the past two decades, there has begun a resurgence of athlete activists who are speaking out about social injustice and inequality. There are countless examples of student-athletes who protested, boycotted, responded to, and made demands about racial issues and incidents on their campuses, including the University of Iowa, University of Texas, Oklahoma University, Oklahoma State University, and University of Missouri (Nietzel, 2020). Student-athletes from the Ohio State University, the University of South Carolina, and others have taken to the streets in support of the Black Lives Matter movement (Nietzel, 2020). In 2020, football players in the PAC-12 athletic conference formed a statement of unity (#weareunited) with demands to protect and support players against both the

COVID-19 pandemic and the pandemic of racial injustice and inequity within college sports. (The Players' Tribune, 2020).

Many contemporary athlete activists have taken to social media platforms such as Facebook, Twitter, and Instagram to express their frustration with racism, police brutality, and other human rights issues. For example, when University of Oklahoma football player Eric Striker saw a video of the racist chant from then campus fraternity Sigma Alpha Epsilon, his first response was on Twitter. Soon after, the university president David Boren severed ties with the fraternity and ordered members to move out of their fraternity home. Although these efforts are important and necessary, they are not guaranteed to end in the student athletes' favor.

Responses to Athlete Activists

Although athletes act with integrity, honor, and sincerity when trying to restore integrity, humanity, and justice to society, many run the risk of being criticized. Often those who gather the courage to voice opinions on issues such as social injustice and political oppression face a hate-filled backlash of scorn and contempt from teammates, coaches, fans, and sponsors (Kaufman, 2008). Consequently, when African Black athletes comment or demonstrate about social issues, examining audience response is important, as the actions of fans and others may affect future advocacy efforts. The reactions to athlete activism vary from coaches, fans, and administrators. Some support the efforts of athlete activists, and others despise their actions due to misperceived notions of identity. Sanderson et al. (2016) found that fans likewise take to social media to express their disagreement with athlete activists; common themes were: renounced their fandom, punishment commentary, racial commentary, and general criticisms (Sanderson et al., 2016).

One of the most publicized recent athlete activist efforts was the boycott of the University of Missouri (Mizzou) football team in 2015, when they stood in solidarity with the Black student organization on campus against racial issues. The football players vowed not to play until certain administrators were held accountable for actions. They garnered support from the coaches, athletic department, state legislators, and even the Governor to find a resolution. The support from these student-athletes not only got the campus community involved but it got the entire state involved. This example, along with many other displays of unity, can inspire more student-athletes to engage as activists. Their celebrity and social media platforms can be leveraged to draw attention to and resolve larger societal issues. Activist athletes deserve our attention because they challenge the expectations of other athletes and society in general (Kaufman, 2008).

CONSIDERATIONS FOR THE FUTURE OF ATHLETE-ACTIVISM

While predominantly White collegiate institutions continue to be unprepared for African Black students and in denial about the legitimacy of African Black students' concerns and interests, they also continue to provide the optimal environment for African Black student and athlete activist collaboration (Edwards, 2016a). Students-athletes are often recognized as leaders in their sport; however, student-athletes have displayed throughout history that they are more than athletes. They are community activists, advocates of equality, and fighters for justice. Much can be learned from student-athlete leaders' passion, unity, and commitment to invoking change. This section outlines tensions, questions, and considerations for understanding, supporting, and advancing student-athlete activism.

Technology

Technological advances have enabled the development of social media platforms, "architected by design to readily support participation, peer-to-peer conversations, collaboration, and community" (Meraz, 2009, p. 682). With the click of a button, athletes can connect at any point in time on Facebook, Twitter, Instagram, and Tik-Tok. This connectivity allows athletes to spread their messages faster between one another, as well as with fans. At the same time, a close examination of the tactics and strategies used by contemporary athlete activists reads like a page from the book of their predecessors: organizing in large groups, constructing a list of demands, and holding steady until resolutions are achieved. These strategies have effectively garnered the attention of those most often considered the sports industry leaders (i.e., coaches, administrators, and governing bodies).

Development Opportunities

In these moments we should also take a pause and reflect on how things have gotten to a point of contention when concerning human rights. We must consider the authenticity of efforts displayed by stakeholders who supported student-athletes in their respective areas of interest. Student-athletes are often limited in the ways they can get involved on their college campuses and within their larger communities. It is common for athletes to do community service or charity work. However, what is unknown is whether or not these athletes chose those opportunities. Stakeholders and overseers within sports can better support the leadership development of student-athletes by giving them more autonomy over their college careers, including time to participate in internships or attend conferences like The Black Student-Athlete Summit. Other opportunities for student-athletes include serving on committees and tasks forces outside of sports. For example, student-athletes could serve on community council boards.

A commercial from the National Collegiate Athletic Association (NCAA) addresses student athletes directly: "There are over 360,000 NCAA student athletes and just about all of us will be going pro in something other than sports. The NCAA reminds us to ask ourselves, 'What will we do?'" (RefineryNYC, 2010). This statement prompts the question: Why, then, are there so few examples of these athletes gaining the same kind of career preparation experiences as other students on college campuses? Experiences such as social activism, participating in internships, and going to professional and academic conferences? It is important to move past any perceived coddling or hyper-focus that prevents student athletes from exploring the development of their own leadership skills through their experiences

Campus Climate

Questions should be raised about the environment (i.e., college campus) in which these student-athletes are being developed: Why are these athletes boycotting or protesting? What created the conditions for this form of leadership? It could be because they feel a sense of personal connection with a victim or issue, which is rooted in a culture reminiscent of their hometown, and at times, their campus community. Are athletes "allowed" to speak up with confidence about the issues that matter to them? Or do the overseers control their words and tone? It is hard to conceive that a person can truly be a leader if they lack the autonomy to operate as so.

Further, how do college campuses create and promote a climate of inclusion and respect of all—aspirational values reflected in many universities' mission statements? Student athletes' voices are part of those included on college campus—at least they should be. Maybe student athletes are tired of having their voices muffled from the locker rooms when they are constantly told in public that they are "students first and athletes second."

Additionally, what kind of change needs to occur so that there is no longer a need to protest these persistent issues? Our society has supposedly progressed since the days of Jim Crow. Yet, today's student athletes are fighting the same battles as collegiate and professional athletes of the past. This means (1) society has not come as far as it imagines, and (2) these issues are not of great concern to anyone other than the athletes. One interpretation of the problem is that as more students and athletes speak out about unjust situations at institutions, it causes concerns with recruiting; this is worth considering.

Leveraging Collective Impact

Student-athletes leveraging their collective power as activist leaders to create deep change that is needed in higher education would be the ultimate expression of leadership. However, student-athletes will need to take full ownership of what a new leadership model looks like at their respective institutions or collectively with the NCAA and its partner institutions. One action could be forming a Players Association or Union similar to professional athletes. The NCAA contests such a proposal, stating that "Student-athletes are not employees, and their participation in college sports is voluntary" (Remy, n.d.). Student-athletes may want to pause on volunteering until an agreement is reached that allows them to have the autonomy to decide whether to be involved in societal matters. However, it would make more sense if student athletes, particularly those in the revenue generating sports, were both compensated and afforded autonomy to engage in civic issues if they so choose.

Financial Impact. If student-athletes took a national stand and decided to forfeit full seasons, it would cause a loss of revenue for institutions of higher education, the NCAA, and corporations. That expression of activist leadership alone could tip the scale in their favor to truly generate change. If universities and corporations are no longer able to profit off the entertainment value offered to fans via sports, then meeting the social justice demands of student-athletes becomes a more appealing avenue. Of course, many student-athletes may fear losing scholarships or playing time; however, there is great strength in numbers, as has been displayed by the Mizzou football team. There also seems to be a good possibility for change when more members of the collective support the cause.

As more collegiate athletes shift their interests to larger social issues, universities are noticing that African Black athletes' protests have a greater financial influence and impact. When African Black athletes, who comprise a significant portion of revenue sports such as basketball and football, collectively amplify their voices and threaten a boycott, universities simply cannot afford to disregard them. Athletic department budgets, most already deep in the red, would collapse if the players followed up on threats to not compete should their demands be disregarded (Nietzel, 2020).

CONCLUSION

As more student-athletes gain a sense of self regarding their rights, plights, and concerns of others they deem in need of support, there will be increased public mobilization and demonstrations. This level of leadership learning should be supported within higher education if stakeholders within athletics/sports genuinely want to develop students into the non-sport professionals they will become. These efforts should also be reinforced if this country is to achieve the "Freedom, Liberty, and Justice for ALL" that it so professes are citizens' inalienable rights.

REFERENCES

Beachy, E. G., Brewer, B. W., Van Raalte, J. L., & Cornelius, A. E. (2018). Associations between activist and athletic identities in college students. *Journal of Sport Behavior*, *41*(4), 369–389.

Bertrand Jones, T., Guthrie, K. L., & Osteen, L. (2016). Critical domains of culturally relevant leadership learning: A call to transform leadership programs. In K. L. Guthrie, T. Bertrand Jones, & L. Osteen (Eds.), *New Directions for Student Leadership: No. 152. Developing culturally relevant leadership learning* (pp. 9–21). Wiley. https://doi.org/10.1002/yd.20205

Cooper, J. N., Macaulay, C., & Rodriguez, S. H. (2019). Race and resistance: A typology of African American sport activism. *International Review for the Sociology of Sport*, *54*(2), 151–181.

Davis, F. J. (2010). *Who is Black?: One nation's definition*. Penn State Press.

Edwards, H. (2016a, November 3). The fourth wave: Black athlete protest in the second decade of the 21st century. Keynote address at annual conference of the North American Society for the Sociology of Sport, Tampa, FL.

Edwards, H. (2016b). The promise and limits of leveraging Black athlete power potential to compel campus change. *Journal of Higher Education Athletics & Innovation*, (1), 4–13.

Gabler, N. (2014, May 30). *NFL: Last sports bastion of White, male conservatives*. Reuters. http://blogs.reuters.com/great-debate/2014/05/30/nfl-last-sports-bastion-of-white-male-conservatives/

Guthrie, K. L., Bertrand Jones, T., Osteen, L., & Hu, S. (2013). *Cultivating leader identity and capacity in students from diverse backgrounds: ASHE Higher Education Report, 39: 4*. Wiley.

Kaufman, P. (2008). Boos, bans, and other backlash: The consequences of being an activist athlete. *Humanity & Society, 32*(3), 215–237. https://doi.org/10.1177/016059760803200302

Kaufman, P., & Wolff, E. A. (2010). Playing and protesting: Sport as a vehicle for social change. *Journal of Sport & Social Issues, 34*(2), 154–175.

Kezar, A., Acuna Avilez, A., Drivalas, Y., & Wheaton, M. M. (2017). Building social change-oriented leadership capacity among student organizations: Developing students and campuses simultaneously. In D. M Rosch (Ed.), *New Directions for Student Leadership: No. 155. The role of student organizations in developing leadership* (pp. 45–57). Wiley. https://doi.org/10.1002/yd.20249

Kluch, Y. (2020). "My story is my activism!": (Re-) Definitions of social justice activism among collegiate athlete activists. *Communication & Sport, 8*(4–5), 566–590.

Martin, G. L., Williams, B. M., Green, B., & Smith, M. J. (2019). Reframing activism as leadership. In G. L. Martin, C. Linder, & B. M. Williams (Eds.), *New Directions for Student Leadership: No. 161. Leadership learning through activism* (pp. 9–24). Wiley. https://doi.org/10.1002/yd.20317

Meraz, S. (2009). "Is there an elite hold? Traditional media to social media agenda setting influence in blogs network." *Journal of Computer-Mediated Communication, 14*(3), 682–707.

Nietzel, M. (2020, June 28). Black athletes are leading the new college protest movement. *Forbes.* https://www.forbes.com/sites/michaeltnietzel/2020/06/28/black-athletes-lead-the-new-college-protest-movement/?sh=7860997c62fa

O'Boyle, I., Murray, D., & Cummins, P. (Eds.). (2015). *Leadership in sport*. Routledge.

Pope, M. L., Smith, D., & Pope, S. (2019). Student athlete activism in a millennial world: Recognizing their voice and expressing their concerns. In M. T. Miller & D. V. Tolliver (Eds.), *Exploring the technological, societal, and institutional dimensions of college student activism* (pp. 167–182).

The Players' Tribune. (2020, August 02). *#WeAreUnited*. https://www.theplayerstribune.com/articles/pac-12-players-covid-19-statement-football-season

RefineryNYC. (2010, January 21). *NCAA commercial* [Video]. YouTube. https://www.youtube.com/watch?v=6ltaRIJ0N2o

Remy, D. (n.d.). *NCAA responds to union proposal*. NCAA. https://www.ncaa.org/about/resources/media-center/press-releases/ncaa-responds-union-proposal

Rost, J. C. (1993). *Leadership for the twenty-first century*. Greenwood.

Ruffin, H. G., II (2014). "Doing the right thing for the sake of doing the right thing": The revolt of the Black athlete and the modern student-athletic movement, 1956-2014. *Western Journal of Black Studies, 38*(4), 260–278.

Sanderson, J., Frederick, E., & Stocz, M. (2016). When athlete activism clashes with group values: Social identity threat management via social media. *Mass Communication and Society, 19*(3), 301–322.

Van Sterkenburg, J., & Knoppers, A. (2004). Dominant discourses about race/ethnicity and gender in sport practice and performance. *International Review for*

the Sociology of Sport, 39(3), 301–321. https://doi.org/10.1177/
1012690204045598

CHAPTER 17

CULTIVATING A SYSTEMS MINDSET THROUGH FEMINIST LEADERSHIP

Brittany Devies and Julie E. Owen

Educators work hard to dispel notions that leadership only refers to those with positional power. Rather, leadership may also be constructed as a relational process between and among people who seek to make a positive difference in the world (Higher Education Research Institute, 1996). Going further, Ospina and Uhl-Bien (2012) describe the "relational turn" in leadership studies where "both leaders and followers are 'relational beings' who constitute each other....in an unfolding dynamic relationship" (p. xix). In this way, leadership is about how people interact, engage, and negotiate with each other and inherently incorporates social context into leadership research (Ospina & Uhl-Bien, 2012). Whether contexts are construed as liberating or toxic makes a difference in how feminist leadership is constructed and perceived. This chapter suggests that cultivating a systems mindset can facilitate the naming and claiming of feminist leadership.

Activist scholar bell hooks (2000) defines feminism as "the struggle to end sexist oppression" (p. viii). This definition does not privilege one

Navigating Complexities in Leadership: Moving Toward Critical Hope, pp. 175–183
www.infoagepub.com
Copyright © 2022 by Information Age Publishing
All rights of reproduction in any form reserved.

gender over others but instead invites the interrogation of sexist structures in the world around us. Additionally, educators must challenge the frequent conflation of sex, gender identity, and gender expression. Gender is far more than one's "manliness" or "womanliness." Leadership educators should invite more complex views that take gender expression, fluidity, and intersectionality into account. Leadership literature that reinforces gender binary approaches hampers gender inclusive feminist praxis (Tillapaugh & Haber-Curran, 2017). Systems mindsets involve acknowledging complex interconnections that eschew binary and dichotomous views of gender (man/woman) and leadership (leader/follower).

This chapter draws heavily on Acaragolu's (2017) conceptualization of systems thinking. She believes people can shift the way they see the world, moving "from a linear, structured mechanical worldview to a dynamic, chaotic, interconnected array of relationships and feedback loops" (para. 5). We invite readers to interrogate how systems thinking might move everyone closer to embracing feminist leadership as a way to move from disconnection to interconnectedness, towards valuing wholeness and cultivating critical hope.

A CRITICAL MOMENT FOR WOMEN IN LEADERSHIP

It is a critical moment for both women and leadership. Even before the COVID-19 pandemic revealed stark gender discrepancies in healthcare, education, and domestic labor, women were calling attention to unaddressed social issues through women's marches, the #MeToo and #SayHerName movements, and the Black Lives Matter movement. Yet attacks on reproductive health and rights, the lack of representation in politics and certain industries, pay disparities, sexual violence, rape culture, and the unequal status of women across the globe persist. Now, more than ever, we need leaders of all gender identities to address these complex, multifaceted problems. For example, in December 2020, women lost all 140,000 jobs amidst the COVID-19 pandemic in the United States, causing some to label it an economic SHE-cession (Connley, 2021). The COVID-19 pandemic is also projected to worsen women's access to family planning services, decrease girl's access to education, limit female representation in politics, harm gender workplace equity, and increase instances of gender-based violence (Holder, 2020).

The ensuing themes will connect insights from complexity theory and systems thinking to conceptions of women and leadership, especially in regards to fostering feminist leadership. Recent examples are offered as possible avenues to engage students in conversations about these themes.

HOW CULTIVATING A SYSTEMS MINDSET
FOSTERS FEMINIST LEADERSHIP

Systems thinking is an approach to complex problem solving and transition, mirroring the circumstances many of us find ourselves in at this moment. While there are many approaches, themes, and actions associated with systems thinking, this chapter is guided by the concepts articulated by Acaroglu (2017), including interconnectedness, synthesis, emergence, feedback loops, causality, and systems mapping.

Move From Disconnection to Interconnectedness, From Isolation to Relationships

In defining interconnectedness from a systems thinking mindset, "we are defining a fundamental principle of life. From this, we can shift the way we see the world, from a linear, structured 'mechanical worldview' to a dynamic, chaotic, interconnected array of relationships and feedback loops" (Acaroglu, 2017, para. 7). Complexity thinking demands interconnectedness, even in an increasingly positioned and polemical world. In order to develop interconnectedness, we must first acknowledge intersectionality. Intersectionality reveals the connections among multiple social identities; it invites us not to reduce individuals to single categories or stereotypes (Crenshaw, 1991). Instead, we must acknowledge the multiple compounding effects of these interactions in how people understand and navigate their own leadership identity, behavior, and effectiveness.

This requires doing our own self-work to understand our own privileged and oppressed identities and how they may show up in leadership. It means refusing to essentialize others and seeking to understand leadership from the lens of multiple social identities, communities, and contexts. It means guarding against burnout and the physical and psychological toll it takes to navigate unwelcoming or even hostile spaces. Developing deeply committed relationships that acknowledge the complex roles and identities of women is essential to feminist leadership. How do we move from calling people out to calling them in (Ross, 2020)? How can we shift from a cancel culture to a connection culture?

For example, we must interrogate recent practices related to "cancel culture." People's tendency to decide a leader's worth based on expressed rather than enacted values has become common practice. Take Vice-President Kamala Harris and Supreme Court Justice Amy Coney Barrett as examples. Both are women who were widely evaluated based on their expressed ideologies before their leadership was ever practiced in their new roles. While their expressed ideologies are vastly different, both have been assessed as leaders through gendered expectations, lenses, and values. It is vital as leadership educators to encourage the upward trend in focusing on the ethical integrity of our leaders while also educating students on the dangers of cancel culture, which fosters disconnection rather than interconnectedness.

Go Beyond Deconstruction to Synthesis and Reconstruction

Complexity thinking invites us to move beyond the long and fraught history of people studying and writing about 'women's leadership.' The typical narrative in this research is women lead in relational and collaborative ways that "emphasize mutual power and influence processes, attend to relationships and tasks, and encourage democratic and participatory forms of decision making" (Kezar & Wheaton, 2017, p. 20). Meanwhile, men's leadership is characterized as assertive, charismatic, and commanding.

In actuality, a synthesis approach to empirical research on gender differences often reveals very small actual differences between men and women's leadership styles, yet these differences are often exaggerated (Eagly & Carli, 2007). Binary views of gender are often extremely resistant to change. In some ways, it feels empowering to say women's leadership is the antidote to all the evils in the world, yet we know the truth is far more complex. We need all people, men, women, and those who identify beyond binary gender labels to work in more inclusive and egalitarian ways. We must stop perpetuating mythologies about women's ways of leading. This perpetuation can be incredibly damaging, especially with how young students are receiving these gendered messages of the leader they can become. One approach to this is to use Dugan's (2017) tools, grounded in critical social theory, for deconstruction (ideological critique, commodification, flow of power, and willful blindness) and reconstruction (disrupting normativity, attending to power, building interest convergence, and cultivating agency) when we collectively reimagine feminist leadership through systems thinking.

Let's embrace recent examples of people challenging traditional gender norms and expectations of gender expression, such as Harry Styles' cover shoot for *Vogue* magazine and the social media backlash it engendered. We cannot only focus on the cover photo as an outward act of challenging binary views of gender expression, but we must also acknowledge the dangerous counterresponse of the "manly men" critique. Both are critical in understanding messaging around gender and leadership for learners; one was an act of leadership to challenge the binaried views of expression. The other was a direct response upholding and affirming binary expectations and oppressive messages for all leadership learners around gender expression.

Shift From Silos to Emergence

Emergence can be understood as

> the natural outcome of things coming together.... Emergence is the outcome of the synergies of the parts; it is about nonlinearity and self-organization and we often use the term "emergence" to describe the outcome of things interacting together. (Acaroglu, 2017, para. 11–12).

Examples of emergence in nature include a snowflake forming from freezing water particles developing into beautiful fractal patterns around a single molecule of matter or a caterpillar transforming into a butterfly.

In leadership, what might emerge when small changes coalesce into bigger ones? Gender and leadership are socially constructed. Messages about the socially acceptable ways to enact gender begin before birth and are accelerated in childhood socialization, through what one is taught by parents and other trusted adults, authoritative religious interpreters, and peers, as well as lessons learned from the media, education, and other systemic forces (Haber-Curran & Sulpizio, 2017; Lorber, 1994). Similarly, what is deemed as leadership is a product of dominant narratives about how people view, interpret, and explain the world around them. Even answers to the questions, "Who is a leader?" and "What is leadership?" are contextualized and crafted by our socialization around identity and power (Dugan, 2017; Owen, 2020). How do we deconstruct biased, binary, and outmoded approaches to gender and leadership while simultaneously holding space to create or reconstruct more equitable and just approaches?

In applying this concept, think of how the leadership of women of color and transwomen were historically excluded from the early waves of feminism yet are now emergent. "Early feminism was directly related to the abolitionist movements, although it remained a predominantly White endeavor" (Owen, 2020, p. 16), with history textbooks focusing almost exclusively on White suffragettes. While the second wave became slightly more inclusive, Alice Walker (1983) created the womanist movement to address the exclusion of women of color in the feminist movement. To not repeat the history of this siloed approach to feminist leadership, we must first teach, address, and reckon with the historical exclusion of the feminist movement. This reckoning can be a first step towards an emergent coming together and reconstructing a more inclusive feminism (Kendall, 2020).

Progress From Linear Thinking
by Developing Circular Feedback Loops

Acaroglu (2017) describes two types of feedback loops, reinforcing and balancing. Reinforcing feedback loops do exactly as they say: they reinforce what is already believed or being said as it continues to gain traction and power. "A balancing feedback loop, however, is where elements within the system balance things out. Nature basically got this down to a tee with the predator/prey situation" (Acaroglu, 2017, para. 18–19). Balancing feedback loops provide a system of checks and balances, similar to the natural evolution of nature (Acaroglu, 2017).

What are the implications of assuming that leadership is not situated in the individual but rather is a function of complex, interacting systems? How would you characterize the difference between directing change and influencing change? What are practical examples of "influence?" How do we invite people to seek and learn from feedback opportunities? Many people naturally approach feedback with trepidation and fear. Instead, we should talk about the gifts inherent in receiving critical feedback and asking, "What do I have to learn here?" We invite people to practice having hard conversations with each other.

Finally, we need to pay special attention to the mental health and well-being of women-identified students and staff. Women suffer from perfectionism at a much greater rate than men (American Association of University Women, 2014) and are nearly twice as likely as men to be diagnosed with an anxiety disorder in their lifetime (National Institute of Mental Health, 2019), which can also hinder their engagement in leadership. We need to go beyond effortless perfection and imposter syndrome to cultivate healthy self-appraisal and developmental goals.

One example of this in practice is Brené Brown's work on learning from feedback. Brown's research reveals that humans' deepest desire is for connection with others (Brown, 2013, 2018). The pandemic and resulting social distancing challenge our access to sources of connection, along with the ways leadership and relationships are enacted. "When we define ourselves by what everyone thinks, it's hard to be brave. When we stop caring about what anyone thinks, we're too armored for authentic connection" (Brown, 2018, p. 22). So how does one balance accepting too much or too little feedback? One tool to do this is called "square squad," in which Brown (2013) challenges people to physically write down the names of people whose opinions and feedback they care deeply about and using that to evaluate the feedback they receive from others. Developing meaningful feedback loops from trusted relationships moves us closer to feminist leadership praxis.

Learn to Map Systems and See the Whole Rather Than Only Discrete Parts

Systems mapping works to "identify and map the elements of 'things' within a system to understand how they interconnect, relate, and act in a complex system, and from here, unique insights and discoveries can be used to develop interventions, shifts, or policy decisions" (Acaroglu, 2017, para. 22). What are the links between leadership and organizational functions such as performance, innovation, adaptation, and building collective identity? How do these functions support women and leadership development? If we redefine leadership as meaning making, how can leaders become 'sense makers' who align feminist language and direction within an organization? Shea and Renn (2017) list three tools of feminist leadership: using and subverting power structures, complicating difference, and enacting social change. "It is not enough to just talk about justice and equity; feminist leaders engage in advocacy and activism to counteract injustice" (Shea & Renn, 2017, p. 88).

Think of the women who organized the Black Lives Matter movement and the women who started #MeToo and #TimesUp. These women channel the collective leadership identity, capacity, and efficacy of their community to create sustainable, positive, social change. They empowered those around them to look at the entire inequitable system alongside the individual stories that spoke to these systems in action. These founders mobilized to combat inequitable systems, seeing the whole rather than only the parts. These movements are brilliant, powerful examples of grassroots mobilization and are some of Gen Z's first introductions to feminist leadership in the media.

CONCLUSION:
VALUING THE WHOLE WHILE MAINTAINING CRITICAL HOPE

Educators should stress the importance of critical hope to leadership. This does not refer to naïve hope, or people who negate the difficulties of sustaining the work necessary to overcome injustice. Rather, learning to sustain hope in the face of struggle is perhaps one of the most essential skills of leadership (Owen, 2020). To maintain hope, we suggest people learn more about the idea of a liberatory consciousness (Love, 2013).

Love (2013) states anyone committed to changing systems and institutions to create great equity and social justice must develop a liberatory consciousness. This kind of thinking enables people to live their lives in oppressive systems and institutions with intentionality and awareness, rather than submit to the forces of socialization. A liberatory consciousness enables people to maintain an awareness of the dynamics of oppression without giving in to despair and hopelessness. It allows us to maintain an awareness of roles played by those in the system without blaming them for the roles they play, while also intentionally challenging systems of oppression. We invite people to work towards this kind of consciousness—after all, as Martin Luther King, Jr. reminds us, "the arc of the moral universe is long, but it bends toward justice."

REFERENCES

Acaroglu, L. (2017, September 7). *Tools for systems thinkers: The 6 fundamental concepts of systems thinking.* Medium. https://medium.com/disruptive-design/tools-for-systems-thinkers-the-6-fundamental-concepts-of-systems-thinking-379cdac3dc6a

American Association of University Women. (2014). *Close the confidence gap.* https://www.aauw.org/2014/05/19/close-the-confidence-gap/

Brown, B. (2013). *Daring greatly: How the courage to be vulnerable transforms the way we live, love, parent and lead.* Penguin Random House.

Brown, B. (2018). *Dare to lead: Brave work. Tough conversations. Whole hearts.* Penguin Random House.

Connley, C. (2021, January 11). *A year ago, women outnumbered men in the U.S. workforce, now they account for 100% of jobs lost in December.* CNBC. https://www.cnbc.com/amp/2021/01/11/women-account-for-100percent-of-jobs-lost-in-december-new-analysis.html

Crenshaw, K. (1991). Mapping the margins: Intersectionality, identity politics, and violence against women of color. *Stanford Law Review, 43,* 1241–1299. https://doi.org/10.2307/1229039

Dugan, J. P. (2017). *Leadership theory: Cultivating critical perspectives.* Jossey-Bass.

Eagly, A. H., & Carli, L. L. (2007). *Through the labyrinth: The truth about how women become leaders.* Harvard Business School Press.

Haber-Curran, P., & Sulpizio, L. (2017). Student leadership development for girls and young women. In D. Tillapaugh & P. Haber-Curran (Eds). *New Directions for Student Leadership: No. 154. Critical perspectives on gender and student leadership* (pp. 33–46). Wiley. https://doi.org/10.1002/yd.20238

Higher Education Research Institute. (1996). *A social change model of leadership development: Guidebook Version III.* National Clearinghouse for Leadership Programs.

Holder, A. (2020, April 6). COVID-19 could set women back decades on gender equality. *U.S. News.* https://www.usnews.com/news/best-countries/articles/

2020-04-06/commentary-coronavirus-pandemic-may-set-women-back-decades-on-equality

hooks, b. (2000). *Feminism is for everybody.* South End Press.

Kendall, M. (2020). *Hood feminism: Notes from the women that a movement forgot.* Viking.

Kezar, A. J., & Wheaton, M. M. (2017). The value of connective leadership: Benefitting from women's approach to leadership while contending with traditional views. *About Campus, 21* (6), 19–26. https://doi.org/10.1002/abc.21274

Lorber, J. (1994). "Night to his day": The social construction of gender. In J. Lorber (Ed.), *Paradoxes of gender* (pp. 54–65). Yale University Press.

Love, B. J. (2013). Developing a liberatory consciousness. In M. Adams, W. J. Blumenfeld, R. Castaneda, H. W. Hackman, M. L. Peters, & X. Zuniga (Eds.), *Readings for diversity and social justice* (3rd ed., pp. 600–605). Routledge.

National Institute of Mental Health. (2019). *Statistics.* https://www.nimh.nih.gov

Owen, J. (2020). *We are the leaders we've been waiting for: Women and leadership development in college.* Stylus.

Ross, L. (2020, November 19). What if instead of calling people out, we called them in? *New York Times.* https://www.nytimes.com/2020/11/19/style/loretta-ross-smith-college-cancel-culture.html

Shea, H. D., & Renn, K. A. (2017). Gender and leadership: A call to action. In D. Tillapaugh & P. Haber-Curran (Eds.), *New Directions for Student Leadership: No. 154. Critical perspectives on gender and student leadership* (pp. 83–94). Wiley. https://doi.org/10.1002/yd.20242

Tillapaugh, D., & Haber-Curran, P. (Eds). (2017). *New Directions for Student Leadership: No. 154. Critical perspectives on gender and student leadership.* Wiley.

Uhl-Bien, M., & Ospina, S. M. (Eds.). (2012). *Advancing relational leadership research: A dialogue among perspectives.* Information Age.

Walker, A. (1983). *In search of our mothers' gardens: Womanist prose.* W. W. Norton.

CHAPTER 18

CRITICAL APPROACHES TO GENDER EQUITY IN LEADERSHIP DEVELOPMENT AND PRACTICE

**R. J. Youngblood, Tess Hobson,
and Roberta Maldonado Franzen**

> There is an incredible lift of invisible labor that women are having to do in every single role they play. It is really hard to get help. It is really, really hard. (Stephanie)

At the time of writing this chapter, the COVID-19 pandemic has continued for over a year and requires leadership developers to confront the pernicious nature of gender inequity. As represented by the opening quote, systems-level social challenges like COVID-19's impact on gender equity are complex and ambiguous (Uhl-Bien et al., 2007). These challenges require leadership to make progress on dismantling inequitable systems and reconstructing a more equitable future. Leadership educators and practitioners need to equip both themselves and learners with critical perspectives, approaches, and tools to address complex social issues and move toward a practice of critical hope.

Navigating Complexities in Leadership: Moving Toward Critical Hope, pp. 185–193
www.infoagepub.com
Copyright © 2022 by Information Age Publishing
All rights of reproduction in any form reserved.

This chapter calls on leadership educators and practitioners to engage in a paradigm shift, consider new ways of knowing, and advance a critical practice. First, this chapter offers an example of a global systemic social challenge that has implications for leadership. Next, using the example of the impact of the COVID-19 pandemic on gender equity, leadership educators are called to shift to collective, relational, and practice paradigms, engage and ground in critical perspectives, and practice critical pedagogy. These three actions are required to develop a systems-level understanding of complex equity issues that move to leadership action.

GENDER EQUALITY: COVID-19 AS A CALL FOR CRITICAL PERSPECTIVES AND APPROACHES

Gender inequities have existed and continue to exist globally. In the context of COVID-19, the pandemic has heightened a systems-level awareness of complex gender equity issues. In some ways, COVID-19 is exposing the long-standing systems and structures that have produced inequities. Leadership educators and practitioners are uniquely positioned to analyze and deconstruct systemic challenges and reconstruct more inclusive systems.

People who identify as women have experienced a heightened, disproportionate negative impact in all areas of private, public, and civic life as a result of COVID-19. U.N. Women (2020a, 2020b) outlines the global financial implications of COVID-19 on the (a) worsening of the poverty gender gap; (b) increase in women's unemployment; (c) disproportionate impact on industries where women are over-represented and in domestic work; d) inequality in the private sphere with unpaid labor; and e) estimated long-lasting consequences on gender equality. Additionally, increases in gender-based violence have been exponential with an estimated 243 million women and girls globally subjugated to sexual and/or physical violence in the first twelve months of COVID-19 (U.N. Women, 2020a; United Nations Development Programme, 2020). During the pandemic, unemployment rates disproportionately impacted women, and many women that remained in the workforce were required to juggle virtual transitions of both working and educating children from home (Horsley, 2020; Milliken et al., 2020; Schneider et al., 2020; U.N. Women, 2020b). The impact in academia has been no exception (Gonzalez & Griffin, 2020). The lack of research projects, journal submissions, and databases logging the initiation of new research projects points to increased gendered disparities (Oleschuk, 2020).

The disparities faced by people who identify as women during the COVID-19 pandemic have been far-reaching. While this example narrows on gender and gendered aspects, it also intersects race, class, ability, sexual orientation, religion, and other social identities. Being attentive to the intersectionality of gender and various social identities recognizes who is disproportionately impacted by COVID-19. Though not perfect, this example can be used to understand the complex challenges that intersect social identities, systems, and equity. A pathway forward is ambiguous. If leadership is required to reimagine and redesign more equitable systems, leadership educators and practitioners need theories, perspectives, methods, frameworks, and practices that are attentive to this reality.

WHAT IS REQUIRED OF LEADERSHIP EDUCATORS AND PRACTITIONERS?

The type of leadership learning and development required to advance equity issues needs to rely on critical perspectives and approaches. In this case, "critical" means more than just thinking deeply or using critical thinking skills to make progress on specific leadership challenges. Critical perspectives and approaches assume that unjust systems lack the necessary capabilities to redirect towards justice on their own (Chandler & Kirsch, 2018). Critical perspectives and approaches challenge boundaries and fundamental assumptions, ask questions that highlight issues of power, and equip practitioners and learners with emancipatory tools, practices, and methodologies. Three actions leadership educators and practitioners can take are to (a) shift to understanding leadership as collective, relational, and a practice, (b) ground in critical frameworks like feminist perspectives and theory, and (c) practice pedagogy that aims to recognize power and dismantle systems.

Shift to Collective, Relational, and Practice Paradigms

To dismantle systemic inequities during COVID-19 and beyond requires leadership educators and practitioners to shift from paradigms that center leadership as individual traits, styles, and virtues to a leadership lens that looks for activity that emerges between groups of people and systems. This shift includes commitments to relational, collective, and practice orientations to leadership that build collective agency and action (Carroll et al., 2008). When leadership action moves away from the individual level, groups are empowered to lead change (Quick, 2017). Two paradigms for leadership educators and practitioners to consider are social change leadership (Ospina et al., 2012) and leadership-as-practice (Carroll et al., 2008; Raelin, 2011, 2016).

Social change leadership emphasizes the role of collective leadership and the interplay between beliefs and behaviors (Ospina & Foldy, 2005). Furthermore, social change leadership surfaces inequity, creates a path forward, identifies equity as a value of social justice, and recognizes the importance of building bridges within the disenfranchised community to address broader concerns (Ospina et al., 2012; Ospina & Foldy, 2005, 2009, 2010). However, as a collective, highlighting mutual concern raises awareness on an issue. To advance movements of social change, leveraging innovation that emerges from those previously not recognized is important to change processes and practice (Pares et al., 2007). People can practice social change by creating intentional processes and practice that identify and diagnose issues together. Social change leadership gives leadership educators and practitioners a space to create a shared vision to make meaningful change. The turn toward practice looks to recognize the leadership activity that emerges in the flow of everyday practice.

Practice models of leadership shift responsibility from an individual to processes in groups that emphasize dialogic, relational, and sociomaterial interaction (Raelin, 2011). Leadership-as-practice recognizes the responsibility to emerge and unleash leadership activity held in group dynamics and interactions (Carroll et al., 2008; Raelin et al., 2018). Leadership-as-practice suggests leadership is an activity and is achieved by being attentive to how interactions create turns of practice that move groups and systems in new directions (Gergen & Herstedand, 2016; Raelin, 2016; Sergi, 2016). Understanding that leadership-as-practice can exist in the everyday interactions among individuals builds collective agency (Ford, 2016; Raelin, 2011, 2016).

In the example about gender inequity in COVID-19, shifting to collective, relational, and practice leadership paradigms provides a framework for recognizing leadership as it emerges in the everyday experiences of individuals and communities practicing resistance. Leadership educators and practitioners can rely on a relational, practice, and collective lens to design learning and development experiences that reject dominant assumptions. Leadership learning and development experiences that account for a relational, practice, and collective lens are more likely to prepare learners to see systems in new ways that account for and recognize systemic operations that perpetuate inequities.

Engage and Ground in Critical Perspectives

Critical perspectives are instrumental to the future of leadership scholarship, education, and practice. Leadership educators and practitioners should be attentive to bodies of literature that interrogate power, identity, and systems. Critical race theory and feminist theory are a few bodies of literature that engage notions of power, work to unpack and disrupt systems, elevate diverse perspectives and knowledge, and recognize intersecting identities. Critical perspectives, approaches, and theories can be deployed in leadership learning, development, and practice to diagnose unjust systems and inform ways that move them towards becoming more just (Collinson, 2014; Ford, 2016; Owen, 2020; Shea & Renn, 2017).

Specifically, feminist theories and perspectives have the potential to offer leadership educators and practitioners new ways to understand leadership learning, development, and practice (Owen, 2020; Shea & Renn, 2017). Feminist theories and perspectives are committed to centering and prioritizing experiences of those whose lives are "marked and marred by structural inequalities" (Davis & Craven, 2016, p. 8). Feminist perspectives question knowledge production, embrace diverse ways of knowing, consider positionality and subjectivity, unpack power structures, interrogate identity construction and intersectionality, and construct reflexive engagement (Davis & Craven, 2016). Leadership educators and practitioners can use critical feminist perspectives to attend to power in ways that unleash broader notions of leadership activity and equip learners to unwind systems that maintain unjust relations by precluding a full account of power and identity.

In the example of gender inequity in COVID-19, by engaging in critical perspectives, leadership educators and practitioners would be prepared to ask questions that get at the systems of power that reproduce inequity. For example, leadership educators and practitioners might deploy critical perspectives to ask: Who is the pandemic disproportionately impacting? How has emotional labor been distributed during the pandemic? Which work has been valued and recognized during the pandemic and what has been left out? Who has continued to have access to opportunities for education, employment, and healthcare? How do we surface invisible stories during the pandemic that shape our knowledge creation and history of the pandemic? Where do we see resistance?

A critical feminist approach to leadership learning, development, and practice (a) recognizes gender as a relevant feature of leadership, (b) acknowledges forms of knowledge historically left out or have been marginalized in dominant leadership studies literature, and (c) creates a reflexive practice helpful to realize equitable pathways of leadership identity, efficacy, and motivation. By engaging in critical perspectives, approaches, and theories, educators can design leadership learning and development experiences with emancipatory potential.

Practice Critical Pedagogy

Critical pedagogy is an important practice for leadership educators and practitioners in addressing systems of inequity because it requires us to build upon and utilize critical perspectives to shape our practice. In other words, it requires us to ask: "What approaches to leadership education will highlight power structures and inequitable systems that require leadership for systemic change?" One example of a critical pedagogical practice that is useful for leadership educators and practitioners is storytelling.

Storytelling offers a way to raise consciousness around issues of social inequity, weave diverse perspectives, build confidence in communities, and move to action (Freire, 2018; Ganz, 2011; Mahoney, 2017). Storytelling serves as a transformational activity that builds capacity and collective identity. Perhaps most importantly, storytelling offers a framework for fighting oppression and engages a critical approach by explicitly highlighting issues of power (Collinson, 2018). Coemerging personal and social accounts through story reconnects and raises consciousness about existing inequalities (Senehi et al., 2009).

Storytelling allows voices that have often been silenced by systems to be heard and provides a more authentic and complete foundation for moving toward shared understanding and action (Ganz, 2011). It provides space for critical reflection that raises consciousness around equity issues and the opportunity to build coalitions (Freire, 2018). Sharing stories has the potential to be a consciousness-raising experience and bring those advantaged by existing systems closer to understanding and acting to address issues that they might feel separated from (Senehi et al., 2009).

Creating spaces for storytelling in leadership education and practice can make visible stories of communities impacted by unjust systems. In practice, and when done intentionally, this might look like incorporating storytelling exercises into the leadership education classroom. Doing so can challenge traditional hierarchies between educators and learners. A storytelling pedagogy communicates the inherent value learners bring and recognizes their knowledge and experience as central to learning. Utilizing the practice of storytelling in relation to the example of gender inequities during the COVID-19 pandemic means surfacing concealed stories, or stories that are often ignored or silenced (Bell, 2010).

A practice of storytelling surfaced the below story from a colleague in higher education:

> I took in a kiddo from foster care in COVID. Things I've noticed as a new parent of a toddler is how hard it was to find childcare and how that affected my work. She was with me as I worked from home. Add to that a kid that has

experienced trauma, it made it really really hard, and it meant that any type of supportive therapeutic services that she would get would be delayed. I had meetings where I held her for an hour while she screamed, and I was on mute and not everyone is as aware of why I was muted on camera or microphone. One of the challenges I've had with my partner is a lack of understanding, just because I work from home, doesn't mean I'm "home" all day. If my partner was home, he would not be taking on all housework like I am during the day. (Tara)

Stories of struggle and hardship during the pandemic, like the one shared by Tara, create and hold the possibility to reimagine social, political, economic, and cultural relations that perpetuate gender inequities. Practicing critical pedagogy, like storytelling, allows leadership educators and practitioners to highlight learners' experiences as they provide space for concealed stories to be heard (Mahoney, 2017).

CONCLUSION

Leadership educators and practitioners should actively seek to understand the changes that need to be made in our organizations, institutions, and communities to create more equitable systems. Shifting to collective, relational, and practice leadership paradigms changes the focus of where we look for leadership activity, what counts as leadership activity, and changes what we teach and learn. Engaging critical perspectives and theory allows us to access a broader spectrum of leadership knowledge. This allows learners to access forms of leadership activity capable of realizing equity. Storytelling as a critical pedagogy allows leadership educators, practitioners, and learners to raise consciousness about inequities. These three actions when practiced in leadership learning and development experiences create the potential and space for critical hope.

REFERENCES

Bell, L. A. (2010). *Storytelling for social justice: Connecting narrative and the arts in antiracist teaching*. Routledge.

Carroll, B., Levy, L., & Richmond, D. (2008). Leadership as practice: Challenging the competency paradigm. *Leadership, 4*(4), 363-379. https://doi.org/10.1177/1742715008095186

Chandler, J., & Kirsch, R. (2018). *Critical leadership theory: Integrating transdisciplinary perspectives*. Palgrave Macmillan.

Collinson, D. (2014). Dichotomies, dialectics and dilemmas: New directions for critical leadership studies? *Leadership, 10*(1), 36–55. https://doi.org/10.1177/1742715013510807

Collinson, M. (2018). What's new about leadership-as-practice? *Leadership*, *14*(3), 363-370. https://doi.org/10.1177/1742715017726879

Davis, D., & Craven, C. (2016). *Feminist ethnography: Thinking through methodologies, challenges, and possibilities*. Rowman & Littlefield.

Ford, J. (2016). Gendered relationships and the problems of diversity in leadership-as-practice. In J. A. Raelin (Ed.) *Leadership-as-practice: Theory and application* (pp. 223-242). Routledge.

Freire, P. (2018). *Pedagogy of the oppressed: 50th anniversary edition*. Bloomsbury.

Ganz, M. (2011). Public narrative, collective action, and power. *Accountability through public opinion* (pp. 273–289). https://doi.org/10.1596/9780821385050_ch18

Gergen, K., & Herstedand, L. (2016). Developing leadership as dialogic practice. In J. A. Raelin (Ed.), *Leadership-as-practice: Theory and application* (pp. 178-197). Routledge.

Gonzalez, L. D., & Griffin K. A. (2020, July 14). *Supporting faculty during & after COVID-19: Don't let go of equity*. Aspire Alliance. https://www.mtu.edu/advance/resources/articles-books/supporting-faculty-during-and-after-covid.pdf

Horsley, S. (2020, October 2). Jobs growth slows sharply in last employment report before election. *NPR*. https://www.npr.org/2020/06/28/883458147/how-coronavirus-could-widen-the-gender-wage-gap

Mahoney, A. (2017). Being at the heart of the matter: Culturally relevant leadership learning, emotions, and storytelling. *Journal of Leadership Studies, 11*(3), 55-60. https://doi.org/10.1002/jls.21546

Milliken, F. J., Kneeland, M. K., & Flynn, E. (2020). Implications of COVID-19 pandemic for gender equity issues at work. *Journal of Management Studies, 57*(8), 1767–1772. https://doi:10.1111/joms.12628

Oleschuk, M. (2020). Gender equity considerations for tenure and promotion during COVID-19. *The Canadian Review of Sociology, 57*(3), 502–515.

Ospina, S., & Foldy, E. (2005). *Toward a framework of social change leadership*. Research Center for Leadership Action. https://wagner.nyu.edu/files/leadership/TowardFrameworkSocialChangeLeadership.pdf

Ospina, S. M., Foldy, E. G., Hadidy, W. E., Dodge, J., Hofmann-Pinilla, A., & Su, C. (2012). Social change leadership as relational leadership. In M. Uhl-Bien & S. M. Ospina (Eds.), *Advancing relationship leadership research* (pp. 255-302). Information Age.

Owen, J. E. (2020). *We are the leaders we've been waiting for: Women and leadership development in college*. Stylus.

Pares, M., Ospine, S. M., & Subirats, J. (2017). *Social innovation and democrative leadership: Communities and social change from below*. Edward Elgar.

Quick, K. S. (2017). Locating and building collective leadership and impact. *Leadership, 13*(4), 445-471. https://doi.org/10.1177/1742715015605348

Raelin, J. A. (2011). From leadership-as-practice to leaderful practice. *Leadership, 7*(2), 195–211. https://doi.org/10.1177/1742715010394808

Raelin, J. A. (Ed.) (2016). *Leadership-as-practice: Theory and application*. Routledge.

Raelin, J. A., Kempster, S., Youngs, H., Carroll, B., & Jackson, B. (2018). Practicing leadership-as-practice in content and manner. *Leadership, 14*(3), 371–383. https://doi.org/10.1177/1742715017752422

Schneider, A., Hsu, A., & Horsley, S. (2020, October 2). Enough already: Multiple demands causing women to abandon workforce. *NPR*. https://www.npr.org/sections/coronavirus-live-updates/2020/10/02/919517914/enough-already-multiple-demands-causing-women-to-abandon-workforce

Senehi, J., Flaherty, M., Sanjana Kirupakaran, C., Kornelsen, L., Matenge, M., & Skarlato, O. (2009). Dreams of our grandmothers: Discovering the call for social justice through storytelling. *Storytelling, Self, Society, 5*(2), 90–106.

Sergi, V. (2016). Who's leading the way?: Investigating the contributions of materiality to leadership-as-practice. In J. A. Raelin (Ed.), *Leadership-as-practice: Theory and application* (pp. 110–131). Routledge.

Shea, H., & Renn, K. (2017). Gender and leadership: A call to action. In D. Tillapaugh & P., Haber-Curran (Eds.), *New Directions for Student Leadership: No. 154. Critical perspectives on gender and student leadership* (pp. 83–94). https://doi.org/10.1002/yd.20242

Uhl-Bien, M., Marion, R., & McKelvey, B. (2007). Complexity leadership theory: Shifting leadership from the industrial age to the knowledge era. *The Leadership Quarterly, 18(4)*, 298–318. https://doi.org10.1016/j.leaqua.2007.04.002

United Nations Development Programme. (2020, May 11). *UNDP brief: Gender based violence and COVID.* https://www.undp.org/content/undp/en/home/librarypage/womens-empowerment/gender-based-violence-and-covid-19.html

U.N. Women. (2020a, April 9). *Policy brief: The impact of COVID-19 on women.* https://www.unwomen.org/-/media/headquarters/attachments/sections/library/publications/2020/policy-brief-the-impact-of-covid-19-on-women-en.pdf?la=en&vs=1406

U.N. Women. (2020b, September 16). *COVID-19 and its economic toll on women: The story behind the numbers.* https://www.unwomen.org/en/news/stories/2020/9/feature-covid-19-economic-impacts-on-women

PART V

GLOBAL CONTEXT

CHAPTER 19

LEADING WITH A GLOBAL MINDSET

Yang Li

Globalization is spreading rapidly and generates a dynamic and complex system. It opens opportunities for global citizens to create, collaborate, and converge across the globe, while the risks and challenges are accompanied when exploiting competency and efficiency in this intricate web. Leaders with a global mindset play an imperative role to respond to the complexities of globalization by recognizing differences, integrating distinctiveness, and transforming the challenges into opportunities (Perruci, 2018). Unfortunately, global issues and crises, such as global climate change, global public health, global migration, poverty, and food insecurity threaten the civilians at home and beyond the borders, which embodies the ineffective leadership in globalization. Leadership stifles to a solely parochial scope and fails to envision the issue at a transnational level while reckoning global crises. Thus, "real" global leaders are urgently needed to transform these challenges into opportunities. Leaders have to intrinsically change their way of thinking to a transitional outlook to navigate in the intricate and uncertain system. A leader's global mindset is the "core foundation" to situate their leadership practice within this complicated global context.

This chapter begins by reviewing complexities in globalization and global leadership. Next, it will unpack concepts of what makes up a global

Navigating Complexities in Leadership: Moving Toward Critical Hope, pp. 197–205
www.infoagepub.com

Copyright © 2022 by Information Age Publishing
All rights of reproduction in any form reserved.

mindset, what are the complexities in it, and how to employ a global mindset in the process of leadership in the uncertain world. This chapter will end with "living in the critical hope" by making recommendations for educators, practitioners, leaders, and global citizens in the complicated globalization context.

COMPLEXITIES IN GLOBALIZATION CONTEXT

Globalization is a continuously transforming process with emerging forces of rising transnationalism, declining nationalism, demised loyalty, and crumbling walls (Perruci, 2018). Tensions surfaced and further evolved while integrating enlarged divergences among "free" units at the transnational level (Levy et al., 2007). Concretely speaking, with the advent of the industrial revolution, interconnection among nations emerged and reinforced, and walls no longer isolated one nation from the interdependent international system. Power was not only defined simply in geographical features, but also global market (Perruci, 2018). Global units, such as citizens, labors, resources, capital, and individuals, therefore "freely" flowed across porous borders. Authority and public interest were not solely constrained by nation or state, but expanded to multinational, international, and global levels, initiating beyond-border collaborations and competitions. Outcomes generated by globalization were multinational corporations and nonprofit organizations (Perruci, 2018). Concurrently, the intention to consolidate the dissimilar cultural and social norms among "free" individuals within these transnational corporations generated tensions, enhancing complexities.

The fusion of technologies and the popularity of "virtual" environments increased complexities by reinforcing the worldwide interdependence at cultural, political, economic, and technological levels (Schwab, 2016). Kutz (2013) elucidated that every component in the digital world is changing across digital spheres with no predictable patterns. It challenged individuals, organizations, and corporations to recognize the fluid differences and integrate from the dynamic divergences. Globalization hence shifted to a high-and-fluid difference and low-integration phrase, which created unprecedented opportunities, innovations, as well as formidable challenges with disruption, chaos, complexity, uncertainty, and ambiguity (Beechler & Javidan, 2007; Govindarajan & Gupta, 2001; Lane et al., 2004; Mendenhall et al., 2012). Only individuals equipped with a new scope of vision that is extensive across boundaries can transform the challenges into opportunities (Beechler & Javidan, 2007; Perruci, 2018).

LEADERSHIP IN COMPLEX GLOBALIZATION

Leadership is the most critical response to global complexities, perceived as an effective way to navigate the challenges and opportunities residing in globalization. Kouzes and Posner (1995) defined leadership as a leader-follower collaboration to work toward a shared aspiration or goal. This definition reveals several key components of leadership: the leader-follower relationship, collaboration, and a shared goal; however, it is not sufficient to illuminate the complexities in the leadership spectrum demanded in the new globalization.

Leading in uncertain and complex globalization requires leaders to understand the concept of differentiation. As mentioned above, globalization is a transformative process featuring the eroding borders, the demise of nationalism, and the rise of transnationalism. As the new revolution emerged, each breakthrough of boundaries added another layer of leadership challenge and tension, pushing leaders one more step out of their current leading scope. Perruci (2018) claimed that the leaders evolved from a parochial perspective to a global vision in the context of globalization by recognizing the increasing distinctiveness involved in their leadership. Perruci (2018) defines leadership in globalization as a leader-follower collaboration within an environmental context shaped by different cultural values and norms, thus addressing diversity and difference.

A second component critical to leadership that responds to the demands of globalization is seeking integration from differentiation. Differentiation between domestic and global interests created conflicts and contradictions for leaders (Perruci, 2018). Leaders without advanced awareness and mindset to integrate from differentiation are easily trapped in the struggle of choosing from the demise of loyalty to the indigenous culture or pursuit of "leading globally." Perruci (2018) clarified that leaders need to understand that leading in globalization does not reject the domestic interest and cultures. Alternatively, global leaders should dedicate to root in the domestic scope, extend leadership beyond the borders to a global spectrum, and eventually achieve an integrated scope of leading. Therefore, Kefalas (1998) proposed that leaders in globalization need to act locally but think globally so that they can "reconcile the global with the local and mediate between the familiar and the foreign" (Levy et al., 2007, p. 240).

"GLOBAL BLINDSET" LEADERSHIP DURING COVID-19 PANDEMIC

Though leadership has been perceived as one of the most effective ways to navigate complexities in globalization, missing parts lead to bad leadership in the global context. The COVID-19 pandemic is a case in point. Ansell et al. (2020) categorized the COVID-19 pandemic as a turbulent crisis to the world which builds yet goes beyond complexity with extra surprising, inconsistent, unpredictable, and uncertain problems (Asselt & Renn, 2011). Admittedly, it is a sheer challenge for leaders to navigate unity versus distinctiveness, global collaboration versus local protection, and parochial or nationalism vision versus global mindset in this dynamic balancing game (Lee, 2020).

Unfortunately, the way world leaders, such as presidents in developed countries, reacted to this turbulence did not manifest their quality in dynamic balancing. Alternative to performing the global collaboration, their leadership is pinpointed as "global blindset" (Levy, 2020). She shed light on the narrow nationalist vision of global leaders, such as concealing the vital information driven by the short-term political and economic gains, downplaying the risk of spread, intensifying racism and xenophobia, and competing for vital medical supplies inside and outside of the nation. Thus, throughout years of efforts to erode the borders and close the gaps among nations, "global" leaders' attitude and actions toward the COVID-19 pandemic brought leadership back to the old times when the national borders loomed large, transnationalism demised, and the scope of leading lied on the parochial realm (Reiche et al., 2020).

Leaders in globalization need to recognize the distinctiveness residing in current complexities, be knowledgeable to balance the conflicts nesting in the differentiation, and seek integration among the divergences. Jeannet (2000) and Gupta and Govindarajan (2002) referred to this cognitive ability as a global mindset that serves as "golden threads" that wind throughout the leadership and complexities in globalization.

LEADING WITH GLOBAL MINDSET IN COMPLEXITIES

What is global mindset? A definition that manifests a collaborative work of scholars is adopted here. A global mindset is one has "a stock of knowledge, cognitive, and psychological attributes" to allow a leader to "combines an openness to and awareness of diversity across cultures and markets with a propensity and ability to synthesize across this diversity" (Gupta & Govindarajan, 2002, p. 117) and "to influence individuals, groups, and organizations from diverse sociocultural systems" (Beechler & Javidan, 2007, p. 152). It is necessary to understand what mindsets reside in global leaders and how those mindsets influence their scope of leadership in globalization.

First, mindset is a cognitive filter that can shape and frame an individual's view of the world. Mathews (2017) identified five key representatives in the cognitive structure: knowledge, personality, motivation, emotion, and attitudes. He described mindset as an orienting, dynamic, and complex meaning-making filter that encompasses not only these representations of cognition, but also the interactions among them. This dynamic meaning-making filter matters in leadership; it is like a wheel that drives or orients leaders to different scopes and directions. And mindset guides leaders depending on the cognitive complexity. Cognitive complexity is the degree of differentiation, articulation, and integration within a cognitive structure (Levy et al., 2007; Weick & Bougon, 1986). Leaders with different cognitive complexity of differentiation and integration produce differential structures in knowledge, personality, motivation, emotion, and attitudes in their leadership to reckon with complexities in globalization (Gupta & Govindarajan, 2002).

Second, an individual's mindset pulls information from the environment and generates different cognitive structures while leading. Thus, context is of pivotal importance on the cognitive dimensions. The complexities of cognitive structure and mindset development are contingent on the diverse information pertaining to the environment (Levy et al., 2007; Mathews, 2017). Put another way, if a leader constrains their information system or environment to a Western-centric realm, then their cognitive complexities and scope of leading will only loop within one single cultural map rather than global cultural maps. This leadership is meant to fail while sailing in the current complexities of globalization, in light of the limited ability to recognize the diversity across borders.

Third, mindset is a critical driver of behavior, yet not behavior. Mathews (2017) claimed that the mindset is an interactive cognitive state leading to external behavioral representations. Though mindset drives discoveries and exploration in different scopes, its emphasis is more on a strategic level. Mindset assists on how to process the information from different scopes of context but not how to incorporate it into performance in the operation (Bleicher, 2011). Thus, leaders need to acknowledge that developing the global mindset is a satisfactory start to navigate the complexities in globalization, yet not sufficient to predict success (Andresen & Bergdolt, 2017). Subsequent behaviors are needed (Rhinesmith, 1992).

Hence, only with the combination of cognitive filter and environment impact, the high level of differentiation and integration can be mirrored in leadership. Global mindset can be manifested in leadership to guide through the complexities created by globalization. Differentiating from distinct realms and integrating from divergent cultural and social norms in the global mindset does not mean to forgo historic roots and cultural heritage, or to precede one culture and value over another one (Andresen & Bergdolt, 2017; Beechler & Javidan, 2007; Perruci, 2018). Leveraging both "local adaptation" and "global standardization" is always a priority in global leadership.

Notably, the influence of a global mindset can spring from one individual's attribute, but spread to individuals and groups across the globe (Perruci, 2018). This reinforces the significance of leadership with a global mindset in the midst of globalization filled with uncertainties and complexities. The global mindset is perceived as a "golden thread" that loops leadership and globalization, manifesting a high level of differentiation and integration from global leaders. Cultivating a global mindset is decisive and urgent to perform global leadership in the complicated era of globalization (Javidan et al., 2007).

CRITICAL HOPE: DEVELOPING GLOBAL MINDSET

For global leaders, the COVID-19 pandemic crisis has been an alarm and an opportunity for reflection and learning. What is underestimated and neglected in their leadership, yet accompanied by a loaded price? Fortunately, a global mindset is a critical hope for leaders and educators to retrieve the missing transnational scope of global leadership and prepare the next generation of global leaders (Levy, 2020; Reiche et al., 2020).

First, "a stock of knowledge, cognitive, and psychological attributes" (Beechler & Javidan, 2007, p. 152) is essential for leaders across the globe to resolve global issues, such as the COVID-19 pandemic. As defined above, the turbulent crisis is characterized as uncertainty, emergency, and ambiguity. Global leaders have to operate with the essential knowledge to navigate the unpredictable emergency, psychological resilience to accept the possibility of change during the uncertainty, and cognitive awareness of diversity and equity to continuously perform leadership to balance the contradictions. Turbulent crisis, such as COVID-19 pandemic, requires leaders to own a global mindset instead of relying on a warehouse of well-trained emergency staff or equipment (Ansell et al., 2020). And the knowledge, cognition, and psychological attributes cannot be cultivated quickly, which further calls for leaders to begin developing and integrating a global mindset into their leadership.

Second, "combining an openness to and awareness of diversity across cultures and markets with a propensity and ability to synthesize across this diversity" (Gupta & Govindarajan, 2002, p. 117) is imperative for global leaders to navigate the complexities and uncertainties within globalization. Leaders must realize that embracing difference can benefit them with fresh eyes to identify problems, a collection of diverse perspectives, and cross-cultural collaborations to find the way out (Perruci, 2018). In addition, only with collaborative efforts can leaders undergird adaptive, flexible responses to different cultural circumstances (Osland et al., 2020).

Third, global identity is fundamental to resolve the imbalance between nationalism and transnationalism, unity and distinctiveness, local adaption and global standardization. The value of and need for strong leaders surfaced during turbulent crisis (Osland et al., 2020). "Global" leaders' identity during the COVID-19 pandemic does not embody their value of transnationalism and unity, but is fundamental to lead through multiple complexities. To develop a global mindset, they have to cultivate their sense of belongingness to mankind as one entity that transcends borders, boundaries, and distinctiveness across the globe, as well as rooting on Indigenous local culture (Arnett, 2002; Erez & Gati, 2004).

Last, to seize the critical hope and possibility of good global leadership, cultivating a global mindset for future leaders is what this world is longing for. Four recommendations are made for educators in the context of higher education by Gupta and Govindarajan (2002): (1) "Instilling students with an explicit and self-conscious articulation of current mindset" to hearten them to fathom their own cultural values and biases"; (2) "cultivating students' curiosity about the world and a commitment to becoming smarter about how the world works"; (3) "exposure students to diversity and novelty" to inspire them to discern the difference among the cultural norms; and (4) incorporating a disciplined teaching attempt to "develop an integrated perspective that weaves together diverse strands of knowledge about culture and markets for students" (p. 120).

These steps can help educators equip students with knowledge and skills to step outside of their comfort zone and shape their leadership mindset to succeed within the complexities of globalization. Students must also recognize that paradigms of globalization are shifting to non-predictable and nonlinear patterns. As future leaders, students thus have to evolve their mindset from a linear pace to 3-D thinking which indicates the simultaneous consideration of hindsight (past), insight (present), and foresight (future). This shift can better prepare them to lead in globalization, transforming disruption and chaos into opportunities (Kutz, 2013).

REFERENCES

Andresen, M., & Bergdolt, F. (2017). A systematic literature review on the definitions of global mindset and cultural intelligence—Merging two different research streams. *The International Journal of Human Resource Management, 28* (1), 170–195.

Ansell, C., Sørensen, E., & Torfing, J. (2020). The COVID-19 pandemic as a game changer for public administration and leadership? The need for robust governance responses to turbulent problems. *Public Management Review.* https://doi.org/10.1080/14719037.2020.1820272

Arnett, J. J. (2002). The psychology of globalization. *American Psychologist, 57,* 774–783.

Asselt, M., & Renn, O. (2011). Risk governance. *Journal of Risk Research, 14*(4), 431–449. https://doi.org/10.1080/13669877.2011.553730.

Beechler, S., & Javidan, M. (2007). Leading with a global mindset. In M. Javidan, R. M. Steers, & M. A. Hitt (Eds.), *The global mindset* (pp. 131–169). Emerald. https://doi.org/10.1016/S1571-5027(07)19006-9

Bleicher, K. (2011). *Das konzept integriertes management.* Campus Verlag.

Erez, M., & Gati, E. (2004). A dynamic, multi-level model of culture: From the micro level of the individual to the macro level of a global culture. *Applied Psychology: International Review, 53,* 583–598.

Govindarajan, V., & Gupta, A. K. (2001). *The quest for global dominance: Transforming global presence into global competitive advantage.* Jossey-Bass.

Gupta, A. K., & Govindarajan, V. (2002). Cultivating a global mindset. *Academy of Management Executive, 16*(1), 116–126.

Javidan, M., Steers, R. M., & Hitt, M. A. (2007). *The global mindset.* Emerald.

Jeannet, J. (2000). *Managing with a global mindset.* Pearson Education.

Kefalas, A. G. (1998). Think globally, act locally. *Thunderbird International Business Review, 40,* 547–562.

Kouzes, J., & Posner, B. (1995). *The leadership challenge: How to make extraordinary things happen in organizations.* Jossey-Bass.

Kutz, M. (2013). *Contextual intelligence: Smart leadership for a constantly changing world.* Lulu Enterprises.

Lane, H., Maznevski, M., & Mendenhall, M. (2004). Globalization: Hercules meets Buddha. In H. V. Lane, M. L. Maznevski, M. E. Mendenhall, & J. McNett (Eds.), *The Blackwell handbook of global management: A guide to managing complexity* (pp. 3–25). Blackwell.

Lee, Y. T. (2020). Dynamic balancing as a core quality for global leaders in crisis time. In J. S. Osland, B. Szkudlarek, M. E. Mendenhall, & B. S. Reiche (Eds.), *Advances in global leadership* (Vol. 13, pp. 15–17). Emerald. https://doi.org/10.1108/S1535-1203202013

Levy, O. (2020). Global epidemic of blindness. In J. S. Osland, B. Szkudlarek, M. E. Mendenhall, & B. S. Reiche (Eds.), *Advances in global leadership* (Vol. 13, pp. 37–39). Emerald. https://doi.org/10.1108/S1535-1203202013

Levy, O., Beechler, S., Taylor, S., & Boyacigiller, N. A. (2007). What we talk about when we talk about 'global mindset': Managerial cognition in multinational corporations. *Journal of International Business Studies, 38,* 231–258.

Mathews, J. (2017). The structure and development of global mindset. *Journal of Organizational Behavior, 16*(4), 7–33.

Mendenhall, M. E., Reicher, B. S., Bird, A., & Osland, J. S. (2012). Defining the 'global' in global leadership. *Journal of World Business, 47*(4), 493–503.

Osland, J. S., Mendenhall, M. E., & Li, M. (2020). *Advances in global leadership.* Emerald.

Perruci, G. (2018). *Global leadership: A transnational perspective.* Routledge.

Reiche, B. S., Mendenhall, M. E., Szkudlarek, B., & Osland, J. S. (2020). At the heart and beyond: What can global leadership researchers learn from perspectives on the COVID-19 pandemic? In J. S., Osland, B. Szkudlarek, M. E. Mendenhall, & B. S. Reiche (Eds.), *Advances in global leadership* (Vol. 13, pp. 261–282). Emerald. https://doi.org/10.1108/S1535-1203202013

Rhinesmith, S. H. (1992). Global mindset for global managers. *Training and Development, 46*(10), 63–69.

Schwab, K. (2016, January 14). The fourth industrial revolution: What it means, how to respond. *World Economic Forum.* www.weforum.org/agenda/2016/01/the-fourth-industrial-revolution-what-it-means-and-how-to-respond

Weick, K. E., & Bougon, M. G. (1986). Organizations as cognitive maps: Charting ways to success and failure. In H. P. Sims & D. A. Gioia (Eds.), *The thinking organization: Dynamics of organizational social cognition* (pp. 102–135). Jossey-Bass.

CHAPTER 20

INTERNATIONAL STUDENT LEADERSHIP DEVELOPMENT

Honoring Cultural Identities to Create Inclusive Environments

Pei Hu

The number of international students enrolled in U.S. higher education institutions has sharply increased over the past two decades, reflecting international student mobility in the context of globalization (Glass et al., 2015; Organisation for Economic Co-operation and Development, 2013). During the 2019–2020 academic year, 1.075 million international students were enrolled in U.S. colleges and universities, contributing around $44 billion to the U.S. economy (Institute of International Education, 2020). Despite the significant numbers of international college students in the United States and their contribution to the U.S. economy, culture, and diversity, leadership practice and research have barely focused on them. To fill the gaps in existing literature and practice on leadership, as well as to engage international students with leadership development opportunities during the COVID-19 pandemic and beyond, this chapter seeks to deconstruct complexities of international student leadership experience to further support their leadership development on U.S. campuses.

Navigating Complexities in Leadership: Moving Toward Critical Hope, pp. 207–217
www.infoagepub.com
Copyright © 2022 by Information Age Publishing
All rights of reproduction in any form reserved.

The stereotype of assuming 'international' as international students' most salient identity leads to the ignorance of the diverse cultural identities represented by this student population (Cecil & Hu, 2021). Leadership is a socially constructed concept that can be defined or perceived differently from a culturally values-based lens (Guthrie et al., 2013). The lack of understanding of international students' cultural identities could limit leadership educators' awareness of the unique needs and potential opportunities for these students' leadership development. This chapter seeks to increase awareness of students' diverse cultural identities and illuminate the complexities of international student leadership development. First, I describe the characteristics of today's international students in the United States. Second, I will discuss the significance of engaging international students in leadership development processes. Third, I propose a conceptual framework for leadership educators to understand and examine international students' leadership experiences on U.S. campuses. Additionally, I provide recommendations for leadership educators to deconstruct these complexities and support international student leadership development through increased understanding of this student population.

CULTURALLY DIVERSE INTERNATIONAL STUDENTS

International Students in the United States

The definition of international students varies in different country's education systems for the purposes of student enrollment data collection (Verbik & Lasanowski, 2007). International students in the United States refer to nonimmigrant degree-seekers in U.S. higher education residing temporarily in the Unites States (Verbik & Lasanowski, 2007). This definition aligns with U.S. Citizenship and Immigration Services standards for being a legal international student in the United States. While the definition of international students is simplified for administration or research initiatives, it ignores the diverse characteristics represented by international student populations.

According to the 2020 Institute for International Education Open Doors Report, 851,957 international students were newly enrolled in U.S. higher education institutions in the 2019–2020 academic year. Of those newly enrolled students, 419,321 were undergraduates, 374,435 were graduate students, and the remaining students were either nondegree seeking or on Optional Practical Training temporary employment status. The total number of international students makes up 5.5% of the total college students in the United States. The top five places of origin of international students in the United States are China, India, South Korea, Saudi Arabia, and Canada. China has remained the top source of international students in the United States for the 11th consecutive year (Institute for International Education, 2020).

The Impacts of COVID-19 on International Students

It is also worth acknowledging the COVID-19 pandemic and its associated impacts on international students in the United States, in particular. On July 6, 2020, within one month before the fall semester started for college students, U.S. Immigration and Customs Enforcement (ICE) announced that international students were not permitted to study or stay in this country if they took online-only courses in the fall 2020 semester (ICE, 2020). Unlike domestic college students, who had the right to enroll in fully online courses during that semester, the ICE order (2020) forced international students to attend at least one in-person course or choose between safety and education during that already extremely stressful time. This order was later amended as the result of a successful lawsuit led by Harvard and MIT (Svrluga & Anderson, 2020). Although international students were temporally relieved from the threat of losing their student statuses in the United States, challenges experienced by international students during and beyond this pandemic still existed, which could not be overlooked. Some unique challenges faced by international students during COVID-19 include academic engagement and success, financial supports, and mental health and well-being.

Academic Engagement and Success

Due to school closures and remote instruction during the pandemic, both international and domestic students encountered similar obstacles to their academic study, including less motivation for engaging in online learning, less interaction with other students, and less learning productivity in an online learning format (Chirikov & Soria, 2020). However, remote course instruction presented additional challenges for international students' academic engagement and success. For example, some international students who returned to their home countries experience time zone differences or technology issues while taking courses offered remotely in the United States (Chirikov & Soria, 2020).

Financial Supports

International students are experiencing more financial barriers, but less financial support than domestic students during the pandemic.

Specifically, with schools and campuses partially closed, there are fewer on-campus job opportunities available for students. International students with F-1 student visas are only legally eligible to work on-campus; thus, the shrinking on-campus job situation due to COVID-19 leaves international students who stay in this country in a much worse financial crisis (Fox, 2020). In addition, international students receive less financial support from the U.S. government and institutions. For instance, these students are not eligible for the Coronavirus Aid, Relief, and Economic Security (CARES) Act financial support.

Mental Health and Well-Being

Unexpected events such as COVID-19 exacerbate language barriers, homesickness, and other mental health-related challenges faced by international students (Waston & Barton, 2020). It is vital to notice that international students have been far away from their central support systems, including their home countries, family, and friends during this pandemic, all of which could affect their mental health and well-being (Lai et al., 2020). Some mental health-related stressors reported by international students in mass media include travel restrictions, housing, safety and immigration status, and lack of social and community support during the pandemic.

Glass et al. (2015) suggest that student leadership development could never be separated from experience and engagement on-campus and beyond. International student leadership development must account for the culturally diverse identities and complex characteristics represented by this student population. It is imperative for leadership educators in U.S. higher education to develop a culturally relevant understanding of international students' experiences and engagement within their institutions. In doing so, start to understand international students from a cultural value lens and create a more culturally inclusive campus environment that engages international students with leadership development opportunities.

INTERSECTING INTERNATIONAL STUDENTS WITH LEADERSHIP

Leadership development of college students is a commonly stated outcome in the U.S. higher education mission (Astin, 1993). International students play an integral role in higher education institutions; therefore, it is of significant importance to include international students in college student leadership development processes. Recent literature demonstrates growing attention to the intersections of leadership and diversity of college students (Guthrie et al., 2013). For instance, Renn and Bilodeau (2005) explored the experiences of lesbian, gay, bisexual, and transgender (LGBT) student leaders using the leadership identity development model (Komives et al., 2006). Baughman and Bruce's (2011) study focused on the unique leadership needs of minority student populations. While these studies emphasize leadership and leadership identity development of students from diverse cultural backgrounds, few studies have explored the leadership experiences of international students.

The literature on international student leadership experience is scarce within international student study or leadership education. Existing studies include Collier and Rosch's (2016) research on the effects of cocurricular leadership programs on international students and Manyibe et al.'s (2013) research on the precollege leadership experience of international African college students. Although these studies shed light on international student leadership development, there are some common limitations of these studies noted by the authors. Specifically, the studies only focused on a small number of subculture groups of international students; thus their findings could not be generalized to leadership experiences of international students from other cultural backgrounds. And, in some ways, a goal of generalization is itself problematic. As previously discussed, the complexities of international student leadership development associated with the cultural identities and diverse experiences represented by these students. A more culturally responsive and relevant approach to research may also be needed.

To develop the intersection of leadership and international student population either in research or practice, leadership educators should understand the socially constructed nature of leadership knowledge and be open to multiple ways of knowing and perceiving leadership. The concept and definitions of leadership in existing literature in the United States reflect a predominately Western perspective (Rost, 1991), potentially distancing students from diverse backgrounds from leadership development opportunities, including international students (Guthrie et al., 2013).

There are no well-known definitions of leader and leadership from international students' perspectives. However, Guthrie and colleagues (2013) suggested that diverse individuals enacting in collectivist, servant, and activist ways could be perceived as leaders within different social and cultural contexts, which extends understandings of leadership from a solely Western perspective. The idea of understanding how students define leadership in a larger social context has been further developed in the culturally relevant leadership learning (CRLL) model (Bertrand Jones et al., 2016). As a framework for leadership educators to transform their leadership programs considering the critical connections of leadership and diversity, the CRLL model provides a possible approach for leadership educators to examine how international students with diverse cultural identities may perceive and enact leadership.

A PROPOSED CONCEPTUAL FRAMEWORK
FOR INTERNATIONAL STUDENT LEADERSHIP DEVELOPMENT

This chapter proposes a conceptual framework combining the CRLL model with Astin's (1993) input-environment-outcome (I-E-O) model to help leadership educators understand and examine international student leadership development. Astin's I-E-O model has been widely used as a traditional assessment design to help institutions get a less biased estimate of student development by considering and measuring student input characteristics (Astin, 1993). In the I-E-O model, inputs and outputs refer to student qualities and characteristics pre- and postcollege. Environment refers to the students' actual college experience. Students' environmental experiences offered a possibility for educators to learn about and then use the findings for educational environment design or change to improve student learning outcomes. With the aim of this chapter to honor international students' cultural identities, understand the complexities of their leadership development experiences, and to create a more inclusive environment to engage these students with leadership process, the I-E-O model serves as an overarching umbrella for these purposes.

The similarities between I-E-O and CRLL (for example, the major components of student identity and environment) make combining these two models possible and reasonable. Specifically, the CRLL model domains include a dynamic interaction between the individual (leader) and leadership process with the constructs of identity, capacity, and efficacy as the bridge; and contextual dimensions of campus climate (Bertrand Jones et al., 2016). The campus climate domains include (a) historical legacy of inclusion/exclusion, (b) compositional diversity, (c) behavioral dimension, (d) organizational/structural dimension, and (e) psychological dimension. The CRLL model helps explain how students with different identities from diverse backgrounds define and learn about leadership in the campus context (Bertrand Jones et al., 2016). This model could be applicable for leadership educators to understand the complexities of international student leadership development and create environments to engage and support these students' leadership development process.

Taken together, Figure 20.1 illustrates a proposed conceptual framework to help understand and examine international students' leadership development within U.S. higher education institutions. The conceptual

Figure 20.1

Conceptual Framework

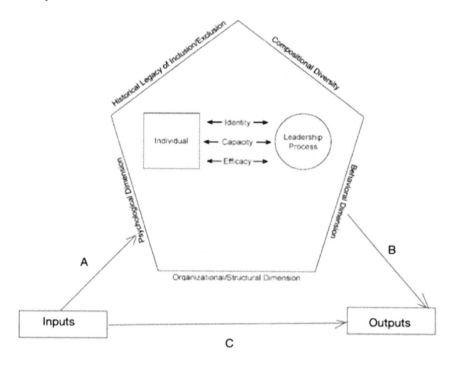

framework consisted of the I-E-O Model and CRLL model while using the CRLL model to replace the environment component originally in the I-E-O model. As the CRLL model mainly focused on institutional environment and how students from diverse backgrounds experience leadership in different institutional contexts, it is reasonable to use the whole CRLL model as the environment component in the overarching I-E-O model. The combination of the I-E-O model and CRLL model formed a framework for leadership educators to fully understand international students' leadership experiences with taking both student cultural identities and the institutional environment factors into account.

RECOMMENDATIONS FOR PRACTICE

The purpose of this chapter was to deconstruct international student leadership complexities and further support international student leadership development. I started by describing international students' presence within U.S. HEIs, highlighting national statistics, and exploring the unique challenges experienced by these students. Next, I underscored the significance of engaging the international student population with leadership development opportunities instead of merely perceiving these students as enrollment numbers or economic revenue. In addition, a combined conceptual framework of the I-E-O model and CRLL model was proposed for leadership educators to understand international students' leadership experiences on U.S. campuses. Several recommendations for leadership practices to create inclusive environments for international student leadership development include:

Recommendation # 1: Interconnecting Leadership With Cultural Identity

As leadership educators, we should be aware of the stereotype of assuming 'international' as international students' most salient identity (Cecil & Hu, 2021) and build awareness of the diverse identities represented by this student population. The complexities regarding international students' cultural identities can make it more challenging for educators and practitioners to understand these students' leadership experiences. Yet, student cultural identity shouldn't be the excuse to exclude international students from leadership processes; instead, it should become a leadership resource to help invite the excluded to a broader collective leadership (Ospina, 2018).

Recommendation # 2: Supporting Student Engagement and Leadership Development

The unique impacts of COVID-19 on international students should prompt the following critical questions: Are our institutional systems supportive for international students at the same level as for domestic students? Do we understand the unique experiences and needs of international students for their engagement and leadership development during the crisis and beyond? How can we be more sensitive to the unique challenges faced by international students? And are there resources to support international students' engagement and leadership development with considering their unique needs?

Recommendation # 3: Theorizing and Practicing Leadership

Applying the I-E-O model and CRLL model as a combined conceptual framework, institutions can intentionally create safe and inclusive environments on campuses to support international students' cultural identity expression and leadership identity exploration. For example, throughout our orientation sessions for international students, professionals could introduce the historical legacy and institutional organizations to our international students to make them feel engaged within the U.S. campuses. Additionally, leadership educators can host sociocultural conversations with international students to understand how they perceive institutional environmental support of their leadership development experiences. This chapter values the complexities of diverse cultural identities represented by international students as they come from different countries with very different cultural backgrounds. These students' cultural identities are related to how they perceive themselves as leaders and see themselves in the leadership process. The combined conceptual framework of I-E-O model and CRLL model provides possible approaches to create safe and welcoming spaces to support these students' cultural identity expression and leadership identity exploration.

Recommendation # 4: Collaborating and Creating Inclusive Environment

There are multiple ways to collaborate. Support of international student leadership development is not just the responsibility of the office of international students (Glass et al., 2015). It requires collaborative work among the whole campus to create a more inclusive environment to meet these students' unique leadership development needs. Honoring the cultural identities of international students to create inclusive environments, collaborations among the office of international students, multicultural office, and leadership centers could be the first effort to support leadership development for international students.

REFERENCES

Astin, A. W. (1993). *What matters most in college: Four critical years revisited.* Jossey-Bass.

Baughman, K. N., & Bruce, J. (2011). The unique leadership needs of minority student populations: Crafting a leadership identity. *Journal of Leadership Education*, *10*(2), 97–115.

Bertrand Jones, T., Guthrie, K. L., & Osteen, L. K. (2016). Critical domains of culturally relevant leadership learning: A call to transform leadership programs. In K. L. Guthrie, T. Bertrand Jones, & L. Osteen (Eds.), *New Directions for Student Leadership: No. 152. Developing culturally relevant leadership learning* (pp. 9-21). Wiley. https://doi.org/10.1002/yd.20205

Cecil, B. G., & Hu, P. (2021). Redefining engagement: Including international students in socially just leadership education. In K. L. Guthrie & V. S. Chunoo

(Eds.), *Shifting the mindset: Socially just leadership education* (139–148). Information Age.

Chirikov, I., & Soria, K. M. (2020). *International students' experiences and concerns during the pandemic*. SERU Consortium, University of California–Berkeley and University of Minnesota. https://escholarship.org/content/qt43q5g2c9/supp/International_Students__Experiences_and_Concerns.pdf

Collier, D. A., & Rosch, D. M. (2016). Effects associated with leadership program participation in international students compared to domestic students. *Journal of Leadership Education, 15*(4), 33–49.

Fox, J. (2020, September 4). *How coronavirus threw America's international students into chaos*. The College Post. https://thecollegepost.com/coronavirus-international-students/

Glass, C. R., Wongtrirat, R., & Buus, S. (2015). *International student engagement: Strategies for creating inclusive, connected, and purposeful campus environments*. Stylus.

Guthrie, K. L., Bertrand Jones, T., Osteen, L., & Hu, S. (2013). *Cultivating leader identity and capacity in students from diverse backgrounds: ASHE Higher Education Report, 39*(4).

Institute of International Education (2020). *Open Doors report on international educational exchange*. Institute of International Education. https://opendoorsdata.org/annual-release/

Komives, S. R., Longerbeam, S. D., Owen, J. E., Mainella, F. C., & Osteen, L. (2006). A leadership identity development model: Application from a grounded theory. *Journal of College Student Development, 47*, 401–418.

Lai, A. Y., Lee, L., Wang, M. P., Feng, Y., Lai, T. T., Ho, L. M., Lam, V. S., Ip, M. S., & Lam, T. H. (2020). Mental health impacts of the COVID-19 pandemic on international university students, related stressors, and coping strategies. *Frontiers in Psychiatry, 11*. https://doi.org/10.3389/fpsyt.2020.584240

Manyibe, B. M., Manyibe, E. O., & Otiso, K. M. (2013). College student leadership development: An examination of precollege leadership development of African students in the United States. *The Journal of Negro Education, 82*(4), 422–432.

Organisation for Economic Co-operation and Development. (2013). *Education indicators in focus*. https://www.oecd.org/education/skills-beyond-school/EDIF%202013--N%C2%B014%20(eng)-Final.pdf

Ospina, S. M. (2018). Toward inclusive leadership scholarship: Inviting the excluded to theorize collective leadership. In B. Carroll, J. Firth, & S. Wilson (Eds.), *After leadership* (pp. 147–156). Taylor & Francis.

Renn, K. A., & Bilodeau, B. L. (2005). Leadership identity development among lesbian, gay, bisexual, and transgender student leaders. *NASPA Journal, 42*(3), 342–367.

Rost, J. C. (1991). *Leadership for the twenty-first century*. Praeger.

Svrluga, S., & Anderson, N. (2020 July 8). Harvard, MIT sue Trump administration to protect student visas, escalating fight over online learning. *The Washington Post*. https://www.washingtonpost.com/education/2020/07/08/harvard-mit-international-students-ice/

U.S. Immigration and Customs Enforcement (2020, July 6). *SEVP modifies temporary exemptions for nonimmigrant students taking online course during fall 2020 semester*. https://www.ice.gov/news/releases/sevp-modifies-temporary-exemptions-nonimmigrant-students-taking-online-courses-during

Verbik, L., & Lasanowski, V. (2007). International student mobility: Patterns and trends. *World Education News and Reviews*, *20*(10), 1–16.

Watson, M., & Barton, G. (2020). Using arts-based methods and reflection to support postgraduate international students' well-being and employability through challenging times. *Journal of International Students, 10*(S2), 101–118.

CHAPTER 21

GRASSROOTS MOVEMENTS IN SENEGAL TO GROW CRITICAL HOPE

Lessons for Higher Education

Trisha Gott, Mary Tolar, Salif Kanoute, and Sedyi Ndiaye

Wicked problems are the most pressing and persistent issues facing our world; they are complex, uncertain, and ungovernable problems that demonstrate a divergence of values among stakeholders. In Senegal, wicked problems include youth engagement, opportunity, and governance, among others. Wicked problems require new ways of understanding and different approaches to progress (Head, 2008; Roberts, 2000). Without clear definition, wicked problems lack a clear pathway forward. Progress requires understanding the problem and working toward solutions through a self-organizing grassroots system (Jantesch, 1980; Roberts, 2000).

Scholars describe emergence within complex adaptive systems; self-organizing refers to a system that developed its own rules, processes, behaviors, and interactions and reflects and builds on those ideals (Stacey, 1996). This chapter explores how the work of leadership learning and development—through higher education and in communities around the

Navigating Complexities in Leadership: Moving Toward Critical Hope, pp. 219–228
www.infoagepub.com
Copyright © 2022 by Information Age Publishing
All rights of reproduction in any form reserved.

globe—can create the conditions for these systems to emerge. We examine grassroots movements where people come together to make progress on an issue. The movements are fundamentally democratic in nature. Batliwala (2002) describes these as movements for the people, by the people that "enjoy high levels of legitimacy and right to representation" (p. 404).

Grassroots efforts emerge when the circumstances are right to lead change, and those leading the change are prepared—or *practiced*—to do so. Movements are not accidental, and higher education can provide the perfect practice field for individuals and collectives to work toward the movement they seek. Through higher education, people can test ideas, try out new practices, build networks, and do so with critical hope, which is necessary to sustain this kind of work. The relevance of higher education hangs in the balance of this kind of practice. The COVID-19 pandemic brought this to the forefront. As an emergent and complex challenge, COVID-19 has presented higher education with opportunities to demonstrate relevance and the ability to respond to these challenges. This chapter connects the role of higher education to the development of global leaders through programs and partnerships, offering examples from our experience with a leadership development program and grassroots movements in Senegal. We suggest that higher education will remain relevant by positioning itself to respond to global complexities.

HIGHER EDUCATION AS A CATALYST FOR LEADING CHANGE

Across history, higher education has claimed multiple purposes, including preparing informed and engaged citizens and growing a robust healthy democracy (Boyer, 1994, Boyer et al., 2015). Institutions incubated movements—places where students go to understand how to lead change for the public good. To develop these skills, innovate and direct change as needed, students would be instructed on the practice of civic engagement about the social good of the community, state, and nation, and develop a collective ethos of care and concern for their neighbors (Addams, 1964; Dewey, 2013). This civic focus connects higher education with the development of grassroots leadership. If students practice civic engagement to lead change on their college campuses, they can bring those practices back to their communities.

The ideological underpinnings of public universities matter to society and to understanding ideas of leadership education and development. Barnett (1994) called on higher education to focus on the knowing, being, and doing components of whole learner development. This call was to move the research and theory of universities to practice with and in communities. These civic purposes are reflected today in the field of leadership studies. Approaches to leadership education represented within leadership-as-practice (Carroll et al., 2008; Raelin, 2011), adaptive leadership (Heifetz et al., 2009), and relational leadership (Cuneliff & Eriksen, 2011; Uhl-Bien, 2011) reflect commitments to leadership as a shared process, relational in nature, and focused on process, practice, and people.

Leadership education and development programs in higher education grounded in these commitments create containers to weave theory and practice and set conditions for institutions and communities to engage, understand, and innovate. These containers allow practitioners to incubate and test ideas of grassroots leadership, and students, professionals, and community practitioners gain momentum in making progress on leading change.

This movement from theory to practice is present in programs like the Mandela Washington Fellowship, which brought this author team together: Kanoute and Ndiaye as participants and Tolar and Gott as facilitators of a U.S. host institution partner. Kanoute and Ndiaye offer two cases of the extension of that mission into the field.

GRASSROOTS MOVEMENTS FOR GLOBAL CHANGE

Kanoute and Ndiaye organize and advance grassroots movements in Senegal. Kanoute works in Ziguinchor and surrounding rural regions in the South of the country marred by a civil war that has left a lasting impact on the community economically and socially. Ndiaye is based in the nation's capital city and urban hub, Dakar, and his work has been through a networked online community of social media activists. Both participated in the Mandela Washington Fellowship Program, an initiative of the U.S. State Department to invest in the leadership development of people across Sub-Saharan Africa. As a grant program that partners with higher education institutes, the Mandela Washington Fellowship program provides a pathway for informal educational interventions to build civic leadership capacity. Kansas State University as a public institution is working toward meeting its public purpose of contributing to the civic good through an intentional organized effort to develop leadership capacity. In the next section, Ndiaye and Kanoute share their work and provide insight about distinct leadership learning and development interventions.

Civic Action as the Means, Leadership Development as the Outcome

I (Sedyi Ndiaye) work among the architects of a social media movement to mobilize activists across Senegal and Sub-Saharan Africa. I am based in Dakar. The movement is continental. It is an effort to mobilize Africans with a shared ideology to join a grassroots effort to build democracy. What began as an online movement to raise awareness and spur public action in monitoring information around voting and elections has grown to in-person train-the-trainer workshops for leadership developers across the region. Recently our team formalized efforts by translating a curriculum into French. We have written a playbook for leadership development extending the network of practitioners making progress in civil society work.

To understand the origins of this grassroots movement, we must reorient our understanding of space to include cyberspace via digital technology as part of the civic space. Cyberspace is a channel to connect people based on their values, points of interest, culture, and ideology. In this space of shared ideology, critical hope blossomed. In Senegal, the past decade has also opened access to the internet. The combination of access, ideology, and a space to connect led to the conditions for a movement. The movement was not accidental but grew from an orientation to activate to lead change.

Understanding access was growing. Youth across Senegal were the primary users of the internet. We saw the Arab Spring as a model for using digital technology to promote democracy, transparency, accountability, and civic engagement. The goal was to raise awareness for critical political questions. Africtivistes raise awareness on social media and digital platforms to create a critical mass around democracy and civic engagement. We use that tool to build an online civic change-makers and cyber-activists community. We used an innovative approach based on digital strategist backgrounds and created an online platform to monitor Senegalese elections. With social media, we engaged people, asked them to vote, recruited e-observers, shared candidate programs, and worked to mitigate internet instability.

The project, named #SUNU2012 spread to Côte d'Ivoire, Ghana, Burkina Faso, and Benin leading to the birth of the Africtivistes—a pan-African cyber league/movement of bloggers, civil society organizations, and journalists who use digital technology to promote democracy, transparency, and accountability. We have over 300 members in 30–40 countries in Africa. The mode for engagement is a cross canal 360 degree approach to share and raise awareness broadly. Present on Facebook, Twitter, and Instagram, the Africtivistes maintain a website to share information and a newsletter to connect as a community. Our work happens primarily online—and uses Over the TOP applications like WhatsApp, Signal, and Telegram to keep a safe, private communication channel. Hashtags have become a mechanism to curate content and invite engagement around a specific question or trend.

We work in the urban area. The questions guiding our work evolved from *how do we use cyberspace to build an online community to lead change*, to *how do we foster connection between civic engagement in cyberspace and real life*, and finally, *how do we build relationships in cyberspace?* We used and continue to use digital media to promote local narratives and to inspire others to do the same.

Interested youth sign up for community-based organizing activities. Once the civic leadership and engagement training is complete, attendees can join the volunteer network to practice what they have learned. While practicing community-based organizing activities (community service), volunteers share the stories about that experience on social media. This is how we move(d) from cyberspace to real-life civic engagement and leadership activity.

We assess this work using digital technology analytics and metrics. We discover how many people have been reached by the narratives shared on social media. Promoting a narrative through digital storytelling via concept, ideology, and cases based in our local context and challenges draws attention to the message of our movement. Others see themselves in the story and take ownership of the concept, ideology, and message.

The Africtivistes practice demonstrates how grassroots movements can take place specific to an urban context and group ideology. Next, let's examine a grassroots movement from a rural community context seeking to mobilize change.

Leadership Development as the Means, Civic Action as the Outcome

I (Salif Kanoute) envisioned advancing a leadership development youth movement in rural Senegal with four colleagues. The primary goal was to change the trajectory of the Casamance region by engaging and empowering the youth. Through meetings in peoples' homes, on the streets, and building trust through personal connections, we are building a movement to reinvigorate a rural region. Leadership development is the means and the goal. The process includes developing a leadership curriculum and ethos that has mobilized thousands of rural youths to make change on their community issues. This group, DECLIC, is an example of a grassroots movement built from a shared ideology. Their motto, "To take the leadership challenge for the common good."

In Africa, youth (aged 18–35) represent over 60% of the population. In sub-Saharan countries like Senegal, many young people look to the government and institutions for help. Youth suffer from a lack of confidence and a lack of opportunity. A weak educational system that does not emphasize leadership development or practical capacity building leads to a lack of awareness of entrepreneurship, employment, project management, civic engagement, and community development. These gaps undermine youths' opportunities to contribute and create a feeling of helplessness toward local challenges. Local success stories are rare. Young people progressively become pessimistic and passive toward their social problems. Youth find themselves in "social danger," looking to the easiest ways to solve individual needs, opening the door to drugs, violence, illegal migration, and extremism. The singular biggest challenge facing Africa is that political systems are not strong enough to respond to the needs of the vulnerable, and many political leaders have different priorities, dismissive of youth in social danger. DECLIC exists to accompany youth in shifting mindsets so they can take on the leadership challenge.

DECLIC's focus and approach are unique to the audience and region. Founded in August 2016, DECLIC (integrated Civic Leadership and Community Development) is an international youth organization of positive, passionate, and talented young leaders from diverse cultural backgrounds, joining forces with local communities to take Africa's Leadership Challenge. DECLIC members are multidisciplinary young professionals and volunteers who bring solid backgrounds in civic engagement, arts, entrepreneurship, management, international development, and humanitarian work. We (Salif and DECLIC) believe that to make progress, the young underprivileged must be change makers in their communities. We develop their leadership and competency so they can fully seize opportunities to improve their lives and communities through lasting projects and distributed sustainable resources. We prioritize youth leadership development, civic engagement, women and children empowerment, social entrepreneurship, and arts and culture. Evidence demonstrates our grassroots effort has grown. In less than 5 years, we grew from five founding members to 50 members; expanded the model in five countries (Senegal, The Gambia, Guinea Bissau, Guinea Conakry and Togo); implemented five youth projects partnering with national and international organizations; engaged +300 VIP (Proximity Intercommunity Volunteers) living in their community throughout Ziguinchor region; trained +3,000 young community leaders; and mobilized more than $300,000 from a beginning budget of $0.

Our grassroots movement began distinctly. Having been raised in and shaped by underprivileged backgrounds, we were (are) inspired by a deep understanding of young people's essential needs and a desire to create change—this is our shared ideology. Our relationship started in person through established connections.

DECLIC builds young people's capacity and resilience so they can address the challenges of Casamance, Senegal, and Africa. The strategy lies on three dimensions: leadership development, organizational development, and community development and is developed through camps, talks, capacity building, monitoring, and coaching youth and women in social danger. Our actions reinforce the spirit of servant leadership, the sense of community, vision, self-improvement, positive action, and sense of service without expecting personal gain. Our quest for the common good consists of an integrated approach, positively affecting all the layers of the community. We build and strengthen bridges between self and people around, institutions, and local leaders. We contribute to the growth of civic engagement through community engagement in design, decision-making, implementation, and follow-up, without discrimination.

LESSONS LEARNED
ACROSS RURAL AND URBAN GRASSROOTS WORK

We learn from the Africtivistes and DECLIC that grassroots leadership looks different based on region, population served, and those engaged in the work. In this case, it looks different based on contexts of rural and urban. Ndiaye's story is of a movement that began online with a shared ideology and moved to building relationships through the online medium. Due to the rurality of Kanoute's work, his movement began with a familial and community approach to organizing. The movement grew from relationships formed by the in-person, high-touch model of meeting in people's homes, with their families, and for the purposes of the youth movement.

In both cases, the movements advance(d) notions of leadership as an activity. Part of the grassroots orientation was an expectation that – online and in-person—the requirement for change was a practice of leadership beyond a role or position. They share ideology around what leadership requires and demonstrate the power of that leadership to move communities forward across different mediums to make progress.

The movements share ideology and an orientation toward critical hope as a key to building and sustaining relationships in communities. Critical hope is a thread that connects movements, weaving together collectives to pursue and sustain change efforts. For the Africtivistes, critical hope was built through the networked online community. With DECLIC, it emerged through the relationships held in the rural community and region. The dovetailing of grassroots movements and critical hope led to shared common elements for sustaining change efforts around wicked leadership challenges. The movements used practices of critical hope to advance their work. Critical hope bolstered both groups to advance from theory to practice, even sustaining the movement when progress slowed.

Africtivistes developed relationships by leaning on a shared ideology to bring together youth using a networked approach to online communities. The people moving the grassroots work forward did not know each other personally, but they knew each other through their agreement on the ideology required to make change in the region. For DECLIC, the relationships among members of the movement came first. The focus on developing relationships came through an understanding of the importance of personal connections in the rural community. Through in-person meetings, family visits, and regular connections in the local context, the group began to share their goals and then their ideology to build DECLIC.

Both relationship to ideology and ideology to relationship are critical organizing pathways in these grassroots movements. The context of rural and urban organizing also represents pieces of how these organizations began and were nurtured into movements. At the core of both pathways was an insistence on critical hope.

Cultivating Critical Hope

Critical hope is the common thread through any connected social movement—it is critical hope held by individuals and the collective that advances reform. Without it, the effort or the ideology may not sustain. Ndiaye experiences critical hope in a networked online community united by ideology. Kanoute sees it in the relationships among rural community members who look to collectively build a new way forward.

In higher education, by engaging the processes and principles of democracy, we create a container for critical hope, grassroots movements, and leadership education and development. As we face global crises of public health, ethnic and racial injustice and violence, and threats to our planet's future, the ideological underpinnings of public universities matter more now than ever. They also shape how we understand ideas of leadership education and development. While Kanoute and Ndiaye were already advancing this work before their time with the Mandela Washington Fellowship, the experience partnering with higher education in the U.S. context provided an important container for them both. They deepened and expanded their approaches to understanding and advancing grassroots leadership learning and development movements during and following the Fellowship program. Programs like the Fellowship connect the movement of research from theory to practice in global communities. Leadership studies and leadership educators can also reflect and advance these civic purposes. To study, to practice, and to build a leadership development movement in Senegal is also an opportunity to deepen global understandings and approaches to leadership learning and development. We can learn about critical hope—in a global context that moves beyond borders to lead change. Finally, we can reflect on the relationships and purposes of higher education as an important link in this chain.

The case studies offered are exemplars of the relevance of leadership learning, development, and practice. Through our ongoing relationships and program partnerships, we have continued to expand capacities to practice leadership for change within our respective communities—local and global. By understanding how two distinct grassroots leadership development movements are imagined, built, and taking root in Senegal, we might reimagine our leadership practices and development efforts in our classrooms and in the field. One way to explore this is through the lens of critical hope.

Paulo Freire suggested that hope was a universal ontological need in education. What does this mean for leadership education? It means the work of leadership education is about shifting orientations to the world, and wicked problems, by introducing concepts of critical hope, and justice. It is about embodying and practicing these ideas as a way of being (Freire & Freire, 1992; Torres-Olave, 2021). Freire & Freire's advancement of critical hope was a practice of the transformation of injustice. Torres-Olave described this as a relevant invitation for ourselves to be with others in how we understand, relate to, and contrast knowing deeply in collective community. In this, the work of educators – especially leadership educators – is in liberating systems of education. By advancing ideas like critical hope and collective, grassroots organizing as core in leadership education, higher education can realize its role as an institution poised to tackle complex global challenges and to serve the common good.

To advance this work, institutions might consider the following ideas. (1) What is required to sustain relationships built during a leadership development program? (2) What is the capacity and commitment to do so? (3) How might your institution explore commitments to critical hope related to leadership development? (4) How does your current programming make room for collective knowing, practice, and grassroots organizing as central to leadership education and development?

REFERENCES

Addams, J. (1964). *Democracy and social ethics*. Belknap Press.

Barnett, R. (1994). *The limits of competence: knowledge, higher education and society*. Open University Press.

Batliwala, S. (2002). Grassroots movements as transnational actors: Implications for global civil society. *VOLUNTAS: International Journal of Voluntary and Non-profit Organizations 13*, 393–409. https://doi.org/10.1023/A:1022014127214

Boyer, E. L. (1994). Creating the new American college. *Chronicle of Higher Education, 40*(27), A48.

Boyer, E. L., Moser, D., Ream, T. C., & Braxton, J. M. (2015). *Scholarship reconsidered: Priorities of the professoriate*. John Wiley & Sons.

Carroll, B., Levy, L., & Richmond, D. (2008). Leadership as practice: Challenging the competency paradigm. *Leadership, 4*(4), 363–379.

Cunliffe, A. L., & Eriksen, M. (2011). Relational leadership. *Human relations, 64*(11), 1425–1449.

Dewey, J. (2013). *The school and society and the child and the curriculum*. University of Chicago Press.

Freire, P., & Freire, A. M. A. (2004). *EPZ pedagogy of hope: Reliving pedagogy of the oppressed*. A&C Black.

Head, B. W. (2008). Wicked problems in public policy. *Public policy, 3*(2), 101.

Heifetz, R. A., Grashow, A., & Linsky, M. (2009). *The practice of adaptive leadership: Tools and tactics for changing your organization and the world*. Harvard Business Press.

Raelin, J. (2011). From leadership-as-practice to leaderful practice. *Leadership, 7*(2), 195–211.

Roberts, N. (2000). Wicked problems and network approaches to resolution. *International Public Management Review, 1*(1), 1–19.

Stacey, R. D. (1996). *Complexity and creativity in organizations*. Berrett-Koehler.

Torres-Olave, B. (2021) Pedagogy of hope: reliving pedagogy of the oppressed, *Educational Review, 73*(1), 128–128. https://doi.org/10.1080/00131911.2020.1766207

Uhl-Bien, M. (2011). Relational leadership theory: Exploring the social processes of leadership and organizing. In P. H. Werhane & M. Painter-Morland (Eds.), *Leadership, gender, and organization* (pp. 75–108). Springer

CHAPTER 22

#EndSARS

Illuminating Leadership Within a Leaderless Movement

Onyedikachi Ekwerike

On October 3, 2020, a video surfaced on Twitter showing alleged Special Anti-Robbery Squad (SARS) officers shooting an unarmed young man in Delta State, Nigeria. This viral video sparked outrage on Nigeria's Twitter, with people using the hashtag #EndSars to express their anger and call for the disbandment or abolition of SARS. In just 2 days, the hashtag #EndSars was trending globally on Twitter.

SARS is a police unit formed in 1992 to curb the menace of armed robbery and kidnapping in Nigeria. The challenge, though, is that this unit has abused its powers and has allegedly terrorized young people—hence the call for abolition. Using the hashtag #EndSars, many young people shared scary stories about their experience with SARS. There seems to be a pattern: extortions, extrajudicial killings, unjust imprisonments, abduction, and brutality are common themes.

I, too, have been a victim of SARS. Five years ago, I was abducted and assaulted by SARS after they wrongly suspected me of being an internet fraudster. When the SARS officers searched my phones and realized they had nothing on me, they threw me out of a moving bus. I suffered bruises,

Navigating Complexities in Leadership: Moving Toward Critical Hope, pp. 229–238
www.infoagepub.com
Copyright © 2022 by Information Age Publishing
All rights of reproduction in any form reserved.

but I was thankful I made it out of their hands, alive. Not many are that lucky.

Five days after the viral video showing the killing of a young man surfaced on Twitter, the call to #EndSars moved offline. On October 8, 2020, thousands of young Nigerians took to the streets nationwide to protest and demand that the government abolish SARS peacefully. As a researcher, what I find fascinating about the #EndSars movement is the absence of formal leaders. The #EndSars movement has no face.

In this chapter, I opine that the absence of formal leaders does not indicate a lack of leadership. First, I provide a brief overview of leaderless movements and how autonomist leadership theory offers one perspective on the type of leadership displayed in leaderless movements. I then suggest that at an ontological level, Drath et al.'s (2008) direction, alignment, and commitment (DAC) framework provides a helpful lens to understand the nature of leadership enacted within leaderless movements such as #EndSars. Lastly, I highlight what implication this has for those who study, practice, and teach/develop leadership.

LEADERLESS SOCIAL MOVEMENTS

Social movements are organized efforts to engage authorities using various strategies to create long-term political and social change (Myer, 2003). These movements often seek to gain the support of both local and international communities, calling attention to widespread injustice (Byrne, 2013). Social movements are spontaneous and can appear disorganized using unconventional methods and tactics to achieve their goals (Byrne, 2013; Myer, 2003). Past social movements have been characterized by strong charismatic leaders who mobilize citizens into action against authorities. For example, the American civil rights movement of the 1950s and 60s is most often associated with leaders like Rosa Parks, Dr. Martin Luther Jr., and Malcolm X. In Nigeria, the 2012 Occupy Nigeria movement was led by the chairman of the Nigerian labor congress, Peter Esele.

Recently though, we have witnessed the rise of leaderless social movements around the world. From the Arab Spring to #MeToo, these movements exhibit nonhierarchical and distributed leadership forms that challenge traditional orientations to leadership. Leaderless social movements leverage social media platforms like Twitter to organize, collaborate, and communicate their goals (Castells, 2015). Social media also provides technological affordance that facilitates the spread of information at lightning speed. For example, Twitter hashtags provide conversational spaces that allow social actors within movements to spread their ideas simultaneously and in ways that are easily accessible.

In leaderless social movements, as the name implies, there are no leaders and no followers. Joosse (2007) argues that leaderless movements foster inclusiveness, and the leaderless structure of the movement allows social actors to engage in political actions while avoiding persecution from authorities. No face, no case! This leaderless form makes it almost impossible for the government or other opposers to contain or control the social movement (Western, 2014).

However, the absence of formal leaders does not indicate a lack of leadership. A close study of the activities of leaderless movements suggests the presence of leadership (Sutherland et al., 2013; Gerbaudo, 2012). Within the context of the #EndSars movement in Nigeria, what I witnessed was collective leadership in action. From my observation, in just 10 days, ordinary citizens set up:

- legal teams to advocate for and bail individuals arrested for protesting;
- medical teams provide ambulances and treatments for protesters who are hurt;
- mental health care for protesters who are traumatized;
- provision of private security for protesters against thugs and hoodlums who might infiltrate the protest and cause trouble;
- feedings arrangements to ensure all protesters get food and water to sustain their energy;
- a call center where protesters/organizers can request any of the above services without charge; and
- a radio station to keep citizens informed.

The nature of leadership displayed within the context of the #EndSars and other leaderless social movements turns the focus of inquiry away from "Who is leading?" to "What exactly is leadership?" and "What does leadership accomplish?" Western (2014) theorizes the type of leadership within leaderless movements as autonomist leadership.

AUTONOMIST LEADERSHIP

Drawing from anarchism and situating it with critical leadership studies, autonomist leadership (Western, 2014) deviates from traditional types of leadership that center on individuals or groups who wield power over followers. Five features of autonomist leadership distinguish it from other types of leadership: spontaneity, autonomy, mutualism, networks, and affect.

Western (2014) explains that spontaneity refers to the spontaneous and flexible nature of leadership within leaderless movements. Leadership is a function of context and can take up various forms depending on the situation. Autonomy refers to the absence of hierarchy within the leaderless movements. There is no one leader or group of leaders; instead, all members of the movement can take up leadership roles at any point to mobilize collective action. Leaders and followers interchange to cocreate this type of leadership. The concept of mutualism refers to the presence of mutual consent and mutual benefits within leaderless movements. Social actors must navigate the tension between personal interests and that of the group.

Autonomist leadership is embedded within networks, which speaks to the fluidity and dispersion of leadership, making it difficult to observe through the traditional leadership lenses. Finally, affect refers to individuals' emotional connection to ideals like freedom and the fight against oppression. Social movements generate powerful collective effects such as hope, solidarity, and love that arise from the idealism, camaraderie, and unity expressed within them. An individual's "affective attachments are reinforced and shaped through the networked conversations and exchanges that take place" (Western, 2014, p., 682).

While autonomist leadership calls attention to the type of leadership enacted within leaderless social movements, the theory does not offer insight into the ontology of leadership within these movements. Ontological assumptions prompt questions like: How should leadership be understood in the context of these leaderless movements? How do we locate leadership? And, what does leadership accomplish? Drath et al.'s (2008) DAC framework provides insight into the nature of leadership enacted within leaderless movements.

DIRECTION, ALIGNMENT, AND COMMITMENT

The dominant perspective of leadership focuses on individuals and the role they play to inspire a collective purpose. It is rooted in what Alvesson (2019) calls a Hollywood ideology of leadership. According to Hollywood ideology, leadership is a product of an all-knowing, strong individual or group of individuals who transforms and influences others to achieve a set goal (Alvesson, 2019). Similarly, Drath et al. (2008) describe a leadership perspective emphasizing leaders, followers, and shared goals as operating from a "tripod" ontology (p. 257). An ontology is beliefs about the nature of a thing in its most basic form, in this case: the nature of leadership.

When an individual believes that leadership at its core is the interaction between leaders, followers, and shared goals, it means they subscribe to the "tripod" ontology (Drath et al., 2008). Although Western (2014) argued that autonomist leadership deviates from mainstream leadership traditions, the theory still reflects a traditional tripod ontology. The autonomist perspective suggests that for a social movement to be sustainable, members of the movement need to take up leadership roles in order to mobilize collective action. Western (2014) argues that leadership roles are not stable, as individuals who take up leadership roles can be followers when the situation calls for it. However, the theory still reflects the assumption that leadership requires leaders, followers, and goals. While the tripod ontology of leadership offers insight, it is not a sufficient lens for understanding leadership in the context of movements like #EndSars, where leadership activity is collaborative and a formal leader is nonexistent (Drath et al., 2008). Leaderless does not mean leader*ship*less.

Drath et al. (2008) suggest an alternative ontological lens, replacing the tripod entities of leader, follower, and shared goals with leadership outcomes of DAC. Leadership, then, is defined as the production of direction, alignment, and commitment (Drath et al., 2008). This means that wherever/whenever a group of people has direction, are in alignment, and demonstrates commitment, you find leadership. Leadership through this lens is viewed as a collective activity and not residing within an individual. Direction is achieved when there is an agreement among a collective on their overarching goal. A group is said to have direction when they have clarity and understanding of their goals and aims. Similarly, alignment is achieved when a collective organizes and coordinates resources that help them achieve their purpose. Lastly, commitment is evident when group members are invested in achieving the group's goal (Drath et al., 2008). Hence, when a group has direction, alignment, and commitment, then leadership is enacted. How then can leadership be understood within the context of the #EndSars movement through a DAC lens?

Direction

Even before Nigerian youths took to the streets, the direction was clear: #EndSars. There was a consensus on Twitter that rot within the police unit SARS was beyond reform. The youths, therefore, called for the abolishment of SARS. The direction was evident, and from my observation, the youths understood what the goal was, #EndSars. There is more to having a shared direction than just knowing what the goal is or understanding the group's mission (Drath et al., 2008). Having shared direction involves agreeing to the value of the direction. Nigerian youths who joined the protest online and, in the streets, agree that abolishing SARS was the right step to take.

According to Drath et al. (2008), a shared direction is not set in stone. It is continuously negotiated and can change based on the context and challenges facing the group. Therefore, it is not surprising that the #End-Sars protests continued despite the President's announcement of the disbandment of SARS. Nigerian youths are now demanding a total reform of the police, compensation for families of people who have lost their lives during the protest, justice for families who have lost loved ones to rogue SARS operatives, and better welfare for police officers.

Alignment

A collective achieves alignment when their work is organized and coordinated (Drath et al., 2008). I have been astonished by the amount of organization and coordination shown during the #EndSars protest. Using the hashtag #EndSars on Twitter, youths have set up legal teams to advocate for and secure the release of individuals arrested during the protest. Youths have also used the hashtag #EndSars to pull resources together to provide food and water for protesters. Nonprofit organizations have collaborated to provide medical support for protesters, both physical and mental healthcare. Achieving this requires significant coordination and organization, proof of alignment.

The hashtag #EndSars provides an online space for collaborating and organizing. The communication theory of affordance suggests that hashtags' help coordinate large-scale discussions that support movements like #EndSars (boyd, 2010; Eddington, 2018; Gibson, 2015). This technological affordance likely enabled #EndSars to achieve a level of coordination under a short period that would have been difficult or impossible without technology, or specifically with the Twitter hashtag.

Commitment

Thousands of young people on the streets for ten consecutive days proved there was commitment. Besides leaving their work and families, people have donated money and other resources to sustain the protest. Drath et al. (2008) argue that commitment is achieved when individuals are willing to allow others to "make demands on their time and energy" (p. 648). The amount of funds donated and energy expended is proof of loyalty to the cause and commitment to ensuring an end to police brutality in Nigeria.

IMPLICATIONS FOR FUTURE

In this section, I discussed implications for future research, practice, and leadership development.

Research

An important question to consider is, how are direction, alignment, and commitment produced? Drath et al. (2008) argue that DAC is an outcome of individual and collective leadership beliefs and practices. Leadership beliefs are the dispositions people have about why and how DAC should be produced. In contrast, leadership practices are patterns of behavior within a collective deployed to achieve DAC (Drath et al., 2008). Therefore, research is needed to understand the leadership beliefs and practices that produced DAC in leaderless social movements like #EndSars. How did these beliefs and practices come into being and become widespread among protesters? How did protesters' leadership beliefs and practices develop and change over time?

Young people are organizing online using platforms like Twitter and implementing offline. Leadership scholars should investigate the role hashtags such as #EndSars play in organizing leaderless social movements. Innovative methods like social network analysis and hermeneutic phenomenological approach (HPA) can help locate and understand how leadership is enacted within these movements.

Practice

For organizers and practitioners, achieving and maintaining DAC is important. Since leaderless social movements often aim to create structural and systemic change, social change leadership practices are valuable (Ospina & Foldy 2015). Social change leadership practices align with the DAC ontology and include prompting cognitive shifts and engaging dialogue about differences (Ospina & Foldy 2015). Prompting cognitive shifts involves changing the way audiences view or understand the crucial elements of the leadership work (direction). It is necessary to get people to think about how the issues that need to be addressed are relevant to them. This helps to create a sense of shared purpose, which in turn fosters alignment and commitment. Engaging dialogue about the difference is crucial in achieving long-term goals. People come from different backgrounds and may have varying interests. It is, therefore, essential to create space to surface and engage these differences. Engaging differences via deliberations that accommodate multiple voices can help a group gain clarity about their direction and help achieve alignment and commitment.

Leadership Development

There are several implications for leadership learning and development. First, the leadership enacted during the #EndSars movement demonstrates that young people have the capacity to create and drive change. Leadership educators in higher education play an important role in developing students' capacity to exercise leadership for change. Indeed, higher education has a responsibility to develop citizens who will play an active role in organizational and civic spaces. As demonstrated during #EndSars, leadership is an activity, one that anyone regardless of titles can participate in. Leadership educators and developers need to consider the ontological perspectives from which they are working.

For example, it is common that leadership education and educators in higher education focus on helping individuals develop skills and competence that will enable them to influence people toward achieving a goal (working from a traditional tripod ontology). These skills, while helpful, do not prepare them to engage effectively in movements that do not recognize leaders. Engaging in collective practices that foster/produce DAC requires a mindset shift. Petrie (2014) uses the term "vertical development" to describe the shifting capacity to think in more complex, systemic, strategic, and interdependent ways (p. 8).

Leadership educators can use various active learning pedagogies, including in-class exercises, self-assessments, peer learning, self-reflection, and action learning projects, to build leadership capacity (Raelin & Raelin, 2006). Leveraging these tools and activities can help learners move from dependent-conformers (team player, leverage/reliant on authority) to interdependent-collaborators (interdependent thinkers, sees systems, patterns and connections, holds multiple perspectives) (Petrie, 2014). What is more, the #EndSars movement can serve as a critical case study to teach leadership as a collective process. When Nigerian leadership educators utilize contextually and culturally relevant case studies or examples, students are more likely to understand and apply ideas they are learning (Bertrand Jones et al., 2016; Ladson-Billings, 1995).

In conclusion, the #EndSars movement is collective leadership in action. The absence of a formal leader does not negate the presence of leadership. On the contrary, the direction, alignment, and commitment of protesters is the enactment of leadership. Therefore, DAC ontology is useful in understanding leaderless movements like #EndSars. What is more, the nature of leadership found within the context of leaderless movements like #EndSars gives hope for the future. For one, it shows that more and more young people are engaging in leadership activities. The nature of the complexities facing our world today requires all hands on deck. Higher education must continue to play its role in developing the leadership capacity of young people so that even without power and positional authority, they can engage in leadership for the common good.

REFERENCES

Alvesson, M. (2019). Waiting for Godot: Eight major problems in the odd field of leadership studies. *Leadership*, *15*(1), 27–43. https://doi.org/10.1177/1742715017736707

Bertrand Jones, T., Guthrie, K. L., & Osteen, L. (2016). Critical domains of culturally Relevant leadership learning: A call to transform leadership programs. In K. L. Guthrie, T. Bertrand Jones, & L. Osteen (Eds.), *New Directions for Student Leadership: No. 152. Developing culturally relevant leadership learning* (pp. 9–21). Wiley. https://doi.org/10.1002/yd.20205

boyd, d. (2010). Social network sites as networked publics: Affordances, dynamics, and implications. In Z. Papacharissi (Ed.), *A networked self: Identity, community, and culture on social network sites* (pp. 39–58). Routledge.

Byrne, P. (2013). *Social movements in Britain*. Routledge.

Castells, M. (2015). *Networks of outrage and hope: Social movements in the internet age.* John Wiley & Sons.

Drath, W. H., McCauley, C. D., Palus, C. J., Van Velsor, E., O'Connor, P. M., & McGuire, J. B. (2008). Direction, alignment, commitment: Toward a more integrative ontology of leadership. *The Leadership Quarterly*, *19*(6), 635–653. https://doi.org/10.1016/j.leaqua.2008.09.003

Eddington, S. M. (2018). The communicative constitution of hate organizations online: A semantic network analysis of "Make America great again". *Social Media + Society*, *4*(3), 1–12. https://doi.org/10.1177/2056305118790763

Gerbaudo, P. (2012). *Tweets and the streets: Social media and contemporary activism.* Pluto Press.

Gibson, J. J. (2015). *The ecological approach to visual perception.* Psychology Press.

Joosse, P. (2007). Leaderless resistance and ideological inclusion: The case of the earth liberation front. *Terrorism and Political Violence*, *19*(3), 351–368. https://doi.org/10.1080/09546550701424042

Ladson-Billings, G. (1995). Toward a theory of culturally relevant pedagogy. *American Educational Research Journal*, *32*(3), 465–491. https://doi.org/10.3102/00028312032003465

Meyer, D. S. (2003). How social movements matter. *Contexts*, *2*(4), 30–35. https://doi.org/10.1525/ctx.2003.2.4.30

Ospina, S., & Foldy, E. (2015). Enacting collective leadership in a shared-power world. In J. L. Perry & R. K. Christensen (Eds.), *Handbook of public administration* (pp. 489–507). Jossey-Bass.

Petrie, N. (2014). Vertical leadership development–part 1 developing leaders for a complex world. *Center for Creative leadership*, 1–13.

Raelin, J. A., & Raelin, J. D. (2006). Developmental action learning: Toward collaborative change. *Action Learning: Research and Practice*, *3*(1), 45–67. https://doi.org/10.1080/14767330600574615

Sutherland, N., Land, C., & Böhm, S. (2013). Anti-leaders(hip) in social movement organizations: The case of autonomous grassroots groups. *Organization*, *21*(6), 759–781. https://doi.org/10.1177/1350508413480254

Western, S. (2014). Autonomist leadership in leaderless movements: anarchists leading the way. *Ephemera: Theory & Politics in Organization*, *14*(4), 673–698.

CHAPTER 23

SEEING THE SUNLIGHT

Critical Hope for the Future

Kathy L. Guthrie and Kerry L. Priest

Navigating through the many, nuanced complexities of multiple pandemics has been exhausting. Most of us have been operating in constant fight, flight, or freeze modes. We lean into the recommendation of several authors in this text that creating space for self-care and supportive community is absolutely essential. As this book illustrates, there is incredible energy created when we gather members of our community together to reflect, learn, and imagine a better future. This is central to fostering critical hope. Critical hope is more than a feeling, it's an action—a leadership practice—at the intersection of social justice and complex adaptive systems. We engage in critical hope when we are able to realistically assess our contexts, environments, and systems through a lens of equity and justice, envision the possibility of a better future, and take courageous action in pursuit of it (Bishundat et al., 2018; Dugan, 2017). In this way, we see critical hope as both the process and outcome of adaptive action (Eoyang & Holladay, 2013). The cover of this book depicts an illustration of sunlight breaking through colorful, complex clouds. This symbolically represents how critical hope helps us to see beauty and possibility in the chaos. When breakthrough happens, hope is a ray of light that illuminates

Navigating Complexities in Leadership: Moving Toward Critical Hope, pp. 239–249
www.infoagepub.com
Copyright © 2022 by Information Age Publishing
All rights of reproduction in any form reserved.

the way forward. As we learn from nature, weather patterns can be unpredictable. But with the right tools we can learn to sensitive, responsive and adaptive to the constant change. In this chapter, we share the light that has emerged from this collaborative inquiry.

MAKING MEANING OF THE DYNAMIC NATURE OF LEADERSHIP

Our praxis goal for this book was to make collective meaning from our diverse lived experiences while being faced with multiple intense complexities. We have felt that individually making meaning of the ongoing, layered complexities is challenging, and sometimes impossible. However, especially in the context of leadership, meaning making and reflection are critical to learn and move forward (Volpe White et al., 2019). To collectively make meaning is challenging because it requires slowing down and listening to multiple perspectives to gain insight. By collectively creating insight from complexity, we are able to move into envisioning new possibilities with hope and courage. As did Chapters 2–6 in this text, we need to further explore the dynamic leadership frames and the interconnectedness of the complexities in which we operate from and within.

Interconnectedness of Multiple, Nuanced Complexities

When thinking about the nuanced and layered complexities we have been experiencing, several metaphors came to mind, but nothing felt exactly right. A visual that came to our minds was that of a spider web. That each silk in the intricate spider web represented a nuanced complexity and the intertwinement with the others were so complicated they could not simply be undone. That when one complexity was attempted to be pulled out for exploration, all the others would go with it because of their interconnectedness. Essentially, you could not pull out one silk strand (or complexity) without the others needing consideration. However, the metaphor of a spider web was not exactly right because of its delicacy. How quickly the intricate web could be destroyed and quickly dissolve does not mirror that of the web of complexities in which we are living in.

As we started reading the brilliance of the chapter authors' voices in this book, we began visualizing a slightly different metaphor. A reflective activity that has been used at the end of a leadership development program, whether that is a training, class, or retreat, is one of a group web. The facilitator has the group circle up and provides a ball of yarn. A member of the group begins the activity by holding onto the end of the ball of yarn and tossing it to someone else in the group. The ball of yarn is then tossed from person to person in the circle with each individual holding onto the yarn when it is tossed to them. Once everyone in the circle has had the yarn tossed to them, it returns to the first person. At the end of the yarn tossing, everyone pulls the yard tight, noticing the intricate web created the interconnectedness of the group. Variations of this activity include when the ball of yarn is tossed to each individual, they share a story, or provide a reflection from a shared experience, or give an interesting fact about themselves. No matter what the variation is, it demonstrates the way people are linked, part of the same team, and connected.

As chapters in this book began to form, we were seeing how authors were using their voices and sharing their stories, like each individual while tossing the ball of yarn. We noticed the ways in which we are all linked and part of a web of complexities. We are all a part of a collective, through our association with higher education, we are also part of a greater whole. We are together teaching, studying, and practicing leadership, not only in a higher education environment, but many other contexts as well.

Situating Leadership in the Complexities

In Chapter 1 we explore how understanding and practicing leadership in complexity requires a systems perspective. Complex adaptive systems are made up of parts (people, things) that interact to create patterns. These patterns influence ongoing behaviors that sustain the system. Systems change requires making some shift in the conditions of the system. Adaptive action is a process by which we observe what is happening in the system, make meaning of it, then take an informed action. When we take an action, we must then observe what happen to the system, thus repeating the process (Eoyang & Holladay, 2013). In complex adaptive systems, there is no way to fully predict or control the interactions or outcomes. But we can make meaning and adapt. Leadership is what emerges from dynamic interactions in a system. Adaptive action is a leadership practice in that it provides a process for us to keep observing, learning, and acting.

LEADERSHIP PRACTICE IN HIGHER EDUCATION

Navigating the complexities highlighted throughout this book requires educators to engage in tough conversations about how leadership practice emerges in the context of higher education. Not only does this require educators, scholars, and practitioners to question how they personally engage in the leadership process, but how they teach leadership and how does their leadership influence the learning of all students. Deconstructing current ways of leadership education is essential to critically looking at how leadership identity, capacity, and efficacy is developed for current and future leaders. Authors in this text have shared useful perspectives and tools to not only critically look at leadership education, but recommendations in changing leadership education by focusing on the possibilities of embracing complexity for positive change. Chapters 7–13 specifically focused on the context of higher education with leadership practice and serving as a partner in this journey.

Deconstructing Leadership Education

Chapter authors highlighted various aspects of the complexities observed and experienced both generally and in the context of higher education. Acknowledging we are all educators by working in higher education situates us in a place of critically examining and changing how leadership learning opportunities are development and delivered. It is essential to consider what knowledge and skills are needed to be included in leadership education to prepare current and future leaders for the complexities they will face.

Appreciating how each of us engage in the role of educator with different experiences, strengths to influence, obstacles to overcome, and lived experiences to learn from, we can not ignore how essential our identity is to navigating the increasing complexities we all face. We need to remember that as we navigate complexities, our students are observing us and learning from our engagement in not only the leadership process, but interaction with the sheer complexity. Our practices as leadership educators become their leadership learning. This, by itself, should be motivation for educators to reflect and deconstruct on how leadership learning opportunities are developed and delivered.

Many chapter authors provided ways to frame leadership learning in possibility and with critical hope for the future. Recommendations are offered as useful guidance in creating contexts for examination of complexities in leadership education to flourish. Although we acknowledge context is critical in how these recommendations may be useful in various learning opportunities, we encourage all educators to think and innovatively act to integrate more of these recommendations then currently seem possible.

Suggestions to Evolve Leadership Education

In Chapter 2, Chelsea D. Shore discussed how individuals need to raise consciousness in the leadership paradigms they used. Paradigms serve as a dynamic lens for viewing not only the practice of leadership, but the complexities of the world. Shore challenged us to think about how we coconstruct the leadership process with others. This coconstruction is also explored in Rian Satterwhite, Katherine Sheridan, and Whitney McIntyre Miller's chapter about the tensions in sustainability leadership. Their tensions model sheds light on how we can embrace the tensions between critique and action to move toward a better future.

At the core of this text, honoring the dynamic leadership frames we all operate from and within, as well as how we live and lead within the tensions is critical for moving forward. This is essential to evolve leadership education, as teaching skills of acknowledging complexities, assessing needs, and practicing leadership in rapidly changing and uncertain environments shifts us from simply surviving in these spaces to thriving in it. The higher education context, which was a focus of this text, is often described as an uncertain, swiftly evolving environment, which can hold people back from making positive change and maintaining the status quo. Chapters in this text explored how emergent strategy, using mass media, honoring emerging student engagement, and powerful observation as pedagogy can be used not only in the leadership practice in higher education, but also creating leadership learning opportunities.

Another consideration in evolving leadership education is how we, as educators, should value partnerships. Julie B. LeBlanc, in Chapter 11, discussed how universities are complex adaptive systems and the importance of honoring the power dynamics with community organizations, especially during intense complex times. Further exploring how higher education can serve as a partner in various communities is needed to evolve what and how we teach leadership. Chapters 12 and 13 provided insight on how higher education can and should partner with agricultural and rural communities and in addressing the challenges of health equity in the United States.

The last part of this text included chapters that help leadership educators complicate the conceptualization of leader with intersections of identities in mind. Chapters 14–22 focused on identities and the global context. It is critical for leadership learning to focus on listening to and learning from the lived experiences of Black students in higher education, the leadership tax place on Black women, the collective impact of athlete activism, feminist leadership, and approaches to gender equity. By learning from these voices, educators can better understand how to center leadership learning in socially just and culturally relevant ways.

The interconnectedness of the global community has never been so evident and Yang Li, in Chapter 19, highlighted the need for leading with a global mindset. One way to embrace the global mindset is to further acknowledge international student leadership development, as Pei Hu did in Chapter 20. Further examples of grassroots movements and leaderless movements in global contexts illuminated strategies of how higher education to grow critical hope in a better, more globally aware future. Recommendations for working through and with the nuanced and layered complexities we encounter are provided in order to create more relevant education and has potential to produce more leaders who can engage in the leadership process in an ever-changing landscape.

MOVING TOWARD CRITICAL HOPE

In this text we have attempted to open conversations about the multiple complexities we are facing in leadership, not only in the practice of leadership, but also in the creation of leadership learning opportunities. We acknowledge we have a long way to go in discussing the multiple layers of complexities we each face in learning and practicing leadership. As stated in Chapter 1, the adaptive action process (Eoyang & Holladay, 2013) is guided by three questions, What? So what? Now what? These questions guide and support individual and collective decision-making and action in complexity. In this section, we move toward: Now what is the path forward as we move toward critical hope in further enhancing our leadership practice and leadership learning opportunities to address the complexities at hand?

To provide further actionable direction to develop leadership education situated in multiple complex context and systems, we offer the following questions to support leadership educators' thinking and engagement in this work. These questions allow for practitioners to reflect on their personal context and move toward critical hope in navigating the complexities we will continue to face. These questions are organized into categories including challenges, to continue development of opportunities for change; innovation, to hopefully spark creativity; community partnerships, to continue diving into how partnerships are critical to progressing forward in this work; and, education, which continue interrogating and learning new ways to facilitate the teaching and learning of current and future leaders.

Challenges

The various complexities discussed in this book are just beginning the conversation of the layered, dynamic nature of leadership. As contextual layers continuously deepen and become more nuanced and complex, they become more difficult to identify and make meaning of. We bring forth challenges tackled in several chapters within this book to continue development and movement toward opportunities for change. To sharpen the focus of navigating multiple complexities in leadership education, we offer the following:

- In coconstructing the leadership process, how do we honor paradigm interplay in the framing of leadership to navigate complexities (Shore, Chapter 2)?
- How can we, as leadership educators, create leadership learning opportunities to address the intersection of life and politics through a biopolitical lens (Kliewer, Chapter 4)?
- As examples of unethical and ineffective leadership increase, how can we learn from these examples to cultivate leaders who center humanity in decision making (Edwards, Chapter 5)?
- How can leadership educators center the experiences of marginalized individuals in navigating the complexities of racial injustice (Ford & Propst, Chapter 14; Brewster, Chapter 15)?
- What critical approaches to gender equality are we using in leadership development and practice (Youngblood et al., Chapter 18)?

We hope the questions provided here can support educators in developing leadership programs that focus on the increasing complexity we face. Although honest answers may lead us to uncomfortable conversations with colleagues in our institutions, and perhaps in our own personal reflection, it is essential to critically challenge the current ways leadership learning opportunities are being provided. These potentially uncomfortable conversations lead to shifting thoughts and therefore actions necessary for positive change toward socially just leadership education. These changes also require relying on partnerships while interrogating and reimaging education to continue deconstruction of current ways and innovation to formulate new ways.

Generative Engagement

Eoyang and Hollady (2013) use the term generative engagement to describe how patterns of reciprocity, authenticity, and justice are shaped when we make the choice to share identities, balance power, and show honor and respect to multiple voices. With the critical challenges we face in the practice of leadership and in leadership education, we must focus on how this work can collectively be done. As leadership educators, we need to concentrate how collaboration with diverse communities is key in progressing forward in this work. Alone, not one perspective or disciplinary framework can solve complex systems oftentimes deeply rooted. Relying on the emerging voices in this book, we offer questions for reflection in how we can refine the ways in which we engage with diverse communities to offer opportunities for leadership learning in new ways to collectively solve complex issues together:

- As leadership educators, what can we learn about navigating complexities by redefining agricultural and rural communities and the practice of leadership in those contexts (Metzger & Plaschka, Chapter 12)?
- From the lens of adaptive and collective leadership, how can we cooperatively address health inequities in diverse communities (Benavides et al., Chapter 13)?
- As leadership educators, how are we partnering with student athletes to learn about leveraging collective impact through activism (Lofton, Chapter 16)?
- How can leadership educators explore a global mindset and amplify the global community to navigate complexity (Li, Chapter 19)?
- How can social movements inform new partnerships and different ways of leading others to find solutions to social issues (Gott et al., Chapter 21; Ekwerike, Chapter 22)?

Collective action requires identifying complex challenges and reaching out to diverse communities for ways to move forward. The questions offered here is a sampling of how we begin moving forward. The emerging voices in this text offered various perspectives, but it takes additional reflection and action together to move forward. Another aspect critical to this collect work is education.

Education

As educators, we all need to continue interrogating and discovering new ways to facilitate learning opportunities for current and future leaders. If education becomes stagnant, then so does the opportunity to learn in dynamic and complex ways. Education is essential to finding new ways to not only look at old problems but solving them in innovative and dynamic ways. To continue to think about how shifting perspective in education and how learning opportunities are created and delivered, we offer the follow questions:

- How can we reimagine scholarship to be more accessible for diverse readers and applicable to current issues? (Dryburgh, Chapter 6)?

- What opportunities are there for students to emerge as leaders during complex times and how are we, as leadership educators, supporting their development (Mainwood, Chapter 9)?

- As leadership educators, how can we intentionally create opportunities to learn from observing to amplify student experiences, accountability, and engagement with the complexities around us (Devies, Chapter 10)?

- Acknowledging universities are complex adaptive systems, how can we reexamine community engagement events in addressing power dynamics in leadership learning opportunities (LeBlanc, Chapter 11)?

- How can educators learn to map systems and cultivate a systems mindset to foster feminist leadership (Devies & Owen, Chapter 17)?

We know these questions are just the beginning in a journey of interrogating how education is framed and delivered. However, we hope the voices in this book enlighten us all in how we can continue to interrogate education and discover new ways to intentional design, deliver, and assess student learning with the increasing complexity we face. Although sincere reflection may lead to discomfort and a call to changing deeply rooted frameworks used in education, it is essential to question whether the current ways leadership is being taught is part of the problem or part of the solution. This evolution requires deconstruction of current ways and innovative thinking in moving forward.

Innovation

We honor that redeveloping leadership learning programs and initiatives is a large task and takes a considerable about of time and energy. However, by focusing on creativity to do this work, we can harness unknown resources, including energy and motivation within ourselves and partners. To think creatively, we offer these questions for reflection:

- By focusing on the tensions between critique and action, how can we center living and leading within these tensions (Satterwhite et al., Chapter 3)?

- What creative ways are leadership educators using emergent strategy to transform leadership learning and practice (Fluker, Chapter 7)?

- How can mass media help leaders and followers embrace and navigate chaos rather than amplifying panic (Kepple, Chapter 8)?
- As leadership educators, how can we expand opportunities for international student leadership development (Hu, Chapter 20)?
- In what ways can we learn from grassroots and leaderless social movements as ways of thinking creatively in navigating complex social issues (Gott et al., Chapter 21; Ekwerike, Chapter 22)?

Considering the current complexities in multiple contexts and observed in the practice of leadership, we generally have been asked to do more with less. In fact, creativity has been required of us, as educators, to meet our goals and objectives in logistical, technical, physical, and emotional areas of our work. As we continue to encourage educators to use diverse perspectives when developing creative ways to teach leadership, we want to also find new ways to do this work with more educators' voices being included and highlighted, especially with the framing of the complexities we continue to face. Only through collectively doing this work and infusing innovative practices will we be able to truly be able to reformulate leadership education.

As this book highlights, navigating is a continuous action that requires commitment, especially in the complexities created by not only a global health pandemic, but incessant oppression, racially motivated murders, political unrest, and countless other complexities we are unable to address here. As educators, we can no longer approach leadership education and the practice of leadership with a framework of stability and certainty. Instead, we need to lean into being sensitive, agile, and responsive to complexity and constant change. We need to center humanity at the points of tension we experience. Together, we can collectively make meaning from the complexities we face and move toward creating a better future. Critical hope will sustain the curiosity we need to discover patterns in seemingly chaotic experiences. By taking care of ourselves and others, relying on our communities of practice, and living in possibility we can shift our mindset from the negativity complexity brings to seeing the beauty in possibility. We not only invite you to continually have these critical conversations with us and others, but to collectively engage in this work together. We need you. The world needs you.

REFERENCES

Bishundat, D., Phillip, D. V., & Gore, W. (2018). Cultivating critical hope: The too often forgotten dimension of critical leadership development. In J. P. Dugan

(Ed.), *New directions for student leadership: No.159. Integrating critical perspectives into leadership development* (pp. 91–102). Wiley & Sons.

Eoyang, G. H., & Holladay, R. J. (2013). *Adaptive action: Leveraging uncertainty in your organizations.* Stanford University Press.

Dugan, J. P. (2017). *Leadership theory: Cultivating critical perspectives.* Jossey-Bass.

Volpe White, J. M., Guthrie, K. L., & Torres, M. (2019). *Thinking to transform: Reflection in leadership learning.* Information Age.

ABOUT THE EDITORS

Kathy L. Guthrie (she/her) is an associate professor of higher education at Florida State University. In addition to teaching in the Higher Education Program, Dr. Guthrie also serves as the director of the Leadership Learning Research Center and coordinates the Undergraduate Certificate in Leadership Studies, which are both partnerships between the College of Education and the Division of Student Affairs. Prior to becoming a faculty member, Kathy served as a student affairs administrator for 10 years in various areas including campus activities, commuter services, community engagement, and leadership development. Kathy's research focuses on leadership learning, socially just leadership education, online teaching and learning, and professional development for student affairs professionals specifically in leadership education. Kathy has developed and taught both undergraduate and graduate courses in leadership and higher education. Kathy has authored/coauthored over 50 refereed journal articles and book chapters, and coedited four issues in the New Directions series. She coauthored *The Role of Leadership Educators: Transforming Leadership; Operationalizing Culturally Relevant Leadership Learning; Engaging in the Leadership Process: Identity, Capacity, and Efficacy of College Students*, and *Thinking to Transform: Reflection in Leadership Learning* and coedited *Changing the Narrative: Socially Just Leadership Education* and *Shifting the Mindset: Socially Just Leadership Education*. She has received awards including NASPA's Robert H. Shaffer Award for Academic Excellence as a graduate faculty member, FSU Transformation Through Teaching Award, American College Personnel Association Contribution of Knowledge award and honored as an American College Personnel Association Diamond Honoree and NASPA Pillar of the Profession. Dr. Guthrie has served on several editorial boards and is currently the associate editor of the *New Directions in Student Leadership* series and on the advisory board for the *Journal of Campus Activities Practice and Scholarship*. Kathy has worked in higher education administrative and faculty roles for over 20 years and loves every minute of her chosen career path. Kathy enjoys spending time with her daughter and husband, where all three of them are affectionately known as Team Guthrie.

Kerry L. Priest (she/her) is an associate professor and director of graduate studies in the Mary Lynn and Warren Staley School of Leadership Studies at Kansas State University. She teaches courses in the undergraduate leadership minor, and teaches and advises in the Leadership Communication Doctoral Program. She is a researcher with the Kansas Leaders Center's Third Floor Research program, and also teaches graduate-level qualitative research methods. Kerry's interdisciplinary research agenda focuses on advancing leadership learning and development, building civic capacity, and leading change. She is interested in leadership learning and development from critical and complex systems lenses, which includes building the capacity of individuals, groups, and communities to engage in collective, relational, adaptive, and socially just leadership practice. Her scholarship explores the intersections between methods of leadership development, practice, and inquiry. She has authored/coauthored numerous peer-reviewed journal publications, book chapters, and conference presentations on leadership identity, leadership educator professional identity development, and critical and community-engaged pedagogies for leadership learning and development. She has coedited several journal special issues and symposiums, including *Being and Becoming a Leadership Educator* in *New Direction for Student Leadership* series. Kerry received the 2018 Outstanding Scholar Award from the Association of Leadership Educators. She is an associate with the Human Systems Dynamics Institute and a member of the International Leadership Association.

ABOUT THE CONTRIBUTORS

Mac T. Benavides is a graduate teaching assistant in the Staley School of Leadership Studies at Kansas State University where he teaches a class encouraging his students to explore topics of power and privilege in leadership activity at the personal and systemic levels. Mac received a master of arts in educational administration from the University of Nebraska and is currently a student in the leadership communication doctoral program at Kansas State University. His research and practice centers around global and domestic intercultural learning; leadership education; and creating inclusive and equitable learning environments at institutions of higher education.

Brittany Brewster (she/her) is a current PhD candidate in the higher education program at Florida State University. She previously served as a higher education practitioner supporting students at the juncture of justice, leadership, and community participation. Brittany's research interests explore the experiences of underrepresented populations in higher education, with a special interest in Black women. Her research applies a critical and intersectional lens to understand and disrupt systemic racism, sexism, and other forms of oppression in postsecondary education policies and practices

Jurdene Coleman (she/her), LCMFT, is a mental health supervisor at a community mental health agency in Kansas. As a community leader, Jurdene is a 2018 graduate of Leadership Manhattan, a local leadership development program through Manhattan Chamber of Commerce and a 2019 graduate of Leadership for Tomorrow, a leadership development program of the Kansas Association of School Boards. Jurdene is pursuing a doctoral degree in leadership communication at Kansas State University studying lived experiences of graduate students of color at predominately White institutions.

Brittany Devies (she/her) is a third year PhD student at Florida State University studying higher education. Brittany is a graduate assistant for the Leadership Learning Research Center, where she works on research and scholarship around collegiate leadership learning. She is also a lead instructor for the Undergraduate Leadership Studies Certificate, including teaching a gender and leadership course. Her research interests include the intersections of gender and leader identity development, culturally relevant leadership learning, and the experiences of women in higher education.

Martinella Dryburgh is the executive director of the Posey Leadership Institute at Austin College in Sherman, TX, where she is also the Leslie B. Crane Chair of Leadership Studies. Dr. Dryburgh research and writing focuses on experiential learning and she has published in the *Journal of Leadership Education*. Martinella earned a PhD in public affairs from The University of Texas at Dallas, a master of liberal arts from Southern Methodist University, and a bachelor of business administration from The University of Texas at Austin.

O'Juan D. Edwards (he/him) is a third-year doctoral student in the higher education program at Florida State University. He serves as a graduate research assistant as well. O'Juan has a decade of experience working in higher education and student affairs administration at Oakland University, Michigan State University, and the University of Maryland, College Park. Additionally, his research interests are sexually transmitted infection prevention amongst undergraduate Black women on college and university campuses.

Onyedikachi (Kachi) Ekwerike is the founder of Postpartum Support Network (PSN) Africa, a leading maternal mental health organization in Nigeria. Dr. Ekwerike earned his PhD in leadership communication from Kansas State University. He is a lecturer of leadership at the Institute of Leadership Advancement in the Terry College of Business, University of Georgia. His research interest revolves around understanding culturally relevant leadership practices of social change leaders in Nigeria. He is passionate about helping social change leaders in Africa develop the capacity to progress on tough challenges facing the continent.

Ciera Fluker (she/her/ella) is a doctoral student in the higher education program at Florida State University. She has worked as an instructional designer for close to a decade creating functional, human resource, and interpersonal skills training. Ciera's research interests are centered around issues of access and success among underrepresented populations of students in higher education. As a first-generation college student and an Afro-Latina scholar, much of her research is informed by her identity and experiences.

Jesse R. Ford is an assistant professor of higher education in the Department of Teacher Education and Higher Education at the University of North Carolina at Greensboro. Dr. Ford's program of research uses culturally responsive frameworks to examine the political and historical socialcultural educational experiences of underrepresented populations in academia. His recent scholarship employs qualitative and quantitative methodologies to tackle inequality in education, particularly within the socialization experiences of underrepresented students, faculty, and administrators across the P–20 pipeline. Jesse's scholarship can be seen in outlets such as *Journal of Black Studies, Education and Urban Society*, and *About Campus*.

Carol Clyde Gallagher (she/her) has completed graduate work in the fields of educational leadership, dispute resolution, gender and women's studies, and executive coaching. After a lengthy career in student affairs, Dr. Gallagher now serves as an assistant professor of organizational leadership at Cottey College, a women's college in Nevada, MO. In addition to her passion for leadership studies and community engagement, she is a competitive billiards player and a lead facilitator for Kiwanis International's Key Leader high school leadership program.

Elizabeth Goryunova is a scholar and practitioner of global leadership, with specific research interests in leadership education, complex problem solving, cross-cultural effectiveness, and global citizenship. Dr. Goryunova is an assistant professor of leadership and organizational studies at the University of Southern Maine, where in addition to teaching and research, she serves on the Faculty Senate Executive Committee, USM Research Advisory Committee, and cochairs USM Core Curriculum Committee. Prior to joining academia, Elizabeth served as president and chief executive officer of the World Trade Center Utah, and as 1 of 10 U.S. Private Sector Liaison Officers to the World Bank Group.

Trisha Gott is an assistant professor and associate director at the Staley School of Leadership Studies. Dr. Gott teaches undergraduate and professional coursework on dimensions of leadership and leadership development. Trisha has worked in higher education for over a decade and has focused her work on practice-based leadership education and development for students and professionals. Since 2016 she has served as coprincipal investigator and codirector for the Mandela Washington Fellowship Civic Engagement and Leadership Institute at Kansas State University.

Trent Grundmeyer currently serves as an associate professor of educational leadership at Drake University in Des Moines, IA. Dr. Grundmeyer research focus includes technology adoption, parent school communication, school law, and hiring practices. Trent teaches multiple classes in the masters, specialist, and doctorate programs at Drake. He served as a secondary principal for nine years and was named Iowa Secondary Principal of the Year in 2013 while leading Indianola High School.

Kathy L. Guthrie (she/her) is associate professor in the higher education program at Florida State University. Dr. Guthrie serves as director of the Leadership Learning Research Center and coordinator of the Undergraduate Certificate in Leadership Studies. She currently serves as associate editor for the *New Directions in Student Leadership* series.

Tess Hobson is a graduate teaching assistant with the Staley School of Leadership Studies and a graduate in student affairs and higher education program at Kansas State University. Dr. Hobson teaches a course about inclusive leadership called Culture and Context of Leadership and coordinates the Edgerley-Franklin Leadership Scholarship Program, which seeks to shape the next generation of social justice leaders. Tess's research interests revolve around the power of storytelling as a pedagogy in developing students' capacity to practice inclusive leadership.

Pei Hu is a doctoral candidate in the higher education program at Florida State University. Pei's research interests focus on leadership education and international student education. Currently, she serves as a graduate assistant for the Leadership Learning Research Center, responsible for research on academic leadership programs across the United States and international student leadership development, as well as teaching in the Undergraduate Certificate in Leadership Studies.

Saya Kakim (she/her) is a doctoral student in the leadership communication interdisciplinary doctoral program at Kansas State University. Saya assists with planning and implementation of cocurriculum activities and community building efforts for diverse and historically underrepresented students in STEM with the Kansas Louis Stokes Alliance for Minority Participation. Her research interests include leadership development, public engagement, deliberation and dialog, and intercultural communication. Saya earned her master's degree from the National Research University Higher School of Economics (Moscow, Russia).

Salif Kanoute is one of the founders of DECLIC, an organization based in the Casamance region of Senegal. He is a social entrepreneur with a background in humanitarian work. Salif's work with DECLIC is focused on mobilizing others by developing human capacity to lead. DECLIC, is a grassroots youth leadership movement built with the motto, "To take the leadership challenge for the common good"

Cassandra R. Kepple (she/her) is a doctoral student in the higher education program at Florida State University. Cassandra works as a research assistant studying how colleges can best support students with autism as well as best advising practices in higher education. Her research interests revolve around specific programming on college campuses that help ensure success for diverse student populations.

Brandon W. Kliewer is an associate professor of civic leadership in the Mary Lynn and Warren Staley School of Leadership Studies at Kansas State University. Dr. Kliewer studies leadership in organizations and democracy through the lens of civic capacity, dialogic process consulting, democratic theory, and systems change. Brandon holds a PhD from The University of Georgia in political science and a master's degree in political science from Virginia Polytechnic Institute and State University.

Julie B. LeBlanc (she/her) is a doctoral candidate in the higher education program at Florida State University. She works in the Leadership Learning Research Center as an instructor for the Undergraduate Certificate in Leadership Studies program. Julie has over seven years of experience designing community engagement and leadership education programs. Her dissertation research focuses on the interconnected relationship between democratic engagement and socially just leadership education and how campuses enact democratic approaches to community engagement to disrupt systems of oppression and contribute to community change.

Yang Li is a current PhD student in the higher education program at Florida State University. Yang earned her MS in global higher education program from the University of Wisconsin-Madison. Yang currently serves as a graduate assistant in the Center for Global Engagement where she assesses programs related to international students' campus experience and involvement. Her current research interest lies in student success, especially international students' success on campuses in the United States.

Sherrina S. Lofton is an alumni and academic advisor at Florida State University. Sherrina holds a bachelor's and master's from California State University, Northridge, and a master's from Florida State University. Her research focuses on the transition out of sports experiences of African Black collegiate and professional athletes.

Marissa Mainwood (she/her) is a doctoral student in the Higher Education Program at Florida State University. Marissa's interests include leadership development, international education, and online learning. Marissa is currently employed in the College of Business as the student engagement coordinator at Florida State University. Prior she was employed in the area of workforce training and continuing education.

Roberta Maldonado Franzen (she/her) is an instructor at the Staley School of Leadership Studies at Kansas State University and has a PhD in leadership communication. Dr. Maldonado Franzen research interest intersects with leadership development and program evaluation. As a first-generation college student, Roberta's approach is to teach students to connect their classroom education to their career development by offering experiences that help them grow and make sense of their learning. Her focus is to create a supportive environment that prepares and empowers others to exercise leadership in their communities and global workplace.

Whitney McIntyre Miller (she/her) is an associate professor of leadership studies at Chapman University. Dr. Miller centers her scholarship on peace leadership and community development and leadership. She has served as the coconvener of the International Leadership Association's Peace Leadership Affinity Group, as a Community Development Society board member, and on the Los Alamitos Unified School District Human Relations Advisory Council.

Susan Metzger (she/her) serves as the senior executive administrator to the dean/director of Kansas State University's College of Agriculture and Kansas State University's Research and Extension. Susan also serves as the associate director for the Kansas Center for Agricultural Resources and the Environment. Susan has broad experience representing Kansas State University and Kansas agriculture. She is also currently a doctoral candidate in the leadership communication program at Kansas State University.

Seydina M. Ndiaye has a background in digital technology and transformation with a MBA in digital marketing and strategy e-business. Seydina is cofounder of AfricTivistes, a cyberleague of cyberactivist, who promote democracy, accountability and civic engagement via digital technology. Seydina is now a social innovator and entrepreneur after cofounding Consortium Jeunesse Senegal (Youth Consortium Senegal) where he is vice president in charge of designing a civic leadership and social transformation program for the youth in popular area.

Julie E. Owen is associate professor of leadership studies at the School of Integrative Studies, George Mason University, where she coordinates the leadership studies major and minor, and teaches interdisciplinary courses on socially responsible leadership, women's development, and community-engaged research. Dr. Owen is also affiliate faculty with the higher education program, and women and gender studies. Julie is the author of numerous scholarly publications, including: *We are the Leaders We've Been Waiting For: Women and Leadership Development in College*. Her research explores the intersections of leadership identity and women's adult development, as well as the scholarship of liberatory leadership teaching and learning.

Russell Plaschka serves the Kansas Department of Agriculture as the agribusiness development director where he leads a team to grow the Kansas agriculture industry and economy. As director, Russell leads the facilitation and outreach to rural communities across the state to help communities navigate community lead economic development. He spent 25 years teaching agriculture and advising FFA members at the secondary level. Russell is also pursuing a doctorate in leadership communications at Kansas State University with research focused on how and why communities determine their interest in growing specific agricultural sectors.

Kerry L. Priest (she/her) is an associate professor and director of graduate studies in the Mary Lynn and Warren Staley School of Leadership Studies at Kansas State University. Dr. Priest teaches courses in the undergraduate leadership minor, and teaches and advises in the leadership communication doctoral program. Kerry's interdisciplinary research agenda focuses on advancing leadership learning and development, building civic capacity, and leading change. She is interested in leadership learning and development from a systems lens, which includes building capacity in individuals, groups, and communities to engage in collective, relational, adaptive, and socially just leadership practice.

Brandy S. Propst (she/her), MEd, with 15 years of experience in higher education, Brandy is a scholar-practitioner who serves as the director of Elon 101 and assistant director of academic advising within the Koenigsberger Learning Center at Elon University. Prior, Brandy has experience in orientation/new student programs, parent/family programs, graduate admissions, and enrollment management. Brandy is also a fourth-year doctoral student in the PhD in educational studies with a concentration in higher education program at The University of North Carolina at Greensboro. Her research interests include the self-care practices of higher education professionals, experiences of Black women student affairs professionals, Black feminist theory, and critical race feminism.

Rian Satterwhite (he/him) serves as director of the Office of Service Learning and Leadership at the University of Nevada, Las Vegas, as well as teaching faculty at Claremont Lincoln University and affiliate faculty at St. Thomas University. Rian coconvenes the International Leadership Association Sustainability Leadership Member Community, serves as cochair of the ILA Leadership Education Academy, sits on the steering committee for Compassionate Las Vegas, and is a board member for the Alliance for Nevada Nonprofits and Nevada CARE Coalition.

Kate Sheridan (she/her) is the director of career development at Chatham University in Pittsburgh, Pennsylvania and has led and coauthored several publications exploring the confluence of leadership, sustainability, peace, and social justice. Kate serves as a member of the International Leadership Association Sustainability Leadership Member Community Steering Committee and is an alumna of Penn State University and the University of San Diego.

Chelsea Shore (she/her) is doctoral student in the higher education program at Florida State University. Chelsea's research uses developmental perspectives and mixed methods to examine how college students develop through institutional mechanisms such as community engagement, registered student organizations, and campus recreation. Chelsea has experience working in student leadership, community college instruction, federally funded research, and currently serves as the graduate assistant for College Recovery Programs.

Mary Tolar (she/her) serves as director of the Staley School of Leadership Studies, Kansas State University, providing learning experiences aligned with the mission of "developing knowledgeable, ethical, caring, inclusive leaders for a diverse and changing world." Dr. Tolar research interests include the art and practice of civic leadership development and women's pathways to leadership. Mary is a Truman Scholar, a Rhodes Scholar, and holds a bachelor's degree in history and doctorate in educational leadership from Kansas State University. In between, she read for her master of letters in modern history from Oxford University, United Kingdom.

Cristina de Mello e Souza Wildermuth is an associate professor at Drake University, where she directs the Master of Science in Leadership Development and teaches courses in leadership, ethics, technology, and instructional design. Originally from Rio de Janeiro, Brazil, Dr. Wildermuth has traveled extensively, conducting leadership development programs in Latin America and Europe. Her main research interests are ethics and international education.

R. J. Youngblood (she/her) is assistant director of the Academic Achievement Center and a PhD candidate in leadership communication at Kansas State University. As a first-generation college graduate, her role in academic success is grounded in a commitment to making equitable spaces for student learning, and her research interests focus on leadership practice that support student success and employee engagement. Her current scholarly agenda is positioned at the intersection of material discursive leadership practice, emergent technologies, and gender.

CPSIA information can be obtained
at www.ICGtesting.com
Printed in the USA
BVHW040554070322
630792BV00003B/12